A Gift for

....

From

_____

Life-Changing
Moments
with God

David
Jeremiah

Published by
THOMAS NELSON™
Since 1798

www.thomasnelson.com

Published in Nashville, Tennessee, by Thomas Nelson, Inc.

All Scripture quotations are taken from the *New King James Version* ©1979, 1980,
1982, 1992, Thomas Nelson, Inc.

Project Developer: Lisa Stilwell
Project Editor: Lisa Guest

Designed by The DesignWorks Group, Sisters, Oregon

ISBN-10: 1–4041–0387–2
ISBN-13: 978–1–4041–0387–0

Printed and bound in China

www.thomasnelson.com

Contents

Some people refer to the Bible as God's "love letter" to us. His Word indeed offers detailed accounts of God's "love in action" in every kind of situation we may encounter in life, whether joyful, trying, abundant, painful, redeeming, forgiving, sinful, victorious . . . the list is all-encompassing. It's His love gift to us to read, to meditate on, to claim for every corner of our lives and ounce of our being.

Through my years of walking with our Lord, I came across a powerful little book compiled by several generations of one family as their response to that "love letter." Family patriarch Samuel Bagster began writing daily devotions by carefully selecting Scripture passages by theme for his family. His son Jonathan continued the practice, and Jonathan's son, Robert, along with his children published them for use by other families. I have found that in addition to reading His Word, this little book, *Daily Light*, has had a profound influence on my life.

A few years ago Anne Graham Lotz, who was similarly blessed by the nearly two-century-old book, published a new edition of the book, using the New King James translation. At a time when I was searching for a practical way to meditate on the Word, I began using Anne's book to incorporate the daily readings into my journal.

My response was to make this collection from God's "love letter" even more personal. I have carefully and prayerfully turned it into devotional prayers. Consider the glorious promise in Revelation that God will wipe away every tear (Revelation 21:4). Now consider that promise recast like this: "Once I'm with You, Lord, I know that my Father will wipe away every tear from my eyes." Yes, that truth will be true for *you*.

Or consider the basic doctrinal truth that we are saved by faith. That truth becomes more personal when we pray it: "I humbly acknowledge that it is by Your grace that I have been saved through faith, and not at all of myself. My salvation is Your gift, Father God; it's not of works, lest I should boast. For I am Your workmanship, created in Christ Jesus for good works, which You prepared beforehand that I should walk in them" (Ephesians 2:8–10).

And then there are God's charges and commands. When we pray them, we can at the same time call on the Lord to enable us to obey: "Awesome Lord, You call me to work out my salvation with fear and trembling. The fear and trembling come easily, but please show me how to work out my salvation. Help me first want to do Your will—and then empower me to do it!" (Philippians 2:12–13).

Within the following pages there are Scripture-based devotional prayers followed by a brief closing prayer that summarizes the theme of the day. My prayer for you is that they will keep you focused on Almighty God, the One who wrote this love letter to you.

Draw close to God by spending time praying these truths revealed in His Word, and in doing so, may you be blessed with a greater understanding of the width and length and depth and height of His faithfulness and never-ending love for you.

DR. DAVID JEREMIAH

January

But one thing I do,

forgetting those things which

are behind I press toward the goal

for the prize of the upward call

of God in Christ Jesus.

One thing I do, forgetting those things
which are behind . . . I press toward the goal for the prize
of the upward call of God in Christ Jesus.

Father, it is Jesus' will that we whom You gave Him may behold His glory which You have given Him.

I know whom I have believed and am persuaded that You are able to keep what I have committed to You until that Day. You who have begun a good work in me will complete it until the day of Jesus Christ.

Your word says, "Do you not know that those who run in a race all run, but one receives the prize?" May I run in such a way that I obtain it. And everyone who competes for the prize is temperate in all things. Now they do it to obtain a perishable crown, but we for an imperishable crown.

So help me lay aside every weight, and the sin which so easily ensnares me, and let me run with endurance the race that is set before me, looking unto Jesus.

I can only keep focused and I can only run this race this year—
this day—in Your power and by Your grace.
Thank You for being with me each step of the way.

PHILIPPIANS 3:13–14; JOHN 17:24; 2 TIMOTHY 1:12;
PHILIPPIANS 1:6; 1 CORINTHIANS 9:24–25; HEBREWS 12:1–2

Sing to the lord a new song.

I sing aloud to You, Lord God, my strength; I make a joyful shout to the God of Jacob. I raise a song and strike the timbrel, the pleasant harp with the lute. You have put a new song in my mouth—praise to my God; many will see it and fear, and will trust in You, Lord.

I can be strong and of good courage . . . not afraid, nor dismayed, for the Lord my God is with me wherever I go. The joy of the Lord is my strength.

Lord God, I know the time, that now it is high time to awake out of sleep; for now my salvation is nearer than when I first believed. Therefore let me cast off the works of darkness and . . . put on the armor of light. Let me walk properly, as in the day, not in revelry and drunkenness, not in lewdness and lust, not in strife and envy. But may I put on the Lord Jesus Christ, and make no provision for the flesh, to fulfill its lusts.

Lord, You are the same yesterday, today, and tomorrow—
and of You I can always sing.
Help me find joy and courage as I sing of Your goodness.

ISAIAH 42:10; PSALM 81:1–2; PSALM 40:3; JOSHUA 1:9;
NEHEMIAH 8:10; ROMANS 13:11–14

He led them forth by the right way.

In the wasteland, a howling wilderness, You encircled Jacob, You instructed him, You kept him as the apple of Your eye. As an eagle... hovers over its young, spreading out its wings, taking them up, carrying them on its wings, so You alone, Lord, led him. Even to my old age, You are He, and even to gray hairs You will carry me! You have made, and You will bear; even You will carry, and will deliver me.

You restore my soul; You lead me in the paths of righteousness for Your name's sake. Yea, though I walk through the valley of the shadow of death, I will fear no evil; for You are with me; Your rod and Your staff, they comfort me.

You, Lord, will guide me continually, and satisfy my soul in drought, and strengthen my bones; I shall be like a watered garden, and like a spring of water, whose waters do not fail. For this is God, my God forever and ever; You will be my guide even to death. None teaches like You!

I face so many decisions—big and little—
in the course of the day, Lord. Enable me to keep my eyes on You,
who will lead me exactly where You want me to go.

PSALM 107:7; DEUTERONOMY 32:10–12; ISAIAH 46:4;
PSALM 23:3–4; ISAIAH 58:11; PSALM 48:14; JOB 36:22

For as yet you have not come to the rest and the inheritance which the Lord your God is giving you.

Heavenly Father, this is not my rest. There remains a rest for the people of God. Behind the veil, where the forerunner has entered for me, even Jesus... who said in His Father's house are many mansions; if it were not so, He would have told me. He went to prepare a place for me. And if He goes and prepares a place for me, He will come again and receive me to Himself; that where He is, there I may be also. With Christ, which is far better.

God will wipe away every tear from my eyes; there shall be no more death, nor sorrow, nor crying. There shall be no more pain. There the wicked cease from troubling, and there the weary are at rest.

So I lay up for myself treasures in heaven . . . for where my treasure is, there my heart will be also. I set my mind on things above, not on things on the earth.

Lord, You know the rest I need—
physical, emotional, mental, even spiritual. Thank You that
You offer me rest today as well as for eternity.

DEUTERONOMY 12:9; MICAH 2:10; HEBREWS 4:9;
HEBREWS 6:19–20; JOHN 14:2–3;
PHILIPPIANS 1:23; REVELATION 21:4; JOB 3:17;
MATTHEW 6:20–21; COLOSSIANS 3:2

We who have believed do enter that rest.

Lord God, they weary themselves to commit iniquity. I see another law in my members, warring against the law of my mind, and bringing me into captivity to the law of sin which is in my members. O wretched man that I am! Who will deliver me from this body of death?

Jesus answers, "Come to Me, all you who labor and are heavy laden," and You will give me rest. Having been justified by faith, I have peace with God through my Lord Jesus Christ, through whom also I have access by faith into this grace in which I stand, and rejoice in hope of the glory of God.

Father, I who have entered Your rest have myself also ceased from my works. Not having my own righteousness, which is from the law, but that which is through faith in Christ, the righteousness which is from You, God, by faith. This is the rest with which You may cause the weary to rest, and, this is the refreshing.

The rest the world offers, Lord, is temporary at best.
May I find true rest in You,
my Good Shepherd and my King.

HEBREWS 4:3; JEREMIAH 9:5; ROMANS 7:23–24;
MATTHEW 11:28; ROMANS 5:1–2;
HEBREWS 4:10; PHILIPPIANS 3:9; ISAIAH 28:12

Let the beauty of the Lord our God be upon us,
and establish the work of our hands for us.

Dear Father, Your beauty . . . Your perfect splendor You bestowed on me. I, with unveiled face, beholding as in a mirror the glory of the Lord, am being transformed into the same image from glory to glory, just as by the Spirit of the Lord. The Spirit of glory and of God rests upon me.

Blessed is every one who fears You, Lord, who walks in Your ways. When I eat the labor of my hands, I shall be happy, and it shall be well with me. I commit my works to You, Lord, and my thoughts will be established.

I work out my own salvation with fear and trembling; for it is You, God, who works in me both to will and to do for Your good pleasure. My Lord Jesus Christ Himself, and my God and Father, who has loved me and given me everlasting consolation and good hope by grace, comforts my heart and establishes me in every good word and work.

Lord God, please transform me by Your Spirit—
enjoying Your beauty, submitting to Your transforming work,
and serving You joyfully in grateful love.

PSALM 90:17; EZEKIEL 16:14; 2 CORINTHIANS 3:18;
1 PETER 4:14; PSALM 128:1–2; PROVERBS 16:3;
PHILIPPIANS 2:12–13; 2 THESSALONIANS 2:16–17

Remember me, my God, for good.

Lord, You remember me, the kindness of my youth, the love of my betrothal, when I went after You in the wilderness. You will remember Your covenant with me in the days of my youth, and You will establish an everlasting covenant with me. You will visit me and perform Your good word toward me. For You know the thoughts that You think toward me, thoughts of peace and not of evil, to give me a future and a hope.

As the heavens are higher than the earth, so are Your ways higher than my ways, and Your thoughts than my thoughts. I would seek You, God, and to You I would commit my cause—who does great things, and unsearchable, marvelous things without number. Many, O Lord my God, are Your wonderful works which You have done; and Your thoughts toward me cannot be recounted to You in order; if I would declare and speak of them, they are more than can be numbered.

You see my sin more clearly than I do, yet You choose to remember me "for good." I praise You for this mercy, this grace.

NEHEMIAH 5:19; JEREMIAH 2:2; EZEKIEL 16:60; JEREMIAH 29:10–11; ISAIAH 55:9; JOB 5:8–9; PSALM 40:5

Those who know Your name will put their trust in You;
for You, Lord, have not forsaken those who seek You.

Your name, Lord, is a strong tower; the righteous run to
it and are safe. I will trust and not be afraid; for You,
Lord, are my strength and my song; You also have
become my salvation.

I have been young, and now am old; yet I have not seen the
righteous forsaken, nor his descendants begging bread. For You,
Lord, love justice, and do not forsake Your saints; we are
preserved forever, but the descendants of the wicked shall Your
His people, for Your great name's sake, because it has pleased
You, Lord, to make us Your people…. You who delivered me
from so great a death, and does deliver me; in whom I trust that
You will still deliver me.

I will be content with such things as I have. For You Yourself
have said, "I will never leave you nor forsake you." So I may
boldly say: "The Lord is my helper; I will not fear. What can
man do to me?"

Lord, You are my Helper and a strong Tower for me,
yet sometimes I do fear. Forgive me—
and teach me to trust You more wholeheartedly.

PSALM 9:10; PROVERBS 18:10; ISAIAH 12:2;
PSALM 37:25; PSALM 37:28; 1 SAMUEL 12:22;
2 CORINTHIANS 1:10; HEBREWS 13:5–6

You have given a banner to those who fear You,
that it may be displayed because of the truth.

Jehovah Nissi: Lord-My-Banner. When my enemy comes in like a flood, Your Spirit, Lord, will lift up a standard against him.

I will rejoice in my salvation, and in the name of my God I will set up my banner! You, Lord, have revealed my righteousness. Let me declare in Zion the work of the Lord my God. I am more than a conqueror through You who loved me. Thanks be to You, God, who gives me the victory through my Lord Jesus Christ.

I will be strong in You, Lord, and in the power of Your might. I will be valiant for the truth . . . and fight Your battles. "Be strong, all you people of the land," You say, "and work; . . . do not fear!" I look at the field, white for harvest. For yet a little while, and You who are coming will come and will not tarry.

Light and dark; spirit and flesh; truth and lies; tolerance and
discrimination . . . The battles are many, Lord. Keep me focused on
You, a rallying point, my guide in conflict, and a banner of victory.

PSALM 60:4; EXODUS 17:15; ISAIAH 59:19; PSALM 20:5;
JEREMIAH 51:10; ROMANS 8:37; 1 CORINTHIANS 15:57;
EPHESIANS 6:10; JEREMIAH 9:3; 1 SAMUEL 18:17;
HAGGAI 2:4–5; JOHN 4:35; HEBREWS 10:37

*May your whole spirit, soul, and body be preserved blameless
at the coming of our Lord Jesus Christ.*

Christ Jesus, You loved the church and gave Yourself for
her . . . that You might present it to Yourself a glorious
church, not having spot or wrinkle or any such thing,
but that she should be holy and without blemish. You I preach,
warning every man and teaching every man in all wisdom, that
every man may be perfect in Christ Jesus.

The peace of God . . . surpasses all understanding. May I let
Your peace rule in my heart, God, as I was also called.

May my Lord Jesus Christ Himself, and my God and
Father, who has loved me and given me everlasting consolation
and good hope by grace, comfort my heart and establish me in
every good word and work. God will also confirm me to the
end, that I may be blameless in the day of our Lord Jesus Christ.

*Help me, Holy God, to cooperate
with Your Spirit's transforming work, with His efforts
to make me holy and blameless.*

1 THESSALONIANS 5:23; EPHESIANS 5:25, 27;
COLOSSIANS 1:28; PHILIPPIANS 4:7; COLOSSIANS 3:15;
2 THESSALONIANS 2:16–17; 1 CORINTHIANS 1:8

Praise is awaiting You, O God, in Zion.

For me You are the one God, the Father, of whom are all things, and I for Him; and one Lord Jesus Christ. All should honor the Son just as they honor You, Father. He who does not honor the Son does not honor You, Father, who sent Him. Therefore by Him let me continually offer the sacrifice of praise to God, that is, the fruit of my lips, giving thanks to His name. Whoever offers praise glorifies You, Lord Jesus; and to him who orders his conduct aright You will show the salvation of God.

The apostle John looked, and beheld, a great multitude which no one could number, of all nations, tribes, peoples, and tongues, standing before the throne and before the Lamb, clothed with white robes, with palm branches in their hands, and crying out with a loud voice, saying, "Salvation belongs to our God who sits on the throne, and to the Lamb!" Amen! Blessing and glory and wisdom, thanksgiving and honor and power and might, be to You my God forever and ever. Amen.

May my words and my life be an ongoing song of joyous praise to You, Almighty God and heavenly Father.

PSALM 65:1; I CORINTHIANS 8:6; JOHN 5:23; HEBREWS 13:15; PSALM 50:23; REVELATION 7:9–10, 12

To God our Savior, who alone is wise.

Father, I am in Christ Jesus, who became for me wisdom from You, God—and righteousness and sanctification and redemption. Can I search out Your deep things? Can I find out the limits of the Almighty? They are higher than heaven—what can I do? Deeper than Sheol—what can I know?

I speak the wisdom of God in a mystery, the hidden wisdom which God ordained before the ages for my glory. The mystery, which from the beginning of the ages has been hidden in You, God, who created all things through Jesus Christ; to the intent that now the manifold wisdom of God might be made known by the church to the principalities and powers in the heavenly places.

If I lack wisdom, I ask of You, God, who gives to all liberally and without reproach, and it will be given to me. Your wisdom that is from above is first pure, then peaceable, gentle, willing to yield, full of mercy and good fruits, without partiality and without hypocrisy.

Lord God, may my life be
characterized by joy in Jesus, who is Your wisdom,
and by the kind of wisdom for each day
that only You can give.

Jude 25; 1 Corinthians 1:30; Job 11:7–8;
1 Corinthians 2:7; Ephesians 3:9–10; James 1:5; James 3:17

*You will keep him in perfect peace, whose mind is stayed on You,
because he trusts in You.*

Jehovah God, I cast my burden on You, and You shall sustain me; You shall never permit the righteous to be moved. I will trust and not be afraid; for You, Lord, are my strength and my song; You also have become my salvation.

Why am I fearful, O me of little faith? May I be anxious for nothing, but in everything by prayer and supplication, with thanksgiving, let my requests be made known to You, God; and Your peace, God, which surpasses all understanding, will guard my heart and mind through Christ Jesus. In quietness and confidence shall be my strength.

The work of righteousness will be peace, and the effect of righteousness, quietness and assurance forever. Jesus leaves His peace with me, His peace He gives to me; not as the world gives does He give to me. So I let not my heart be troubled, neither let it be afraid. Peace comes from Jesus who is and who was and who is to come.

*I believe, Lord God. Help my unbelief
so that I may experience the peace You long for me to know
as I put my trust in You.*

ISAIAH 26:3; PSALM 55:22; ISAIAH 12:2; MATTHEW 8:26;
PHILIPPIANS 4:6–7; ISAIAH 30:15; ISAIAH 32:17

My Father is greater than I.

In prayer, I say, "My Father in heaven"... Jesus' Father and my Father... Jesus' God and my God.

As You, Father, gave Jesus commandment, so He does. The words Jesus speaks to me He does not speak on His own authority; but You, Father, who dwells in Him do the works.

Father, You love the Son, and have given all things into His hand. You have given Him authority over all flesh, that He should give eternal life to as many as You have given Him.

His disciple said, "Lord, show us the Father, and it is sufficient for us." Jesus said to him, "He who has seen Me has seen the Father; so how can you say, 'Show us the Father'? Do you not believe that I am in the Father, and the Father in Me?" Jesus and You—God, His Father—are one. As You, Father, loved Jesus, He also has loved me; so I choose to abide in His love. If I keep His commandments, I will abide in His love, just as He has kept Your commandments and abides in Your love.

Father God, teach me to obey
Jesus' commandments and to abide in His love.

JOHN 14:28; LUKE 11:2; JOHN 20:17;
JOHN 14:31; JOHN 14:10; JOHN 3:35; JOHN 17:2;
JOHN 14:8–10; JOHN 10:30; JOHN 15:9–10

My soul clings to the dust;
revive me according to Your word.

Father, I was raised with Christ, I seek those things which are above, where Christ is, sitting at Your right hand. I set my mind on things above, not on things on the earth. For my life is hidden with Christ in You. For my citizenship is in heaven . . . I eagerly await my Savior, Jesus Christ who will transform my lowly body . . . conformed to His glorious body, according to the working which He is able even to subdue all things to Himself.

Yet now my flesh lusts against Your Spirit, and the Spirit against my flesh; and these are contrary to one another, so that I do not do the things that I wish. I am a debtor—not to the flesh, to live according to the flesh. For if I live according to the flesh I will die; but if by the Spirit I put to death the deeds of the body, I will live. As a sojourner and pilgrim, I am to abstain from fleshly lusts which war against the soul.

Lord, alone I can't live the way You want me to live.
I need the truth of Your Word and of Your powerful Spirit.

PSALM 119:25; COLOSSIANS 3:1–3; PHILIPPIANS 3:20–21;
GALATIANS 5:17; ROMANS 8:12–13; 1 PETER 2:11

It pleased the Father that in Him
all the fullness should dwell.

Y ou, Father God, love the Son, and have given all things
into His hand. You have highly exalted Him and given
Him the name which is above every name, that, in His
name, Jesus, every knee should bow, of those in heaven, and of
those on earth, and of those under the earth, and that every
tongue should confess that Jesus Christ is Lord, to Your glory,
Father God. Jesus is far above all principality and power and
might and dominion, and every name that is named, not only in
this age but also in that which is to come. By Him all things
were created that are in heaven and that are on earth, visible and
invisible, whether thrones or dominions or principalities or
powers. All things were created through Him and for Him.

Christ died and rose and lived again, that He might be
Lord of both the dead and the living. I am complete in Him . . .
the head of all principality and power. Of His fullness I have
received.

Father, Jesus alone is worthy of praise!
I am complete in Him but I need Your help to live like it
and glorify You in all I say and do.

COLOSSIANS 1:19; JOHN 3:35; PHILIPPIANS 2:9–11;
EPHESIANS 1:21; COLOSSIANS 1:16; ROMANS 14:9;
COLOSSIANS 2:10; JOHN 1:16

*But You have lovingly delivered
my soul from the pit of corruption.*

Lord God, You sent Your only begotten Son into the world, that I might live through Him. In this is love, not that I loved You, but that You loved me and sent Your Son to be the propitiation for my sins.

Who is a God like You, pardoning iniquity and passing over the transgression of the remnant of Your heritage? You do not retain Your anger forever, because You delight in mercy. You will again have compassion on me, and will subdue my iniquities. You will cast all my sins into the depths of the sea. O Lord my God, I cried out to You, and You healed me. O Lord, You brought my soul up from the grave; You have kept me alive. When my soul fainted within me, I remembered You, Lord; and my prayer went up to You, into Your holy temple. I waited patiently for You, Lord. You brought me up out of a horrible pit, out of the miry clay, and set my feet upon a rock, and established my steps.

*Lord God, Your compassion and mercy
are obvious in the gift of Your Son for me. I praise You,
my Deliverer and my Rock.*

ISAIAH 38:17; 1 JOHN 4:9–10; MICAH 7:18–19;
PSALM 30:2–3; JONAH 2:7; PSALM 40:1–2

[Christ] was to come.

Lord Jesus, You were made a little lower than the angels for the suffering of death so that You, by the grace of God, might taste death for everyone. You died for all. As by one man's disobedience many were made sinners, so also by Your obedience many will be made righteous.

The first man, Adam, became a living being. You Jesus, the last Adam, became a life-giving spirit. The spiritual is not first, but the natural. . . . God said, "Let Us make man in Our image, according to Our likeness." So God created man in His own image; in Your image, God, You created us. God has spoken to us by You, His Son, the brightness of His glory, and the express image of His person. God has given You, Jesus, authority over all flesh.

The first man was of the earth, made of dust; You, the second Man, are the Lord from heaven. As was the man of dust, so also are those who are made of dust; and as You, the heavenly Man, are, so also are those who are heavenly.

Jesus, You came, died, and rose again—
so I could be made new.
Thank You.

ROMANS 5:14; HEBREWS 2:9; 2 CORINTHIANS 5:14;
ROMANS 5:19; 1 CORINTHIANS 15:45–46; GENESIS 1:26–27;
HEBREWS 1:1–3; JOHN 17:2; 1 CORINTHIANS 15:47–48

Serving the Lord with all humility.

J esus, You teach that whoever desires to become great, let him be a servant. And whoever desires to be first, let him be a slave—just as You, the Son of Man, did not come to be served, but to serve, and to give Your life a ransom for many.

If I think myself to be something, when I am nothing, I deceive myself. Through Your grace to me . . . I am not to think of myself more highly than I ought to think, but to think soberly, as God has dealt to me a measure of faith. When I have done all those things which I am commanded, I say, "I am an unprofitable servant. I have done what was my duty. . . ." My boasting is this: I conducted myself in the world in simplicity and godly sincerity, not with fleshly wisdom but by the grace of God. I have this treasure in an earthen vessel, that the excellence of the power may be of God and not of me.

Jesus, help me to live according to Your kingdom values: to serve rather than seeking to be served; to find my value in Your steadfast love rather than in the affirmation of fickle people.

ACTS 20:19; MATTHEW 20:26–28; GALATIANS 6:3; ROMANS 12:3; LUKE 17:10; 2 CORINTHIANS 1:12; 2 CORINTHIANS 4:7

His name will be called Wonderful.

Mighty God, Your Word became flesh and dwelt among people, and we beheld His glory, the glory as of the only begotten of the Father, full of grace and truth. You have magnified Your word above all Your name.

I call His name "Immanuel," . . . "God with us." I call His name "Jesus," for He saves me from my sins.

I honor the Son just as I honor You, Father. You have highly exalted Him and given Him the name which is above every name. Far above all principality and power and might and dominion, and every name that is named, not only in this age but also in that which is to come. And You put all things under His feet. As for You, Almighty God, we cannot find You. . . . What is Your name, and what is Your Son's name? Jesus . . . a name written that no one knew except Himself: KING OF KINGS AND LORD OF LORDS.

Jesus, my wonderful Savior and Friend,
enable me to live this day—and every day—in a way that
honors You as King of kings and Lord of lords!

ISAIAH 9:6; JOHN 1:14; PSALM 138:2; MATTHEW 1:23;
MATTHEW 1:21; JOHN 5:23; PHILIPPIANS 2:9;
EPHESIANS 1:21–22; PROVERBS 30:4; REVELATION 19:12, 16

Every branch in Me that does not bear fruit
He takes away.

Lord God, You are like a refiner's fire and like launderers' soap. You will sit as a refiner and a purifier of silver; Lord, as You will purify the sons of Levi and purge them as gold and silver, that they may offer to You an offering in righteousness, so purify and purge me.

Father, I glory in tribulations, knowing that tribulation produces perseverance; and perseverance, character; and character, hope. Now hope does not disappoint, because Your love has been poured out in my heart by the Holy Spirit who was given to me. If I endure chastening, You deal with me as with a son; for what son is there whom a father does not chasten? But if I am without chastening, of which all have become partakers, then I am illegitimate and not a son. Now no chastening seems to be joyful for the present, but painful; nevertheless, afterward it yields the peaceable fruit of righteousness to those who have been trained by it. Therefore strengthen my hands which hang down, and my feeble knees.

I long to bear fruit for Your kingdom, Lord.
May I therefore let Your refining and chastening
do its good work in me.

JOHN 15:2; MALACHI 3:2–3; ROMANS 5:3–5;
HEBREWS 12:7–8, 11–12

For this is God, our God forever and ever;
He will be our guide even to death.

O Lord, You are my God. I will exalt You, I will praise Your name, for You have done wonderful things; Your counsels of old are faithfulness and truth. You are . . . my inheritance and my cup.

You restore my soul; You lead me in the paths of righteousness for Your name's sake. Yea, though I walk through the valley of the shadow of death, I will fear no evil; for You are with me; Your rod and Your staff, they comfort me. You hold me by my right hand. You will guide me with Your counsel, and afterward receive me to glory. Whom have I in heaven but You? And there is none upon earth that I desire besides You. My flesh and my heart fail; but You, God, are the strength of my heart and my portion forever. My heart shall rejoice in You, because I have trusted in Your holy name. You, Lord, will perfect that which concerns me; Your mercy, O Lord, endures forever; do not forsake the works of Your hands.

God, You are my Guide, Shepherd, Counselor;
the source of joy, mercy, and love.
I praise You forever!

Psalm 48:14; Isaiah 25:1; Psalm 23:3–4;
Psalm 73:23–26; Psalm 33:21; Psalm 138:8

Hope does not disappoint.

Mighty Lord, I shall not be ashamed as I wait for You. Blessed am I who trusts in You, Lord, and whose hope is You. You will keep me in perfect peace, whose mind is stayed on You, because I trust in You. I will trust in You, Lord, forever, for in You is everlasting strength. My soul waits silently for You alone, for my expectation is from You. You only are my rock and my salvation; You are my defense; I shall not be moved. I am not ashamed, for I know whom I have believed.

You, God, determining to show more abundantly the immutability of Your counsel, confirmed it by an oath, that by two immutable things, in which it is impossible for You to lie, I might have strong consolation, who has fled for refuge to lay hold of the hope set before me. This hope I have as an anchor of my soul, both sure and steadfast, and which enters Your Presence behind the veil, where the forerunner has entered for me, even Jesus.

Thank You for Your immutable word
which gives settled peace and assurance to my hope for today and
forever because Jesus has gone before me into Your presence.

ROMANS 5:5; ISAIAH 49:23; JEREMIAH 17:7; ISAIAH 26:3–4;
PSALM 62:5–6; 2 TIMOTHY 1:12; HEBREWS 6:17–20

The Lord is at hand.

Y ou, Lord Jesus, will descend from heaven with a shout, with the voice of an archangel, and with the trumpet of God. And the dead in Christ will rise first. Then we who are alive and remain shall be caught up together with them in the clouds to meet You in the air. And thus I shall always be with You, Lord. You, Jesus, who testify to these things say, "Surely I am coming quickly." Amen. Even so, come, Lord Jesus!

Therefore, beloved by You and looking forward to these things, may I be diligent to be found by You in peace, without spot and blameless. May I abstain from every form of evil. Now may the God of peace Himself sanctify me completely; and may my whole spirit, soul, and body be preserved blameless at Your coming, my Lord Jesus Christ. You who call me are faithful, who also will do it.

May I also be patient and establish my heart, for Your coming, Lord Jesus, is at hand.

Sovereign God, with joyful anticipation
I look forward to the culmination of history as Jesus returns
victorious over sin and death to reign forever. As I wait, help me
become more worthy to reign with Him.

PHILIPPIANS 4:5; 1 THESSALONIANS 4:16–18; REVELATION 22:20;
2 PETER 3:14; 1 THESSALONIANS 5:22–24; JAMES 5:8

*The righteousness of God,
through faith in Jesus Christ, to all
and on all who believe.*

God, You made Jesus who knew no sin to be sin for me, that I might become Your righteousness in Him. Christ has redeemed me from the curse of the law, having become a curse for me. Christ Jesus became for me wisdom from You—and righteousness and sanctification and redemption. Not by works of righteousness which I have done, but according to Your mercy You saved me, through the washing of regeneration and renewing of the Holy Spirit, whom You poured out on me abundantly through Jesus Christ my Savior.

I also count all things loss for the excellence of the knowledge of Christ Jesus my Lord, for whom I have suffered the loss of all things, and count them as rubbish, that I may gain Christ and be found in Him, not having my own righteousness, which is from the law, but that which is through faith in Christ, the righteousness which is from You, Lord God, by faith.

*Thank You, God, that I am righteous in Christ!
May knowing Jesus better be my focus in life.*

———————

ROMANS 3:22; 2 CORINTHIANS 5:21; GALATIANS 3:13;
1 CORINTHIANS 1:30; TITUS 3:5–6; PHILIPPIANS 3:8–9

Therefore let us go forth to Him,
outside the camp, bearing His reproach.
For here we have no continuing city,
but we seek the one to come.

Lord Jesus, may I not think it strange concerning the fiery trial which is to try me, as though some strange thing happened to me; but rejoice to the extent that I partake of Your sufferings, that when Your glory is revealed, I may also be glad with exceeding joy. As I am a partaker of the sufferings, so also I will partake of the consolation.

If I am reproached for Your name, Jesus, blessed am I, for the Spirit of glory and of God rests upon me. On nonbelievers' part You are blasphemed, but on my part may You be glorified.

May I be like Peter who departed from the presence of the council, rejoicing that he was counted worthy to suffer shame for Your name. May I be like Moses, choosing rather to suffer affliction with the people of God than to enjoy the passing pleasures of sin, esteeming the reproach of Christ greater riches than the treasures in Egypt; for he looked to the reward.

If I am ever found worthy to suffer for Your name,
Jesus, may I rejoice!

HEBREWS 13:13–14; I PETER 4:12–13; 2 CORINTHIANS 1:7;
I PETER 4:14; ACTS 5:41; HEBREWS 11:25–26

*You know that He was manifested to take away our sins,
and in Him there is no sin.*

God, in these last days, You have spoken to us by Your Son, who being the brightness of Your glory and the express image of Your person, and upholding all things by the word of His power, when He had by Himself purged our sins, sat down on high at Your right hand, Majesty. You made Him who knew no sin to be sin for me, that I might become Your righteousness in Him.

So may I conduct myself throughout the time of my stay here in fear; knowing that I was not redeemed with corruptible things, like silver or gold . . . but with the precious blood of Christ, as of a lamb without blemish and without spot. He indeed was foreordained before the foundation of the world, but was manifest in these last times for me. The love of Christ constrains me, because I judge thus: that if Christ died for all, then all died; and He died for all, that I who live should live no longer for myself, but for Him who died for me and rose again.

Teach me to live for You, Jesus, and no longer for myself.

---

1 JOHN 3:5; HEBREWS 1:1–3; 2 CORINTHIANS 5:21;
1 PETER 1:17–20; 2 CORINTHIANS 5:14–15

As your days, so shall your strength be.

Father, when they arrest me and deliver me up, I will not worry beforehand, or premeditate what I will speak. But whatever is given me in that hour, I will speak that; for it is not I who speak, but the Holy Spirit. I do not worry about tomorrow, for tomorrow will worry about its own things. Sufficient for the day is its own trouble.

You, the God of Israel, give strength and power to Your people. Blessed be God! You give power to the weak, and to those who have no might You increase strength. Your grace is sufficient for me, for Your strength is made perfect in weakness. Therefore most gladly I will rather boast in my infirmities, that the power of Christ may rest upon me. Therefore I take pleasure in infirmities, in reproaches, in needs, in persecutions, in distresses, for Christ's sake. For when I am weak, then I am strong. I can do all things through Christ who strengthens me. O my soul, march on in strength!

May I know Your strength, Lord, whenever I am weak.

DEUTERONOMY 33:25; MARK 13:11; MATTHEW 6:34;
PSALM 68:35; ISAIAH 40:29; 2 CORINTHIANS 12:9–10;
PHILIPPIANS 4:13; JUDGES 5:21

You-Are-the-God-Who-Sees.

O Lord, You have searched me and known me. You know my sitting down and my rising up; You understand my thought afar off. You comprehend my path and my lying down, and are acquainted with all my ways. For there is not a word on my tongue, but behold, O Lord, You know it altogether. . . . Such knowledge is too wonderful for me; it is high, I cannot attain it.

Your eyes, Lord, are in every place, keeping watch on the evil and the good. The ways of man are before Your eyes, and You ponder all our paths. God, You know my heart. Your eyes, O Lord, run to and fro throughout the whole earth, to show Yourself strong on behalf of those whose heart is loyal to You.

Jesus knew all men, and had no need that anyone should testify of man, for He knew what was in man. Lord, You know all things; You know that I love You.

It's frightening to think how well You know me, Lord.
You see the sins I try to hide—and the sins I'm so comfortable with
that I don't recognize them as sin. Yet You love me!
Teach me to love you better!

———————

GENESIS 16:13; PSALM 139:1–4, 6; PROVERBS 15:3;
PROVERBS 5:21; LUKE 16:15; 2 CHRONICLES 16:9;
JOHN 2:24–25; JOHN 21:17

*Let us run with endurance the race
that is set before us, looking unto Jesus, the author
and finisher of our faith.*

If I desire to come after You, Lord Jesus, let me deny myself, and take up my cross daily, and follow You. Whoever of us does not forsake all that we have cannot be Your disciple. Therefore let me cast off the works of darkness.

Everyone who competes for the prize is temperate in all things. Now they do it to obtain a perishable crown, but I for an imperishable crown. Therefore I run thus: not with uncertainty. Thus I fight: not as one who beats the air. But I discipline my body and bring it into subjection, lest, when I have preached to others, I myself should become disqualified. One thing I do, forgetting those things which are behind and reaching forward to those things which are ahead, I press toward the goal for the prize of the upward call of God in Christ Jesus. Let me know, let me pursue the knowledge of the Lord.

*Lord God, help me keep my eyes on Jesus as I run this race of life.
I want to deny myself and follow You,
relying on Your strength and direction each step of the way.*

HEBREWS 12:1–2; LUKE 9:23; LUKE 14:33; ROMANS 13:12;
1 CORINTHIANS 9:25–27; PHILIPPIANS 3:13–14; HOSEA 6:3

*If you do not drive out the inhabitants
of the land from before you, . . . those whom you let remain
shall be irritants in your eyes and thorns in your sides,
and they shall harass you in the land where you dwell.*

I will fight the good fight of faith. The weapons of my warfare are not carnal but mighty in You, Lord God, for pulling down strongholds, casting down arguments and bringing every thought into captivity to the obedience of Christ.

I am a debtor—not to the flesh, to live according to the flesh. For if I live according to the flesh I will die; but if by Your Spirit I put to death the deeds of the body, I will live.

The flesh lusts against the Spirit, and the Spirit against the flesh; and these are contrary to one another, so that I do not do the things that I wish. I see another law in my members, warring against the law of my mind, and bringing me into captivity to the law of sin that is in my members. I am more than a conqueror through Him who loved me.

*Teach me, Lord, to live in the power of Your Spirit
so that I might fight well the fight of faith.*

NUMBERS 33:55; 1 TIMOTHY 6:12; 2 CORINTHIANS 10:4–5;
ROMANS 8:12–13; GALATIANS 5:17; ROMANS 7:23; ROMANS 8:37

February

Permit it to be so now,

for thus it is fitting for us to

fulfill all righteousness.

I delight to do Your will,

O my God, and Your law is

within my heart.

Whom having not seen you love.

I walk by faith, not by sight. I love You, God, because You first loved me. I have known and believed the love that You have for me. You are love, and I who abide in love abide in You, and You in me. In You I also trusted, after I heard the word of truth, the gospel of my salvation; in whom also, having believed, I was sealed with the Holy Spirit of promise. To me You willed to make known what are the riches of the glory of this mystery among the Gentiles: which is Christ in me, the hope of glory.

If I say, "I love God," and hate my brother, I am a liar; for I who do not love my brother whom I have seen, how can I love God whom I have not seen?

Jesus said, "Thomas, because you have seen Me, you have believed. Blessed are those who have not seen and yet have believed." Blessed am I who put my trust in You, Lord God.

Enable me, Lord, to abide in You more fully . . .
to love my brother more wholeheartedly . . .
and to trust You more completely
so that I may know Your blessings.

1 PETER 1:8; 2 CORINTHIANS 5:7; 1 JOHN 4:19;
1 JOHN 4:16; EPHESIANS 1:13; COLOSSIANS 1:27;
1 JOHN 4:20; JOHN 20:29; PSALM 2:12

Oh, . . . that You would keep me from evil.

J esus, why do I sleep? You call me to rise and pray, lest I enter into temptation. My spirit indeed is willing, but my flesh is weak.

Two things I request of You, God: (please, before I die) remove falsehood and lies far from me; give me neither poverty nor riches—feed me with the food You allotted to me; lest I be full and deny You, and say, "Who is the Lord?" Or lest I be poor and steal, and profane God's name.

You, Lord, shall preserve me from all evil; You shall preserve my soul. You will deliver me from the hand of the wicked, and You will redeem me from the grip of the terrible. I who have been born of God keep myself, and the wicked one does not touch me.

Because I have kept Your command to persevere, You also will keep me from the hour of trial which shall come upon the whole world, to test those who dwell on the earth. You, Lord, know how to deliver the godly out of temptations.

Please help me cooperate with You, Lord,
as You keep me from evil and deliver me
from temptations.

1 CHRONICLES 4:10; LUKE 22:46; MATTHEW 26:41;
PROVERBS 30:7–9; PSALM 121:7; JEREMIAH 15:21; 1 JOHN 5:18;
REVELATION 3:10; 2 PETER 2:9

"Be strong . . . and work; for I am with you,"
says the Lord of hosts.

Jesus, You are the vine, I a branch. I who abide in You, and You in me, bear much fruit; for without You I can do nothing. I can do all things through Christ who strengthens me. I will be strong in You, Lord, and in the power of Your might. Your joy, Lord, is my strength.

You, Lord of Hosts have said: "Let your hands be strong, you who have been hearing in these days these words by the mouth of the prophets." Strengthen my weak hands, and make firm my feeble knees. You say, "Be strong, do not fear!" And, I "go in this might."

If God is for me, who can be against me? Therefore, as I have received mercy, I do not lose heart.

Let me not grow weary while doing good, for in due season I shall reap if I do not lose heart. Thanks be to God, who gives me the victory through You, my Lord Jesus Christ.

As I abide in You, Lord, may I know Your strength, Your joy,
freedom from fear, and energy for serving You.

HAGGAI 2:4; JOHN 15:5; PHILIPPIANS 4:13; EPHESIANS 6:10;
NEHEMIAH 8:10; ZECHARIAH 8:9; ISAIAH 35:3–4;
JUDGES 6:14; ROMANS 8:10; 2 CORINTHIANS 4:1;
GALATIANS 6:9; 1 CORINTHIANS 15:57

The Lord has said to you,
"You shall not return that way again."

Father, truly if I, as Israel, call to mind that country from which I have come out, I would have opportunity to return. But I desire a better . . . a heavenly country. By faith, I rather suffer affliction . . . than enjoy passing pleasures of sin, esteeming the reproach of Christ greater. . . . Justified, I live by faith; but if I draw back, Your soul has no pleasure in me. But I am not of those who draw back to perdition, but of those who believe to the saving of the soul. If I put my hand to the plow, and look back, I am not fit for Your kingdom, God.

Oh, forbid that I should glory except in the cross of my Lord Jesus Christ, by whom the world has been crucified to me, and I to the world. You say, "Come out from among them and be separate." If I do not touch what is unclean, You will receive me."

You who have begun a good work in me will complete it until the day of Jesus Christ.

Continue transforming me, I pray—
to turn from sin, and obey Your commands.

DEUTERONOMY 17:16; HEBREWS 11:15–16, 25–26;
HEBREWS 10:38–39; LUKE 9:62; GALATIANS 6:14;
2 CORINTHIANS 6:17; PHILIPPIANS 1:6

*I have come that they may have life, and that they
may have it more abundantly.*

God, You commanded that when we would eat...
we would die. Eve took...ate and...also gave to
her husband... and he ate. The wages of sin is
death, but Your gift is eternal life in Christ Jesus my Lord.

By one man's offense death reigned through the one, much
more I who receive abundance of grace and of the gift of
righteousness will reign in life through the One, Jesus Christ.
Since by man came death, by Man also came the resurrection of
the dead. For in Adam I die, even so in Christ I shall be made
alive. My Savior Jesus Christ . . . abolished death and brought
life and immortality to light through the gospel.

You have given me eternal life, and this life is in Your Son.
I who have the Son have life; anyone who does not have the
Son does not have life. For You, Father, did not send Your Son into
the world to condemn the world, but that the world through
Jesus might be saved.

*You forgive sins, give abundant life,
and have abolished death! Hallelujah!*

JOHN 10:10; GENESIS 2:16–17; GENESIS 3:6;
ROMANS 6:23; ROMANS 5:17; 1 CORINTHIANS 15:21–22;
2 TIMOTHY 1:10; 1 JOHN 5:11–12; JOHN 3:17

The grace of our Lord was exceedingly abundant,
with faith and love which are in Christ Jesus.

Lord Jesus, I know Your grace that though You were rich, yet for my sake You became poor, that I through Your poverty might become rich. Where sin abounded, grace abounded much more.

In coming ages the Father might show the exceeding riches of His grace in His kindness toward me in You, Jesus. For by grace I have been saved through faith, and that not of myself; it is God's gift, not of works, lest I should boast. Knowing that I am not justified by the works of the law but by faith in You, Jesus, I have believed in You, that I might be justified by faith in You and not by the works of the law; for by the works of the law no flesh shall be justified. According to God's mercy . . . He saved me, through the washing of regeneration and renewing of the Holy Spirit, whom He poured out on me abundantly through You, Jesus Christ my Savior.

Father God, You bless me abundantly
with grace and faith and love! I praise You for Jesus and
the gift of salvation by faith! To You be the glory!

1 TIMOTHY 1:14; 2 CORINTHIANS 8:9; ROMANS 5:20;
EPHESIANS 2:7, 9; GALATIANS 2:16; TITUS 3:5–6

When you have eaten and are full, . . .
you shall bless the Lord your God
for the good land which He has given you.

Lord God, I am aware not to forget You. One of the ten paralytics, a Samaritan, saw that he was healed, returned, and with a loud voice glorified God, and fell down on his face at Jesus' feet, giving Him thanks. Jesus said, "Were there not ten cleansed? But where are the nine? Were there not any found who returned to give glory to God except this foreigner?"

Lord God, every one of Your creatures is good, and nothing is to be refused if it is received with thanksgiving; for it is sanctified by Your word and prayer. I who eat, eat to You, Lord, for I give You thanks. Your blessing, Lord, makes me rich, and You add no sorrow with it.

My soul blesses You, Lord; and with all that is within me, I bless Your holy name! My soul blesses You, Lord, who forgives all my iniquities, who crowns me with lovingkindness and tender mercies.

May I always be prompt with my thanks
and sincere in my gratitude, Lord God.
May all that is within me bless Your holy name!

DEUTERONOMY 8:10–11; LUKE 17:15–18;
1 TIMOTHY 4:4–5; ROMANS 14:6; PROVERBS 10:22;
PSALM 103:1–4

*No longer do I call you servants, for a
servant does not know what his master is doing;
but I have called you friends.*

You, Lord God, said, "Shall I hide from Abraham what I am doing?" It has been given to me to know the mysteries of Your kingdom. You, Lord God, have revealed them to me through Your Spirit. For Your Spirit searches all things, yes, the deep things of God. . . the hidden wisdom which You ordained before the ages for my glory.

I am blessed, for You chose me, and cause me to approach You, that I may dwell in Your courts. I shall be satisfied with the goodness of Your house, Your holy temple. Your secret is with me; I fear You, and You have shown me Your covenant. Jesus has given to me the words which You have given Him. I have received them, and have known surely that He came forth from You. I believe that You sent Jesus.

Father, I am Your friend if I do whatever You command me.

*Friendship with the Almighty and with His Son, Jesus—
Lord, thank You for that privilege and joy! Enable me to honor You
with faithful obedience and steadfast love.*

JOHN 15:15; GENESIS 18:17; MATTHEW 13:11;
1 CORINTHIANS 2:10; 1 CORINTHIANS 2:7; PSALM 65:4;
PSALM 25:14; JOHN 17:8; JOHN 15:14

Now he is comforted.

The sun shall no longer go down, nor shall the moon withdraw itself; for You, mighty Lord, will be my everlasting light, and the days of my mourning shall be ended. You will swallow up death forever, and You, Lord God, will wipe away tears from all faces; the rebuke of Your people You will take away from all the earth. These are the ones who come out of the great tribulation, and washed their robes and made them white in the blood of Jesus the Lamb. Therefore they are before Your throne, Lord God, and serve You day and night in Your temple. You who sit on the throne will dwell among them. They shall neither hunger anymore nor thirst anymore; the sun shall not strike them, nor any heat; for the Lamb in the midst of the throne will shepherd them and lead them to living fountains of waters. And You, Lord God, will wipe away every tear from my eyes; there shall be no more death, nor sorrow, nor crying; and there shall be no more pain, for the former things have passed away.

What a glorious promise and picture of hope!
I thank You, Lord God, for this promise of comfort eternal that
awaits fulfillment when Jesus returns to reign!

LUKE 16:25; ISAIAH 60:20; ISAIAH 25:8;
REVELATION 7:14–17; REVELATION 21:4

The lamp of the body is the eye. Therefore, when your eye is good,
your whole body also is full of light.

My natural self does not receive the things of Your Spirit, God, for they are foolishness to me; nor can I know them, because they are spiritually discerned. Open my eyes, Lord, that I may see wondrous things from Your law.

Jesus is the light of the world. I, following Him shall not walk in darkness, but have the light of life. And with an unveiled face, beholding as in a mirror Your glory, Lord, I am being transformed into the same image by the Spirit of the Lord. It is You, God, who commanded light to shine out of darkness, who has shone in my heart to give the light of the knowledge of Your glory in the face of Jesus Christ.

You, the God of my Lord Jesus Christ and the Father of glory, give me the spirit of wisdom and revelation in the knowledge of You, that I may know the hope of Your calling, the riches of the glory of Your inheritance in the saints.

Open my eyes, Lord God:
I want to see Jesus and Your truth more clearly.

LUKE 11:34; 1 CORINTHIANS 2:14; PSALM 119:18;
JOHN 8:12; 2 CORINTHIANS 3:18;
2 CORINTHIANS 4:6; EPHESIANS 1:17–18

Then those who feared the Lord spoke to one another,
and the Lord listened and heard them; so a book of remembrance
was written before Him for those who fear the Lord
and who meditate on His name.

So it was, while the two believers conversed and reasoned, that You, Lord Jesus, drew near and went with them. Where two or three are gathered together in Your name, You are there in the midst of us. . . Your fellow workers, whose names are in the Book of Life.

May Your word, Christ Jesus, dwell in me richly in all wisdom, teaching and admonishing others in psalms and hymns and spiritual songs, singing with grace in my heart to the Lord. May we believers exhort one another daily, while it is called "Today," lest any of us be hardened through the deceitfulness of sin.

Every idle word I may speak, I will give account of it in the day of judgment. For by my words I will be justified, and by my words I will be condemned. Behold, it is written before You. . . You will repay.

Make me sensitive to Your presence with me today,
Lord Jesus, that I may honor You
with my actions, my words, my thoughts.

MALACHI 3:16; LUKE 24:15; MATTHEW 18:20;
PHILIPPIANS 4:3; COLOSSIANS 3:16; HEBREWS 3:13;
MATTHEW 12:36–37; ISAIAH 65:6

"They shall be Mine," says the Lord of hosts,
"on the day that I make them My jewels."

Jesus, You have manifested God's name to all whom He has given You out of the world. We were His, He gave us to You, and we have kept His word. You pray for us . . . not for the world but for us whom God has given You. All Yours are God's, all God's are Yours; to glorify You. You desire that we also whom God gave You may be with You where You are, that we may behold Your glory which God has given You; for He loved You before the foundation of the world.

You will come again and receive me to Yourself. You come, in that Day, to be glorified in Your saints and admired among all of us who believe. Then those of us who are alive and remain shall be caught up in the clouds to meet You in the air. And thus we shall always be with You, Lord. I shall also be a crown of glory and a royal diadem in Your hand, my God.

I am Yours—and always will be!
What amazing love and hope and joy!
Thank You for choosing me and loving me.

MALACHI 3:17; JOHN 17:6, 9–10, 24; JOHN 14:3;
2 THESSALONIANS 1:10; 1 THESSALONIANS 4:17; ISAIAH 62:3

On the likeness of the throne was a likeness with the appearance of a man high above it.

Christ Jesus, You came in my likeness. You were, in appearance, as man. Inasmuch then as the children have partaken of flesh and blood, You Yourself likewise shared in the same, that through death You might destroy him who had the power of death.

You are He who lives, and was dead, and You are alive forevermore. You, having been raised from the dead, die no more. Death no longer has dominion over You. For the death that You died, You died to sin once for all; but the life that You live, You live to God. . . . Should I see You ascend to where You were before? God raised You from the dead and seated You at His right hand in the heavenly places. In You dwells all the fullness of the Godhead bodily.

Though You were crucified in weakness, yet You live by the power of God. I shall live with You, Jesus, by the power of God.

Risen and ascended Jesus, Victor over death,
You are King of kings and Lord of Lords!
I stand in awe of You!.

EZEKIEL 1:26; 1 TIMOTHY 2:5; PHILIPPIANS 2:7–8;
HEBREWS 2:14; REVELATION 1:18; ROMANS 6:9–10; JOHN 6:62;
EPHESIANS 1:20; COLOSSIANS 2:9; 2 CORINTHIANS 13:4

Permit it to be so now, for thus
it is fitting for us to fulfill all righteousness. . . .
I delight to do Your will, O my God,
and Your law is within my heart.

Jesus did not come to destroy the Law or the Prophets. He did not come to destroy but to fulfill. For assuredly, Jesus said, till heaven and earth pass away, one jot or one tittle will by no means pass from the law till all is fulfilled. You, Lord, are well pleased for Your righteousness' sake; You exalt the law and make it honorable. Unless my righteousness exceeds the righteousness of the scribes and Pharisees, I will by no means enter the kingdom of heaven.

What the law could not do in that it was weak through the flesh, You, Lord God, did by sending Your own Son in the likeness of sinful flesh, on account of my sin: Jesus condemned sin in the flesh, that the righteous requirement of the law might be fulfilled in us who do not walk according to the flesh but according to the Spirit. Christ is the end of the law for righteousness to everyone who believes.

Lord Jesus, thank You for coming
to fulfill the Law so that
Your righteousness might be mine.

MATTHEW 3:15; PSALM 40:8; MATTHEW 5:17–18;
ISAIAH 42:21; MATTHEW 5:20; ROMANS 8:3–4; ROMANS 10:4

Who can say, "I have made my heart clean"?

You, Lord, look down from heaven upon us children of men, to see if any understand, any seek You. We have all turned aside, we have together become corrupt . . . none does good, no, not one. We in the flesh cannot please You, God.

To will is present with me, but how to perform what is good I do not find. For the good that I will to do, I do not do; but the evil I will not to do, that I practice. I am like an unclean thing, and all my righteousnesses are like filthy rags; I fade as a leaf, and my iniquities, like the wind, have taken me away.

Your Scripture confined all under sin that Your faith promise in Jesus might be given to me. God, in Christ, You reconciled the world to Yourself, not imputing our trespasses. . . .

If I say that I have no sin, I deceive myself, and the truth is not in me. If I confess my sins, You are faithful and just to forgive me my sins and to cleanse me from all unrighteousness.

Thank You, Lord God, for cleansing
all my unrighteousness through Christ Jesus.

PROVERBS 20:9; PSALM 14:2–3; ROMANS 8:8;
ROMANS 7:18–19; ISAIAH 64:6;
GALATIANS 3:22; 2 CORINTHIANS 5:19; 1 JOHN 1:8–9

Your name is ointment poured forth.

Jesus Christ, You loved me and gave Yourself for me, an offering and a sacrifice to God for a sweet-smelling aroma. Therefore, to me who believes, You are precious. God also has highly exalted You and given You the name which is above every name, that at Your name, Jesus, every knee should bow. In You dwells all the fullness of the Godhead bodily.

If I love You, I will keep Your commandments. The love of God has been poured out in my heart by the Holy Spirit who was given to me. The house was filled with the fragrance of the oil. They realized that they had been with Jesus.

O Lord, my Lord, how excellent is Your name in all the earth, You who set Your glory above the heavens! Immanuel . . . God with us. Your name will be called Wonderful, Counselor, Mighty God, Everlasting Father, Prince of Peace. Your name, Lord, is a strong tower; we who are righteous run to it and are safe.

I praise Your name, Lord Jesus, and bow before You, marveling at Your love and grace!

SONG OF SOLOMON 1:3; EPHESIANS 5:2; 1 PETER 2:7;
PHILIPPIANS 2:9–10; COLOSSIANS 2:9; JOHN 14:15;
ROMANS 5:5; JOHN 12:3; ACTS 4:13; PSALM 8:1;
MATTHEW 1:23; ISAIAH 9:6; PROVERBS 18:10

*The whole bull he shall carry outside the camp
to a clean place, where the ashes are poured out,
and burn it on wood with fire.*

They took You, Jesus, and led You away. And You, bearing Your cross, went out to a place called the Place of a Skull, which is called in Hebrew, Golgotha, where they crucified You. The bodies of those animals, whose blood is brought into the sanctuary by the high priest for sin, are burned outside the camp. Therefore You also, that You might sanctify the people with Your own blood, suffered outside the gate. Therefore let me go forth to You, outside the gate, bearing Your reproach, the fellowship of Your sufferings.

I rejoice to the extent that I partake of Your sufferings, Jesus, that when Your glory is revealed, I may also be glad with exceeding joy. My light affliction, which is but for a moment, is working for me a far more exceeding and eternal weight of glory.

*Your death was brutal; Your suffering, excruciating;
Your love, immeasurable. May I willingly suffer
on Your behalf, my King and my Lord—
and then may I joyfully celebrate Your future glory.*

LEVITICUS 4:12; JOHN 19:16, 18; HEBREWS 13:11–13;
PHILIPPIANS 3:8–10; 1 PETER 4:13; 2 CORINTHIANS 4:17

You are my hope in the day of doom.

Loving Father, there are many who say, "Who will show us any good?" Lord, lift up the light of Your countenance upon us. I will sing of Your power; yes, I will sing aloud of Your mercy in the morning; for You have been my defense and refuge in the day of my trouble.

You hid Your face, and I was troubled. I cried out to You, O Lord; and to You, Lord, I made supplication: "What profit is there in my blood, when I go down to the pit? Will the dust praise You? Will it declare Your truth? Hear, O Lord, and have mercy on me; Lord, be my helper!"

You say, Lord God and my Redeemer, that for a mere moment You have forsaken me, but with great mercies You will gather me. With a little wrath You hid Your face from me for a moment; but with everlasting kindness You will have mercy on me. Sorrow will be turned into joy. Weeping may endure for a night, but joy comes in the morning.

What hope I have in You, my Redeemer—
in You who brings joy after sorrow, who offers mercy after wrath,
who serves as my Refuge in trouble.

JEREMIAH 17:17; PSALM 4:6; PSALM 59:16;
PSALM 30:6, 8–10; ISAIAH 54:7–8;
JOHN 16:20; PSALM 30:5

*The Lord gives wisdom; from His mouth
come knowledge and understanding.*

Enable me, Lord, to trust in You with all my heart, and lean not on my own understanding. If I lack wisdom, let me ask of You, God, who give to all liberally and without reproach, and it will be given to me. The foolishness of God is wiser than men, and the weakness of God is stronger than men. You, God, have chosen the foolish things of the world to put to shame the wise. That no flesh should glory in Your presence.

The entrance of Your words gives light; it gives understanding to the simple. Your word I have hidden in my heart, that I might not sin against You.

All bore witness to Jesus, Your Son, and marveled at the gracious words which proceeded out of His mouth. No man ever spoke like this Man! Because of You, Lord God, I am in Christ Jesus, who became for me Your wisdom—and righteousness and sanctification and redemption.

*May I always look to You, Lord God,
for wisdom and understanding,
that I might live in a way that
pleases and glorifies You.*

PROVERBS 2:6; PROVERBS 3:5; JAMES 1:5; 1 CORINTHIANS 1:25;
1 CORINTHIANS 1:27, 29; PSALM 119:130; PSALM 119:11;
LUKE 4:22; JOHN 7:46; 1 CORINTHIANS 1:30

He shall see the labor of His soul, and be satisfied.

Jesus said, "It is finished!" Bowing His head, He gave up His spirit. Father God, You made Jesus who knew no sin to be sin for me, that I might become righteous in Him.

This people You have formed for Yourself; we shall declare Your praise. Now Your manifold wisdom might be made known by the church to the principalities and powers in the heavenly places, according to the eternal purpose which You accomplished in Him, Christ Jesus my Lord. In the ages to come You might show the exceeding riches of Your grace in Your kindness toward me in Christ Jesus.

Having believed, I was sealed with the Holy Spirit of promise, who is the guarantee of my inheritance, to the praise of His glory. I am part of a chosen generation, a royal priesthood, a holy nation, Your own special people, that I may proclaim the praises of You who called me out of darkness into Your marvelous light.

When Jesus' work on the cross was finished,
my life eternal with You, my heavenly Father, began.
Thank You for sending Jesus to die and make this relationship
possible. May my life proclaim Your praises.

ISAIAH 53:11; JOHN 19:30; 2 CORINTHIANS 5:21;
ISAIAH 43:21; EPHESIANS 3:10–11; EPHESIANS 2:7;
EPHESIANS 1:13–14; 1 PETER 2:9

I am the Lord who sanctifies you.

You are the Lord my God, who has separated me from the peoples. I shall be holy to You, for You, Lord, are holy, and have separated me from the peoples, that I should be Yours.

I am sanctified by You, Father God . . . sanctified by Your truth. Your word is truth. May You, the God of peace, sanctify me completely; and may my whole spirit, soul, and body be preserved blameless at the coming of my Lord Jesus Christ.

So that He might sanctify me with His own blood, Jesus suffered outside the gate. My Savior Jesus Christ gave Himself for me, that He might redeem me from every lawless deed and purify for Himself His own special people, zealous for good works. Both Jesus who sanctifies and those of us who are being sanctified are all of one . . . He is not ashamed to call us brethren. For my sake Jesus sanctified Himself, that I also may be sanctified by the truth . . . in sanctification of the Spirit for obedience.

Lord Jesus, help me to obey Your true Word and to be zealous that good works demonstrate my sanctification.

LEVITICUS 20:8; LEVITICUS 20:24, 26; JUDE 1; JOHN 17:17; 1 THESSALONIANS 5:23; HEBREWS 13:12; TITUS 2:13–14; HEBREWS 2:11; JOHN 17:19: 1 PETER 1:2

*Who is the man that fears the Lord? Him shall He teach
in the way He chooses.*

Your word, Lord God, calls my eye the lamp of my body
. . . if it is good, my whole body is full of light.
Your word is a lamp to my feet and a light to my path.
My ears hear a word behind me, saying, "This is the way, walk in
it," whenever I turn to the right hand or whenever I turn to the
left. You will instruct me and teach me in the way I should go;
You will guide me with Your eye. Not like the horse or the mule,
have no understanding, and must be harnessed with bit and
bridle, else they will not come near me. Many sorrows shall be to
the wicked; but I trust in You, Lord; Your mercy surrounds me.
I will be glad in You, Lord, and rejoice; I shout for joy, I who am
upright in heart!

O Lord, I know the way of man is not in himself; it is not
in me who walks to direct my own steps.

*I want to follow Your path in this life, Lord.
Keep me following Your leading and obeying to Your instructions,
constantly aware of Your loving mercy.*

PSALM 25:12; MATTHEW 6:22; PSALM 119:105;
ISAIAH 30:21; PSALM 32:8–11; JEREMIAH 10:23

*The blood of sprinkling that speaks better things
than that of Abel.*

Lord Jesus, You are the Lamb of God who takes away the sin of the world—my sin! You are the Lamb slain from the foundation of the world. For it is not possible that the blood of bulls and goats could take away my sins. Therefore, when You came into the world, You said: "Sacrifice and offering God did not desire, but a body He has prepared for Me." By that will I have been sanctified through the offering of Your body, Jesus, once for all. Abel brought of the firstborn of his flock and of their fat. And the Lord respected Abel and his offering. Christ, You have loved me and given Yourself for me, an offering and a sacrifice to God for a sweet-smelling aroma.

Let me draw near with a true heart in full assurance of faith, having my heart sprinkled from an evil conscience and my body washed with pure water. May I have boldness to enter the Holiest by Your blood, Lord Jesus.

*Cleansed by Your blood, Jesus—
offered once for all—I give myself to You.
Draw me closer to You in faith's full assurance.*

HEBREWS 12:24; JOHN 1:29; REVELATION 13:8;
HEBREWS 10:4–5, 10; GENESIS 4:4; EPHESIANS 5:2;
HEBREWS 10:22; HEBREWS 10:19

Thus says the Lord God: "I will also let the house of Israel inquire of Me to do this for them."

Lord, You said I do not have because I do not ask and "Ask, and it will be given to you; seek, and you will find; knock, and it will be opened to you. For everyone who asks receives, and he who seeks finds, and to him who knocks it will be opened." I have this confidence in You, that if I ask anything according to Your will, You hear me. If I lack wisdom, I will ask You, who gives to all liberally and without reproach, and it will be given to me. If I open my mouth You promise to fill it, so I ought always to pray and not lose heart.

Your eyes, Lord, are on the righteous, and Your ears are open to my cry. You hear, and deliver me out of all my troubles. I will ask in Your name . . . for the Father Himself loves me, because I have loved You, Jesus. I will ask in Your name, and I will receive, that my joy may be full.

Teach me, Father God, to ask according to Your will— with boldness and confidence.

EZEKIEL 36:37; JAMES 4:2; MATTHEW 7:7–8;
1 JOHN 5:14–15; JAMES 1:5;
LUKE 18:1; PSALM 34:15, 17; JOHN 16:26, 24

Resist the devil and he will flee from you.

When the enemy comes in like a flood, Your Spirit, Lord, lifts up a standard against him. "Away with you, Satan! For it is written, 'You shall worship the Lord your God, and Him only you shall serve.'" The devil left Jesus, and angels came and ministered to Him.

Enable me to be strong in You, Lord, and in the power of Your might. I put on the whole armor of God . . . to stand against the wiles of the devil. I will have no fellowship with the unfruitful works of darkness, but rather expose them. Lest Satan should take advantage of me; for I am not ignorant of his devices. I will be sober and vigilant; because my adversary the devil walks about like a roaring lion, seeking whom he may devour. I resist him, steadfast in the faith, knowing that the same sufferings are experienced by my brotherhood in the world. This is the victory that has overcome the world—my faith.

Who shall bring a charge against me? God is my justifier!

Remind me that, in You, Lord God, I am stronger than Satan. Thank You for my protection and his defeat.

JAMES 4:7; ISAIAH 59:19; MATTHEW 4:10–11;
EPHESIANS 6:10–11; EPHESIANS 5:11; 2 CORINTHIANS 2:11;
1 PETER 5:8–9; 1 JOHN 5:4; ROMANS 8:33

Let us search out and examine our ways,
and turn back to the Lord.

Examine me, O Lord, and prove me; try my mind and
heart. You desire truth in my inward parts, and in my
hidden part You will make me know wisdom. I thought
about my ways, and turned my feet to Your testimonies. I made
haste, and did not delay to keep Your commandments. I will
examine myself, and so let me eat of the bread and drink of
the cup.

If I confess my sins, You are faithful and just to forgive my
sins and to cleanse me from all unrighteousness. I have an
Advocate with You, Father, Jesus Christ the righteous. He Himself
is the propitiation for my sins. Therefore I have boldness to enter
the Holiest by the blood of Jesus, by a new and living way which
He consecrated for me, through the veil, that is, His flesh, and
having a High Priest over Your house, Father God, let me draw
near with a true heart in full assurance of faith, having my heart
sprinkled from an evil conscience and my body washed with
pure water.

Father God, please help me to like sin less—
and to love You more.

LAMENTATIONS 3:40; PSALM 26:2; PSALM 51:6;
PSALM 119:59–60; 1 CORINTHIANS 11:28; 1 JOHN 1:9;
1 JOHN 2:1–2; HEBREWS 10:19–22

Reckon yourselves to be dead indeed to sin,
but alive to God in Christ Jesus our Lord.

I hear Your word, Lord Jesus, and believe in God who sent You; I have everlasting life, and shall not come into judgment. . . . I have passed from death into life. . . . dead to the law . . . I live to God. I am crucified with Christ; I no longer live, but Christ lives in me; and the life which I now live in the flesh I live by faith in the Son of God, who loved me and gave Himself for me.

Because You live, Jesus, I will live also. You give me eternal life; I shall never perish; neither shall anyone snatch me out of Your hand. God, who has given me to You, is greater than all; and no one is able to snatch me out of His hand. You and Father are one.

If then I was raised with You, Lord Jesus, I seek those things which are above, where You are, sitting at the right hand of God. . . . For I died, and my life is hidden with You in God.

Lord Jesus, I live now by faith in Your loving sacrifice.
Help me to seek eternal things, alone.

ROMANS 6:11; JOHN 5:24; GALATIANS 2:19–20;
JOHN 14:19; JOHN 10:28–30; COLOSSIANS 3:1–3

*For God so loved the world
that He gave His only begotten Son,
that whoever believes in Him should not perish
but have everlasting life.*

God, You reconciled me to Yourself through Jesus Christ, and have given me the ministry of reconciliation, that is, that You were in Christ reconciling the world to Yourself, not imputing my trespasses to me, and have committed to me the word of reconciliation. Now then, I am an ambassador for Christ, as though You were pleading through me: "I implore you on Christ's behalf, be reconciled to God. For God made Jesus who knew no sin to be sin for us, that we might become the righteousness of God in Him." God, You are love. In this Your love was manifested toward me, that You have sent Your only begotten Son into the world, that I might live through Him. In this is love, not that I loved You, but that You loved me and sent Your Son to be the propitiation for my sins. If God so loved me, I also ought to love others.

*Lord God, help me to love others with your love—
and then speak through me to them
about Your loving plan of reconciliation.*

JOHN 3:16; 2 CORINTHIANS 5:18–21; 1 JOHN 4:8–11

*Do not boast about tomorrow, for you do not know
what a day may bring forth.*

Father, now is the accepted time. . . the time of salvation.
Jesus taught: "A little while longer the light is with you.
Walk while you have the light, lest darkness overtake you;
he who walks in darkness does not know where he is going.
While you have the light, believe in the light, that you may
become sons of light."

Whatever my hand finds to do, may I do it with my
might; for there is no work or device or knowledge or wisdom
in the grave.

"You have many goods. Take your ease; eat, drink, and be
merry," said the foolish man. That night his soul was required of
him; whose will his things be? If I lay up treasure for myself, and
am not rich toward God, I am foolish.

What is my life? It is a vapor that appears for a little time
and then vanishes away. The world is passing away and its lust;
but I who do the will of God abide forever.

*Lord, Your eternal perspective reminds me of life's brevity.
Help me to walk in Your light
and to serve You wisely, with all my might.*

PROVERBS 27:1; 2 CORINTHIANS 6:2;
JOHN 12:35–36; ECCLESIASTES 9:10; LUKE 12:19–21;
JAMES 4:14; 1 JOHN 2:17

March

The Lord make His face

shine upon you,

and be gracious to you;

the Lord lift up

His countenance upon you,

and give you peace.

The fruit of the Spirit is love.

Lord God, You are love, and I who abide in love abide in You, and You in me. Your love has been poured out in my heart by Your Holy Spirit who was given to me. To me who believes, Jesus is precious. I love You because You first loved me. The love of Christ constrains me, because I judge thus: that if One died for me, then I died; and He died for me, that I who live should live no longer for myself, but for Him who died for me and rose again.

I myself am taught by You, Lord God, to love others and Jesus commands me to love others as You have loved me. Above all things I am to have fervent love for others, for love will cover a multitude of sins. May I walk in love, as Christ also has loved me and given Himself for me, an offering and a sacrifice to You, Lord God, for a sweet-smelling aroma.

Lord God, enable me to love people the way You love—
selflessly, sacrificially, and even when I'm not loved in return.

GALATIANS 5:22; 1 JOHN 4:16; ROMANS 5:5; 1 PETER 2:7;
1 JOHN 4:19; 2 CORINTHIANS 5:14–15; 1 THESSALONIANS 4:9;
JOHN 15:12; 1 PETER 4:8; EPHESIANS 5:2

God has caused me to be fruitful
in the land of my affliction.

Blessed be Your name, Almighty God and Father of my Lord Jesus Christ, the Father of mercies and God of all comfort, You who comforts me in all my tribulation, that I may be able to comfort those who are in any trouble, with the comfort with which I myself am comforted by You. For as the sufferings of Christ abound in me, so my consolation also abounds through Christ.

Now for a little while, if need be, I have been grieved by various trials, that the genuineness of my faith, being much more precious than gold that perishes, though it is tested by fire, may be found to praise, honor, and glory at the revelation of Jesus Christ. You, Lord, stood with me and strengthened me.

When I suffer according to Your will, Father God, I commit my soul to You in doing good, as to my faithful Creator.

In Your economy, God,
You use hard times for our good and the good of others.
I believe; help my unbelief.

GENESIS 41:52; 2 CORINTHIANS 1:3–5; 1 PETER 1:6–7;
2 TIMOTHY 4:17; 1 PETER 4:19

*Trust in the Lord with all your heart, and lean not
on your own understanding; in all your ways acknowledge Him,
and He shall direct your paths.*

I trust in You at all times; I pour out my heart before You;
You, Lord God, are a refuge for me.

You will instruct me and teach me in the way I should
go; You will guide me with Your eye. I will not be like the horse
or like the mule, which have no understanding, which must be
harnessed with bit and bridle. . . . Many sorrows will be to the
wicked; but as I trust in You, Lord, mercy shall surround me.
My ears shall hear a word behind me, saying, "This is the way,
walk in it," whenever I turn to the right hand or to the left.

If Your Presence does not go with me, do not bring me up
from here. For how then will it be known that Your people and
I have found grace in Your sight, except You go with us? So Your
people and I, shall be separate from all the people who are upon
the face of the earth.

*Thank You, Father God, that You not only direct my path,
but that You go with me. May I listen for Your voice.*

PROVERBS 3:5–6; PSALM 62:8; PSALM 32:8–10;
ISAIAH 30:21; EXODUS 33:15–16

Set your mind on things above,
not on things on the earth.

Father, I chose to not love the world or the things in the world because if I love the world, Your love is not in me. I will not lay up for myself treasures on earth, where moth and rust destroy and where thieves break in and steal; but lay up my treasures in heaven, where neither moth nor rust destroys and thieves do not break in and steal. For where my treasure is, so is my heart also.

I walk by faith, not by sight. I do not lose heart. Even though my outward man is perishing, yet my inward man is being renewed day by day. For my light affliction, which is but for a moment, is working for me a far more exceeding, eternal weight of glory, while I do not look at the things which are seen, but at the things which are not seen. For the things which are seen are temporary, but the things which are not seen are eternal. An inheritance incorruptible and undefiled and that does not fade away is reserved in heaven for me.

Increase my faith to focus my sights on Your love
and my investments in eternal treasure.

COLOSSIANS 3:2; 1 JOHN 2:15; MATTHEW 6:19–21;
2 CORINTHIANS 5:7; 2 CORINTHIANS 4:16–18; 1 PETER 1:4

O Lord, I am oppressed; undertake for me!

Unto You I lift up my eyes, O Lord who dwells in the heavens. For as the eyes of servants look to the hand of their masters, as the eyes of a maid to the hand of her mistress, so my eyes look to You, my Lord God. Hear my cry, O God; attend to my prayer. From the end of the earth I will cry to You, when my heart is overwhelmed; lead me to the rock that is higher than I. For You have been a shelter for me, and a strong tower from the enemy. I will abide in Your tabernacle forever: I will trust in the shelter of Your wings. You have been a strength to the poor, a strength to the needy in his distress, a refuge from the storm.

Christ suffered for me, leaving me an example, that I should follow His steps: who committed no sin, nor was deceit found in His mouth; who, when He was reviled, did not revile in return; when He suffered, He did not threaten, but committed Himself to Him who judges righteously.

May I follow Jesus' example, Lord God,
and trust myself to Your care—
whatever the circumstances of life.

ISAIAH 38:14; PSALM 123:1–2; PSALM 61:1–4; ISAIAH 25:4;
1 PETER 2:21–23

He . . . preserves the way of His saints.

You, Lord God, go before me to search out a place for me to pitch my tents, to show me the way I should go, in the fire by night and in the cloud by day. As an eagle stirs up its nest, hovers over its young, spreading out its wings, taking them up, carrying them on its wings, so You, Lord, alone lead me. My steps are ordered by You, Lord, and You delight in my way. Though I fall, I shall not be utterly cast down; for You uphold me with Your hand. Many are the afflictions of the righteous, but You, Lord, deliver me out of them all. For You know the way of the righteous, but the way of the ungodly shall perish. I know that all things work together for good to those who love You, to those who are the called according to Your purpose. So, You are with me, Lord God, to help me and to fight my battles.

You, Lord God . . . my Mighty One, will save; You will rejoice over me with gladness.

May I follow Your lead today,
trusting You're working my life's circumstances for good.

PROVERBS 2:8; DEUTERONOMY 1:32–33;
DEUTERONOMY 32:11–12; PSALM 37:23–24; PSALM 34:19;
PSALM 1:6; ROMANS 8:28;
2 CHRONICLES 32:8; EPHESIANS 3:17

Your Maker is your husband,
the Lord of hosts is His name.

Lord, this is a great mystery . . . concerning Christ and the church.

I shall no longer be termed Forsaken . . . but I shall be called Hephzibah [My Delight in Her], for You, Lord, delight in me. As the bridegroom rejoices over the bride, so shall you, my God, rejoice over me. You have sent Jesus to comfort me in mourning, to console those who mourn in Zion, to give us beauty for ashes, the oil of joy for mourning, the garment of praise for the spirit of heaviness.

I will greatly rejoice in You, Lord, my soul shall be joyful in You, my God; for You have clothed me with the garments of salvation . . . as a bridegroom decks himself with ornaments, and as a bride adorns herself with her jewels.

Lord, You will betroth me to You forever; yes, You will betroth me to You in righteousness and justice, in lovingkindness and mercy.

Who shall separate me from the love of Christ?

You are a holy God who delights in His sinful but
forgiven people! What amazing love from a compassionate,
faithful, righteous, loving, and merciful God!

ISAIAH 54:5; EPHESIANS 5:32; ISAIAH 62:4–5; ISAIAH 61:1–3;
ISAIAH 61:10; HOSEA 2:19; ROMANS 8:35

You have cast all my sins behind Your back.

Father, who is a God like You, pardoning iniquity and passing over the transgression of the remnant of Your heritage? You do not retain Your anger forever, because You delight in mercy. You will again have compassion on me, and will subdue my iniquities. You will cast all my sins into the depths of the sea.

For a mere moment You have forsaken me, but with great mercies You will gather me. With a little wrath You hid Your face from me for a moment; but with everlasting kindness You will have mercy on me, You say, my Lord, my Redeemer. You will forgive my iniquity, and my sin You will remember no more.

Father, I am blessed! My transgression is forgiven, my sin is covered. I am blessed! You, Lord, do not impute my iniquity, and in my spirit there is no deceit. The blood of Jesus Christ His Son cleanses me from all sin.

I am totally unworthy of Your grace and forgiveness, Lord. May I never be numb to the marvelous truth that Your Son's death cleanses me from all my sin.

ISAIAH 38:17; MICAH 7:18–19; ISAIAH 54:7–8; JEREMIAH 31:34; PSALM 32:1–2; 1 JOHN 1:7

The living God, who gives us richly all things to enjoy.

Living God, I must beware not to forget You, Lord my God, by not keeping Your commandments, Your judgments, and Your statutes which You command me today, lest—when I have eaten and am full, and have built a beautiful house and dwell in it . . . when my heart is lifted up, and I forget the Lord my God. . . . For it is You who gives me power to get wealth.

Unless You, Lord, build the house, I labor in vain to build it; unless You, Lord, guard the city, the watchman stays awake in vain. It is vain for me to rise up early, to sit up late, to eat the bread of sorrows; for You give me sleep. I did not gain possession of the land by my own sword, nor did my own arm save me; but it was Your right hand, Your arm, and the light of Your countenance, because You favored me. Many say, "Who will show us any good?" You, Lord, lift up the light of Your countenance upon me.

In obedience, and with thanksgiving
for all that I have, Lord, I remember that it is
all given by Your loving favor.

---

1 TIMOTHY 6:17; DEUTERONOMY 8:11–12, 14, 18;
PSALM 127:1–2; PSALM 44:3; PSALM 4:6

The Lord-Will-Provide.

Mighty God, You have provided for Yourself the lamb.... Certainly then, Lord God, Your hand is not shortened, that it cannot save; nor Your ear heavy, that it cannot hear. My Deliverer comes out of Zion, and He will turn away ungodliness from Jacob.

Happy am I who have the God of Jacob for my help, whose hope is in You, the Lord my God. Your eye, O Lord my God, is on me; I fear You, on me: I hope in Your mercy, to deliver my soul from death.

You, my God, shall supply all my need according to Your riches in glory by Christ Jesus. You Yourself have said, "I will never leave you nor forsake you." So I may boldly say: "The Lord is my helper; I will not fear. What can man do to me?" You, Lord, are my strength and my shield; my heart trusts in You, and I am helped; therefore my heart greatly rejoices, and with my song I will praise You.

Lord, You provided a lamb for Abraham and the Lamb for me!
And You provide for me in countless ways from day to day.
Great is Your faithfulness! I praise You and thank You!

GENESIS 22:14; GENESIS 22:8; ISAIAH 59:1; ROMANS 11:26;
PSALM 146:5; PSALM 33:18–19; PHILIPPIANS 4:19;
HEBREWS 13:5–6; PSALM 28:7

The Lord bless you and keep you.

Your blessing, Lord God, makes me rich, and You add no sorrow with it. You, O Lord, will bless the righteous; with favor You will surround me as with a shield.

You will not allow my foot to be moved; You who keeps me will not slumber. Behold, You who keeps Israel shall neither slumber nor sleep. You, Lord, are my keeper; You, Lord, are my shade at my right hand. You, Lord, shall preserve me from all evil; You shall preserve my soul. You, Lord, shall preserve my going out and my coming in from this time forth, and even forevermore. You, Lord, keep me . . . lest any hurt me, You keep me night and day.

Holy Father, keep through Your name all those whom You have given to Jesus. While He was with us in the world, He kept us in Your name. Those You gave to Him He has kept.

You, Lord, will deliver me from every evil work and preserve me for Your heavenly kingdom. To You be glory forever and ever. Amen!

Thank You, Almighty Lord and heavenly Father,
for keeping me close to You—for keeping me safe, protected,
and preserved for Your eternal kingdom.

NUMBERS 6:24; PROVERBS 10:22; PSALM 5:12;
PSALM 121:3–5, 7–8; ISAIAH 27:3;
JOHN 17:11–12; 2 TIMOTHY 4:18

The Lord make His face shine upon you,
and be gracious to you;
the Lord lift up His countenance upon you,
and give you peace.

None has seen You at any time, Lord God. Your only begotten Son, Jesus, who is with You now, has declared You. And He is the brightness of Your glory and the express image of Your person. The god of this age has blinded the minds of those who do not believe, lest the light of the gospel of the glory of Christ, Your image, God, should shine on them.

Make Your face shine upon Your servant; save me for Your mercies' sake. Do not let me be ashamed, O Lord, for I have called upon You, who, by Your favor You have made my mountain stand strong; You hid Your face, and I was troubled. I am blessed! I know the joyful sound! I walk, my Lord, in the light of Your countenance.

You, Lord, will give strength to Your people; You, Lord, will bless me with peace.

So I am of good cheer! It is You; I will not be afraid.

Gracious God, thank You for revealing Yourself to me through Jesus,
saving me, and blessing me with strength and peace!

NUMBERS 6:25–26; JOHN 1:18; HEBREWS 1:3;
2 CORINTHIANS 4:4; PSALM 31:16–17; PSALM 30:7;
PSALM 89:15; PSALM 29:11; MATTHEW 14:27

There is one God and one Mediator between God and men,
the Man Christ Jesus.

Since I am flesh and blood, You Yourself, Lord Jesus,
likewise shared flesh and blood.

You said, "Look to Me and be saved all you ends of
the earth!" For You are God, and there is no other. I look to You!
I am saved!

I have an Advocate with the Father: You, Jesus Christ the
righteous. In You, Christ Jesus, I who once was far off have been
brought near by Your blood. For You Yourself are my peace.
With Your own blood You entered the Most Holy Place once for
all, having obtained eternal redemption. And for this reason You
are the Mediator of the new covenant, by means of death, for the
redemption of the transgressions under the first covenant, that
those like me who are called may receive the promise of the
eternal inheritance. You are also able to save to the uttermost
those like me who come to God through You, since You ever live
to make intercession for us.

The Incarnation, the Resurrection, my salvation—
Lord God, what an amazing plan.
Lord Jesus, what an act of incredible love!

---

1 TIMOTHY 2:5; HEBREWS 2:14; ISAIAH 45:22; 1 JOHN 2:1;
EPHESIANS 2:13–14; HEBREWS 9:12, 15; HEBREWS 7:25

Adorn the doctrine of God our Savior in all things.

Lord God, may my conduct be worthy of the gospel of Christ. May I abstain from every form of evil. If I am reproached for the name of Christ, I am blessed. But may I never suffer as a murderer, a thief, an evildoer, or as a busybody in other people's matters. May I become blameless and harmless, Your child without fault in the midst of a crooked and perverse generation, among whom I shine as a light in the world. May my light so shine before men, that they may see my good works and glorify You, my Father in heaven.

I will bind mercy and truth around my neck, write them on the tablet of my heart, and so find favor and high esteem in Your sight and in the sight of man. Whatever things are true, whatever things are noble, whatever things are just, whatever things are pure, whatever things are lovely, whatever things are of good report, if there is any virtue and if there is anything praiseworthy— I will meditate on these things.

Transform my meditations ... Keep me from evil ...
And let me shine as Your light.

TITUS 2:10; PHILIPPIANS 1:27; 1 THESSALONIANS 5:22;
1 PETER 4:14–15; PHILIPPIANS 2:15; MATTHEW 5:16;
PROVERBS 3:3–4; PHILIPPIANS 4:8

Perfect through sufferings.

Lord Jesus, You prayed, "My soul is exceedingly sorrowful, even to death. Stay here and watch with Me." You went a little farther and fell on Your face, and prayed, saying, "O My Father, if it is possible, let this cup pass from Me; nevertheless, not as I will, but as You will." And being in agony, You prayed more earnestly. Then Your sweat became like great drops of blood falling down to the ground. . . .

The pains of death surrounded me, and the pangs of Sheol laid hold of me; I found trouble and sorrow. Reproach has broken my heart, and I am full of heaviness; I looked for someone to take pity, but there was none; and for comforters, but I found none. Look on my right hand and see, for there is no one who acknowledges me; refuge has failed me; no one cares for my soul.

You, Jesus, were despised and rejected by men, a Man of sorrows and acquainted with grief. And I hid, as it were, my face from You; You were despised, and I did not esteem You.

You know suffering, my Savior—
the fact that You suffered for me humbles me.
You know my pains and pangs and
You alone are my Refuge.

HEBREWS 2:10; MATTHEW 26:38–39; LUKE 22:44;
PSALM 116:3; PSALM 69:20; PSALM 142:4; ISAIAH 53:3

What is your life? It is even a vapor that appears for a little time and then vanishes away.

Father, now my days are swifter than a runner; they flee away, they see no good. They pass by like swift ships, like an eagle swooping on its prey. You carry our days away like a flood; they are like a sleep. In the morning days are like grass which grows up: in the morning it flourishes and grows up; in the evening it is cut down and withers. I am born of woman and have few days, full of trouble. I come forth like a flower and fade away.

The world is passing away, and the lust of it; but if I who do Your will, Lord God, I abide forever. All will perish, but You, Lord God, will endure; yes, all will grow old like a garment; like a cloak You will change us, and we will be changed. But You are the same, and Your years will have no end, like Jesus Christ, the same yesterday, today, and forever.

My life is a vapor, Lord, yet in You I have the promise of eternity and, therefore, significance for today.

JAMES 4:14; JOB 9:25–26; PSALM 90:5–6; JOB 14:1–2; 1 JOHN 2:17; PSALM 102:26–27; HEBREWS 13:8

*He shall put his hand on the head of the burnt offering,
and it will be accepted on his behalf to make atonement for him.*

Lord, I was not redeemed with corruptible things, like silver or gold, from my aimless conduct received by tradition from my fathers, but with the precious blood of Christ, as of a lamb without blemish and without spot. Jesus Himself bore my sins in His own body on the tree.

Holy God, You made me accepted in the Beloved.

As a living stone, I am built up into a spiritual house, a holy priesthood, to offer up spiritual sacrifices acceptable to You through Jesus Christ. Therefore, by Your mercies, Lord God, I present my body a living sacrifice, holy, acceptable to You, which is my reasonable service.

Now to You, Lord God, who is able to keep me from stumbling, and to present me faultless before the presence of Your glory with exceeding joy, to You, God my Savior, who alone is wise, be glory and majesty, dominion and power, both now and forever.

*Almighty God, I am humbled by the fact that
Your Son sacrificed His holy life on
behalf of sinners like me. In response I
present myself as a living sacrifice, with thanksgiving!*

LEVITICUS 1:4; 1 PETER 1:18–19; 1 PETER 2:24;
EPHESIANS 1:6; 1 PETER 2:5; ROMANS 12:1; JUDE 24–25

My eyes fail from looking upward.

Have mercy on me, O Lord, for I am weak; O Lord, heal me, for my bones are troubled. My soul also is greatly troubled; but You, O Lord—how long? Return, O Lord, deliver me! Oh, save me for Your mercies' sake! My heart is severely pained within me, and the terrors of death have fallen upon me. Fearfulness and trembling have come upon me, and horror has overwhelmed me. Oh, that I had wings like a dove! For then I would fly away and be at rest.

I have need of endurance.

While Jesus' disciples looked steadfastly toward heaven as He went up, two men stood by them in white apparel, who also said, "Men of Galilee, why do you stand gazing up into heaven? This same Jesus, who was taken up from you into heaven, will so come in like manner as you saw Him go into heaven." My citizenship is in heaven, from which I also eagerly wait for the Savior, the Lord Jesus Christ . . . the blessed hope and glorious appearing of my great God and Savior Jesus Christ.

Lord Jesus, while I wait for Your return,
enable me to endure life's troubles confidently.
Even so, come, Lord Jesus.

ISAIAH 38:14; PSALM 6:2–4; PSALM 55:4–6; HEBREWS 10:36;
ACTS 1:10–11; PHILIPPIANS 3:20; TITUS 2:13

God, having raised up His Servant Jesus,
sent Him to bless you, in turning away every one of you
from your iniquities.

I praise You, gracious God, Father of my Lord Jesus Christ, who according to Your abundant mercy has begotten me again to a living hope through the resurrection of Jesus Christ from the dead. Saved by His life.

My Savior Jesus Christ gave Himself for me, that He might redeem me from every lawless deed and purify for Himself His own special people, zealous for good works. As You who called me are holy, I also am to be holy in all my conduct, because it is written, "Be holy, for I am holy."

You, the God and Father of my Lord Jesus Christ, have blessed me with every spiritual blessing in the heavenly places in Christ. In Jesus dwells all the fullness of the Godhead bodily; and I am complete in Him. Of His fullness I have received, and grace for grace.

Lord God, You who did not spare Your own Son, but delivered Him up for us all, how shall You not with Him also freely give me all things?

Great are Your holiness, Your grace, Your mercy,
my wonderful God!

ACTS 3:26; 1 PETER 1:3; ROMANS 5:10; TITUS 2:13–14;
1 PETER 1:15–16; EPHESIANS 1:3; COLOSSIANS 2:9–10;
JOHN 1:16; ROMANS 8:32

The entrance of Your words gives light.

Y ou, Lord God, are light and in You is no darkness at all. . . . You, Almighty God, commanded light to shine out of darkness, have shone in my heart to give the light of the knowledge of Your glory in the face of Jesus Christ. The Word was God. In Him was life, and the life was the light of men. If I walk in the light as You, Lord God, are in the light, I have fellowship with other believers, and the blood of Jesus Christ Your Son cleanses me from all sin.

Your word I have hidden in my heart, that I might not sin against You. I am already clean because of the word which Jesus has spoken to me.

I was once darkness, but now I am light in the Lord. May I walk as a child of light. I am part of a chosen generation, a royal priesthood, a holy nation, Your own special people, that I may proclaim the praises of You who called me out of darkness into Your marvelous light.

You know the darkness of this fallen world
and the darkness of my sin nature.
Keep me walking in Your light, Lord God.

PSALM 119:130; 1 JOHN 1:5; 2 CORINTHIANS 4:6;
JOHN 1:1, 4; 1 JOHN 1:7; PSALM 119:11; JOHN 15:3;
EPHESIANS 5:8; 1 PETER 2:9

Be watchful, and strengthen the things which remain,
that are ready to die.

The end of all things is at hand; therefore, Lord God, help me be serious and watchful in my prayers. May I be sober and vigilant; because my adversary the devil walks about like a roaring lion, seeking whom he may devour. I take heed to myself, and diligently keep myself, lest I forget the things my eyes have seen, and lest they depart from my heart all the days of my life. The just shall live by faith; but if I draw back, You have no pleasure in me. But I am not of those who draw back to perdition, but of those who believe to the saving of the soul.

What You say to me, You say to all: Watch!

Yet I fear not, for You are with me; I will not be dismayed, for You are my God. You will strengthen me, yes, You will help me, You will uphold me with Your righteous right hand. You, the Lord my God, will hold my right hand.

Maranatha! Come, Lord Jesus!
But, as I wait, empower me to be faithful to You.

REVELATION 3:2; I PETER 4:7; I PETER 5:8;
DEUTERONOMY 4:9; HEBREWS 10:38–39;
MARK 13:37; ISAIAH 41:10, 13

Lot lifted his eyes and saw all the plain of Jordan,
that it was well watered everywhere (before the Lord destroyed
Sodom and Gomorrah) like the garden of the Lord.
Then Lot chose for himself all the plain of Jordan.

Omniscient Lord, You called Lot, righteous Lot . . . that righteous man.

May I not be deceived, Lord God, for You are not mocked; for whatever I sow, that I will also reap. I remember what Lot's wife reaped.

I will not be unequally yoked together with unbelievers. For what fellowship has righteousness with lawlessness? And what communion has light with darkness? Therefore I come out from among them and am separate, as You say, Lord. I do not touch what is unclean. I will not be a partaker with them. For I was once darkness, but now I am light in the Lord. Enable me to walk as a child of light, finding out what is acceptable to You, my Lord. And I will have no fellowship with the unfruitful works of darkness, but rather expose them.

Lord, I was once darkness, but now I am light in You.
In Your power, may I keep walking in the light.

GENESIS 13:10–11; 2 PETER 2:7–8; GALATIANS 6:7; LUKE 17:32; 2 CORINTHIANS 6:14, 17; EPHESIANS 5:7–8, 10–11

Holy, holy, holy, Lord God Almighty.

You, Lord God, are holy, enthroned in praises. You said to Moses, "Do not draw near this place . . . the place where you stand is holy ground." Moreover You said, "I am the God of your father—of Abraham, of Isaac, and the God of Jacob." And Moses hid his face, for he was afraid. . . . To whom then will I liken You, or to whom shall You be equal? You are the Holy One. You are the Lord my God, the Holy One of Israel, my Savior. You . . . are the Lord, and besides You there is no savior.

As You who called me are holy, I also will be holy in all my conduct, because it is written, "Be holy, for I am holy." My body is the temple of the Holy Spirit who is in me, whom I have from You, Lord God, and I am not my own. I am Your temple, O living God. You have said that You will dwell in me and walk among Your people. You will be my God, and I Yours. Can two walk together, unless they are agreed?

Holy Almighty God, I am Yours alone.

REVELATION 4:8; PSALM 22:3; EXODUS 3:5–6; ISAIAH 40:25;
ISAIAH 43:3, 11; 1 PETER 1:15–16; 1 CORINTHIANS 6:19;
2 CORINTHIANS 6:16; AMOS 3:3

[Abraham] believed in the Lord,
and He accounted it to him for righteousness.

Lord God, Abraham did not waver at Your promise through
unbelief, but was strengthened in faith, giving glory to You,
and being fully convinced that what You had promised
You were also able to perform. And therefore "it was accounted
to him for righteousness." Now it was not written for his sake
alone that it was imputed to him, but also for me. It shall be
imputed to me who believes in You who raised up Jesus my Lord
from the dead.

The promise that he would be the heir of the world was not
to Abraham or to his seed through the law, but through the
righteousness of faith.

The just shall live by faith. Let me hold fast the confession
of my hope without wavering, for You who promised are faithful.
My God, You are in heaven; You do whatever You please.
With You, Almighty God, nothing will be impossible. As Mary
was blessed for believing in the fulfillment of those things which
You, my Lord, told her, so I believe.

Keep me steadfast in my faith, Lord, discerning the doubts the
enemy would sow and mindful of Your great faithfulness in the past.

GENESIS 15:6; ROMANS 4:20–24; ROMANS 4:13; ROMANS 1:17;
HEBREWS 10:23; PSALM 115:3; LUKE 1:37, 45

I will never leave you nor forsake you.

Lord, I may boldly say: "You are my helper; I will not fear. What can man do to me?"

You are with me and will keep me wherever I go, and will bring me back to this land; for You will not leave me until You have done what You have spoken to me. So I can be strong and of good courage, I do not fear nor am I afraid for You, my Lord God, are the One who goes with me. You will not leave me nor forsake me.

Demas forsook Paul, having loved this world. No one stood with Paul, but all forsook him. May it not be charged against them. But You, Lord, stood with Paul and strengthened him. When my father and my mother forsake me, You, Lord, will take care of me.

Lord, You are with me always, even to the end of the age. You are He who lives, and was dead, You are alive forevermore. You will not leave me an orphan; You will come to me. You give to me Your peace!

Lord, may I live confident in Your care
for me and Your presence with me.

HEBREWS 13:5; HEBREWS 13:6; GENESIS 28:15; DEUTERONOMY 31:6; 2 TIMOTHY 4:10, 16–17; PSALM 27:10; MATTHEW 28:20; REVELATION 1:18; JOHN 14:18; JOHN 14:27

*The kingdom of heaven is like a man traveling to a far country,
who called his own servants and delivered his goods to them . . .
to each according to his own ability.*

Father, Your Word says that the one to whom I present
myself as a slave to obey, I am that one's slave whom
I obey.

One and the same Spirit works all these things, distributing
to each one of us believers individually as He wills. The
manifestation of Your Spirit, Lord God, is given to me for the
profit of all. As I have received a gift, I am to minister it to
others, as a good steward of Your manifold grace. It is required
of me, a steward, that I be found faithful. For to me whom
much is given, from me much will be required; and to me, much
has been committed; of me more will be asked.

Who is sufficient for these things? I can do all things
through Your Son, Jesus Christ, who strengthens me.

*Lord God, thank You for entrusting me with gifts
by which to serve Your church. Guide me and strengthen me
as I use them for Your glory.*

MATTHEW 25:14–15; ROMANS 6:16; 1 CORINTHIANS 12:11, 7;
1 PETER 4:10; 1 CORINTHIANS 4:2; LUKE 12:48;
2 CORINTHIANS 2:16; PHILIPPIANS 4:13

He who sows righteousness will
have a sure reward.

Lord, Jesus' parable says: After a long time the lord of those servants came and settled accounts with them. He who had received five talents came and brought five other talents, saying, "Lord, you delivered to me five talents; I have gained five more talents besides them." His lord said to him, "Well done, good and faithful servant; you were faithful over a few things, I will make you ruler over many things. Enter into the joy of your lord."

Lord God, like that servant, I must appear before the judgment seat of Christ, that I may receive the things done in the body, according to what I have done, whether good or bad.

May I truly say: I have fought the good fight, I have finished the race, I have kept the faith; there is laid up for me the crown of righteousness, which You, Lord God, the righteous Judge, will give to me on that Day, and not to me only but also to all who have loved Your appearing.

You are coming quickly! May I hold fast what I have, that no one may take my crown.

Help me, Lord, to exercise faithful stewardship: obeying You,
fighting the good fight, and keeping the faith!

PROVERBS 11:18; MATTHEW 25:19–21; 2 CORINTHIANS 5:10;
2 TIMOTHY 4:7–8; REVELATION 3:11

Be strong and of
good courage.

Oh, Lord, You are my light and my salvation; whom shall I fear? You, Lord, are the strength of my life; of whom shall I be afraid? You give power to the weak, and to those like me who have no might You increase strength. Even the youths shall faint and be weary, and the young men shall utterly fall, but those like me who wait on You, Lord, shall renew our strength; I shall mount up with wings like an eagle, I shall run and not be weary, I shall walk and not faint. My flesh and my heart fail; but You, Lord God, are the strength of my heart and my portion forever.

If You, Lord God, are for me, who can be against me? You, Lord, are on my side; I will not fear. What can man do to me? Through You I will push down my enemies; through Your name I will trample those who rise up against me. I am more than a conqueror through Jesus who loved me.

So I arise and begin working, and You, Lord, are with me.

Your presence and Your power enable me, Lord,
to be strong and of good courage!

JOSHUA 1:18; PSALM 27:1; ISAIAH 40:29–31;
PSALM 73:26; ROMANS 8:31; PSALM 118:6; PSALM 44:5;
ROMANS 8:37; 1 CHRONICLES 22:16

Come, you blessed of My Father,
inherit the kingdom prepared for you
from the foundation of the world.

I do not fear, Father God, for it is Your good pleasure to give me Your kingdom. Have You not chosen the poor of this world to be rich in faith and heirs of the kingdom which You promised to those of us who love You? As one of Your heirs, Lord God, and joint heirs with Christ, if I suffer with Him, I may also be glorified together with Him.

You, Father God, love me, because I have loved Jesus. And You are not ashamed to be called my God, for You have prepared a city for me.

If I overcome I shall inherit all things, and You will be my God and I shall be Your son. There is laid up for me the crown of righteousness, which the Lord Jesus, my righteous Judge, will give to me on that Day, and not to me only but also to all who have loved His appearing. You who have begun a good work in me will complete it until the day of Jesus Christ.

Participating in Your kingdom, sharing Your glory,
wearing a crown—thank You, God, for these promises!

MATTHEW 25:34; LUKE 12:32; JAMES 2:5; ROMANS 8:17;
JOHN 16:27; HEBREWS 11:16; REVELATION 21:7;
2 TIMOTHY 4:8; PHILIPPIANS 1:6

*Isaac went out to
meditate in the field in the evening.*

Oh, Lord, let the words of my mouth and the
meditation of my heart be acceptable in Your sight,
my strength and my Redeemer.

When I consider Your heavens, the work of Your fingers, the moon and the stars, which You have ordained, what am I that You are mindful of me, and that You visit me? Your works, Lord God, are great, studied by all who have pleasure in them.

I am blessed when I walk not in the counsel of the ungodly, nor stand in the path of sinners, nor sit in the seat of the scornful; but delight in Your law, and in Your law I meditate day and night. This Book of the Law shall not depart from my mouth, but I shall meditate in it day and night. My soul shall be satisfied as with marrow and fatness, and my mouth shall praise You, Lord God, with joyful lips. I remember You on my bed, I meditate on You in the night watches.

*Lord, teach me to crave the nourishment
that comes from feasting and meditating on Your Word.*

GENESIS 24:63; PSALM 19:14; PSALM 8:3–4; PSALM 111:2;
PSALM 1:1–2; JOSHUA 1:8; PSALM 63:5–6

*My God shall supply all your need
according to His riches in glory
by Christ Jesus.*

Bountiful God, I seek first Your kingdom, Lord God, and Your righteousness, and all things shall be added to me. You who did not spare Your own Son, but delivered Him up for me, how shall You not with Him also freely give me all things? All things are mine: whether Paul or Apollos or Cephas, or the world or life or death, or things present or things to come—all are mine. And I am Christ's, and Christ is Yours, Lord God, as having nothing, and yet possessing all things.

You, Lord God, are my shepherd; I shall not want. You, Lord, are a sun and shield; You will give grace and glory; no good thing will You withhold from those who walk uprightly. You, the living God, give me richly all things to enjoy. You are able to make all grace abound toward me, that I, always having all sufficiency in all things, may have an abundance for every good work.

*The blessing of being Your child is
beyond description! Thank You,
my faithful Shepherd, for Your gracious
and generous provision.*

PHILIPPIANS 4:19; MATTHEW 6:33; ROMANS 8:32;
1 CORINTHIANS 3:21–23; 2 CORINTHIANS 6:10; PSALM 23:1;
PSALM 84:11; 1 TIMOTHY 6:17; 2 CORINTHIANS 9:8.

April

Do not be afraid;

I am the First and

the Last.

The fruit of the Spirit is . . . joy.

Lord God, You grant me joy in the Holy Spirit . . . joy inexpressible and full of glory.

So even when I'm sorrowful, I am always rejoicing; I can be exceedingly joyful in all my tribulation. I also glory in tribulations.

Your Son Jesus, the author and finisher of my faith, for the joy that was set before Him endured the cross, despising the shame. He spoke these things that His joy may remain in me, and that my joy may be full. As His sufferings abound in me, so my consolation also abounds through Him.

So Lord, I rejoice in You always. Again You say to me, "Rejoice!" The joy of the Lord—joy in You, Lord God—is my strength.

In Your presence is fullness of joy; at Your right hand are pleasures forevermore. For Your Son, the Lamb, in the midst of the throne will shepherd me and lead me to living fountains of waters. And You, Lord God, will wipe away every tear from my eyes.

Lord of joy, teach me to rejoice in You always.

GALATIANS 5:22; ROMANS 14:17; 1 PETER 1:8;
2 CORINTHIANS 6:10; 7:4; ROMANS 5:3; HEBREWS 12:2;
JOHN 15:11; 2 CORINTHIANS 1:5; PHILIPPIANS 4:4;
NEHEMIAH 8:10; PSALM 16:11; REVELATION 7:17

If you return to the Lord with all your hearts,
then put away the foreign gods and the Ashtoreths from among you,
and prepare your hearts for the Lord, and serve Him only.

Father, You command me, Your child, to keep myself from idols. "Come out from among them and be separate," You say. If I do not touch what is unclean, You will receive me. You will be a Father to me, and I shall be Your child, a child of the Lord Almighty. I cannot serve You and mammon.

So I shall worship no other god, for You, Lord, whose name is Jealous, are a jealous God. I will serve You with a loyal heart and with a willing mind; for You, Lord, search my heart and understand all the intent of my thoughts.

Surely You desire truth in the inward parts, and in the hidden part You will make me to know wisdom. For man looks at the outward appearance, but You, Lord, look at the heart. If my heart does not condemn me, I have confidence toward You, Lord God.

You know the idols that compete for my
wholehearted devotion to You.
Help me turn from them and serve only You.

---

1 SAMUEL 7:3; 1 JOHN 5:21; 2 CORINTHIANS 6:17–18;
MATTHEW 6:24; EXODUS 34:14; 1 CHRONICLES 28:9;
PSALM 51:6; 1 SAMUEL 16:7; 1 JOHN 3:21

Beloved, do not forget this one thing,
that with the Lord one day is as a thousand years,
and a thousand years as one day. The Lord is not slack
concerning His promise, as some count slackness.

Lord God, Your thoughts are not my thoughts, nor are my ways Your ways. For as the heavens are higher than the earth, so are Your ways higher than my ways, and Your thoughts than my thoughts. For as the rain comes down, and the snow from heaven, and do not return there, but water the earth, so shall Your word be that goes forth from your mouth; it shall not return to You void, but it shall accomplish what You please, and it shall prosper in the thing for which You sent it.

For You have committed us all to disobedience, that You might have mercy on us all. Oh, the depth of the riches both of Your wisdom and knowledge, Lord God! How unsearchable are Your judgments and Your ways past finding out!

I praise You, God, who are infinite in wisdom and love,
in power and justice, in mercy and grace!

2 PETER 3:8–9; ISAIAH 55:8–11; ROMANS 11:32–33

Do not be afraid;
I am the First and the Last.

Lord, I have not come to the mountain that may be touched and that burned with fire, and to blackness and darkness and tempest, but I have come to Mount Zion to You, my Holy God, the Judge of all, to the spirits of just men made perfect, to Jesus the Mediator of the new covenant. Jesus, Your Son, is the author and finisher of my faith. I do not have a High Priest who cannot sympathize with my weaknesses, but He was in all points tempted as I am, yet without sin. Let me therefore come boldly to Your throne of grace, that I may obtain mercy and find grace to help in time of need.

You, Lord God, the King of Israel, and my Redeemer, the Lord of hosts, say: "I am the First and I am the Last; besides Me there is no God." You are Mighty God, Everlasting Father, Prince of Peace.

Are You not from everlasting, O Lord my God, my Holy One? Who is God, except You, Lord? And who is a rock, except You my God?

Thank You for calling me to know You,
Mighty God and Everlasting Father!

REVELATION 1:17; HEBREWS 12:18, 22–24; HEBREWS 12:2;
HEBREWS 4:15–16; ISAIAH 44:6; ISAIAH 9:6;
HABAKKUK 1:12; 2 SAMUEL 22:32

I will not let You go unless You bless me!

Lord God, You invite me to take hold of Your strength, that I may make peace with You; and I shall make peace with You. I long for You to say, "Great is your faith! Let it be to you as you desire." According to my faith let it be to me. Let me ask in faith, with no doubting, for if I doubt I am like a wave of the sea driven and tossed by the wind. Then let me not suppose that I will receive anything from You, Lord.

As the two men drew near to Emmaus . . . Jesus indicated that He would have gone farther. But they constrained Him, saying, "Abide with us." So abide with me. But He vanished from their sight. And they said, "Did not our heart burn within us while He talked with us on the road, and while He opened the Scriptures to us?" If I have found grace in Your sight, show me now Your way, that I may know You and that I have grace in Your sight. Your Presence will go with me, and You will give me rest.

Lord God, Your presence with me gives me strength.

GENESIS 32:26; ISAIAH 27:5; MATTHEW 15:28;
MATTHEW 9:29; JAMES 1:6–7;
LUKE 24:28–29, 31–32; EXODUS 33:13–14

He always lives to make intercession.

Who is He who condemns me, Lord God? It is Christ who died who also makes intercession for me. Christ has not entered the holy places made with hands, which are copies of the true, but into heaven itself, now to appear in Your presence for me.

If I sin, I have an Advocate with You, Father God: Jesus Christ the righteous. You are the one God, and there is one Mediator between You and men, the Man Christ Jesus. Seeing then that I have a great High Priest who has passed through the heavens, Jesus the Son of God, let me hold fast my confession. For I do not have a High Priest who cannot sympathize with my weaknesses, but was in all points tempted as I am, yet without sin. Let me therefore come boldly to the throne of grace, that I may obtain mercy and find grace to help in time of need. Through Jesus I have access by one Spirit to You, my heavenly Father.

Lord God, it's amazing to me that Your Son—
whom my sin sent to the cross—intercedes for me as I journey
through life. Keep me faithful to my Savior and Lord!

HEBREWS 7:25; ROMANS 8:34; HEBREWS 9:24; I JOHN 2:1;
I TIMOTHY 2:5; HEBREWS 4:14–16; EPHESIANS 2:18.

As sorrowful, yet always rejoicing; as poor, yet making many rich;
as having nothing, and yet possessing all things.

I rejoice in hope of Your glory, Lord God. And not only that, but I also glory in tribulations. I am filled with comfort. I am exceedingly joyful in all my tribulation. Believing, I rejoice with joy inexpressible.

In a great trial of affliction may the abundance of my joy—like the Macedonians'—abound in the riches of liberality despite poverty. To me, who is less than the least of all the saints, this grace was given, that I should preach among the Gentiles the unsearchable riches of Christ, and to make all see what is the fellowship of the mystery, which from the beginning of the ages has been hidden in You, Lord God, who created all things through Jesus Christ.

Lord God, You have chosen the poor of this world to be rich in faith and heirs of the kingdom which You promised to those who love You. You, my God, are able to make all grace abound toward me, that I, always having all sufficiency in all things, have an abundance for every good work.

Lord, use me for Your kingdom work, I pray!

2 CORINTHIANS 6:10; ROMANS 5:2–3; 2 CORINTHIANS 7:4;
1 PETER 1:8; 2 CORINTHIANS 8:2; EPHESIANS 3:8–9;
JAMES 2:5; 2 CORINTHIANS 9:8

You were enriched in everything by Him.

Jesus, when I was still without strength, You died for me, the ungodly. The Father who did not spare You, His own Son, but delivered You up for me, how shall He not with You also freely give me all things?

In You, Jesus, dwells all the fullness of the Godhead bodily; and I am complete in You, the head of all principality and power.

So I abide in You, Jesus, and You in me. As the branch cannot bear fruit of itself, unless it abides in the vine, neither can I, unless I abide in You. You are the vine, I am a branch. I abiding in You, and You in me, bear much fruit; for without You I can do nothing. To will is present with me, but how to perform good I do not find. To me grace was given according to the measure of Your gift.

If I abide in You, Jesus, and Your words abide in me, I will ask what I desire, and it shall be done for me. May Your word, Jesus, dwell in me richly in all wisdom.

As I abide in You, Jesus, enable me to do Your good each day.

---

1 CORINTHIANS 1:5; ROMANS 5:6; ROMANS 8:32;
COLOSSIANS 2:9–10; JOHN 15:4–5; ROMANS 7:18;
EPHESIANS 4:7; JOHN 15:7; COLOSSIANS 3:16

Fear not, for I have redeemed you.

I do not fear, Lord God, for I will not be ashamed; neither be disgraced, for I will not be put to shame; for I will forget the shame of my youth, and will not remember the reproach of my widowhood anymore. For You, my Maker, are my husband, the Lord of hosts is Your name; and You, the Holy One of Israel, are my Redeemer. You have blotted out, like a thick cloud, my transgressions and my sins. So I return to You, for You have redeemed me . . . with the precious blood of Christ, a lamb without blemish or spot.

You, my Redeemer, are strong; the Lord of hosts is Your name. You will thoroughly plead my case. You, Father God, who have given me to Jesus, are greater than all; and no one is able to snatch me out of Your hand.

I am blessed with grace and peace from You, Father God, and from my Lord Jesus Christ, who gave Himself for my sins, that He might deliver me from this present evil age, according to Your will, my God and Father, to whom be glory forever and ever. Amen.

Redeemer God, I praise You
for the forgiveness and hope You grant me!

ISAIAH 43:1; ISAIAH 54:4–5; ISAIAH 44:22; 1 PETER 1:19;
JEREMIAH 50:34; JOHN 10:29; GALATIANS 1:3–5

I am dark, but lovely.

Lord God, I was brought forth in iniquity, and in sin my mother conceived me. Yet You say, "Your fame went out among the nations because of your beauty, for it was perfect through My splendor which I had bestowed on you."

I am sinful, O Lord! But You say, "You are fair, my love! Behold, you are fair!"

I abhor myself, and repent in dust and ashes. You say, "You are all fair, my love, and there is no spot in you."

I find then a law, that evil is present with me, the one who wills to do good. But I am of good cheer; my sins are forgiven me.

I know that in me (that is, in my flesh) nothing good dwells. Yet I am complete in Jesus . . . perfect in Christ Jesus.

I was washed, I was sanctified, I was justified in the name of my Lord Jesus and by the Spirit of my God . . . that I may proclaim Your praises who called me out of darkness into Your marvelous light.

I praise You, Lord, for loving this sinner and making me clean!

Song of Solomon 1:5; Psalm 51:5; Ezekiel 16:14;
Luke 5:8; Song of Solomon 4:1; Job 42:6;
Song of Solomon 4:7; Romans 7:21; Matthew 9:2;
Romans 7:18; Colossians 2:10; Colossians 1:28;
1 Corinthians 6:11; 1 Peter 2:9

In the multitude of words sin is not lacking,
but he who restrains his lips is wise.

Father, You warn me, to be swift to hear, slow to speak, slow to wrath. He who is slow to anger is better than the mighty, and he who rules his spirit than he who takes a city. If I do not stumble in word, I am a perfect man, able also to bridle the whole body. For by my words I will be justified, and by my words I will be condemned. Set a guard, O Lord, over my mouth; keep watch over the door of my lips.

Your Son, Jesus, suffered for me, leaving me an example, that I should follow His steps: who committed no sin, nor was deceit found in His mouth; when He was reviled, did not revile in return; when He suffered, He did not threaten, but committed Himself to You who judge, righteously. I consider Him who endured such hostility from sinners against Himself, lest I become weary and discouraged in my soul.

In my mouth may there be found no deceit, for I am without fault before Your throne.

Lord, only in Your power and
by Your grace can I learn to control my tongue.

PROVERBS 10:19; JAMES 1:19; PROVERBS 16:32;
JAMES 3:2; MATTHEW 12:37; PSALM 141:3; I PETER 2:21–23;
HEBREWS 12:3; REVELATION 14:5

What the law could not do in that it was weak through the flesh,
God did by sending His own Son in the likeness of sinful flesh,
on account of sin: He condemned sin in the flesh.

Holy God, the law, a shadow of the good things to come, and not the very image of the things, can never with these same sacrifices, which are offered continually year by year, make those of us who approach You perfect. For then would sacrifices not have ceased to be offered? By You, Lord, I who believes am justified from all things from which I could not be justified by the law of Moses.

Inasmuch as I have partaken of flesh and blood, Jesus Himself likewise shared in the same, that through death He might destroy him who had the power of death, that is, the devil, and release me who through fear of death was all my lifetime subject to bondage. For indeed He does not give aid to angels, but He does give aid to me, the seed of Abraham. Therefore, in all things He had to be made like me, His brethren.

I thank You for Your Law that shows me my sin.
Even more, I thank You for Your forgiveness
through the perfect sacrifice of Your Son.

ROMANS 8:3; HEBREWS 10:1–2;
ACTS 13:39; HEBREWS 2:14–17

Honor the Lord with your possessions,
and with the firstfruits of all your increase.

Lord God, You warn me that if I sow sparingly I will also reap sparingly, and if I sow bountifully I will also reap bountifully. So on the first day of the week let me lay something aside, storing up as I may prosper.

God, You are not unjust to forget my work and labor of love which I have shown toward Your name, in that I have ministered to the saints, and do minister.

By Your mercies, Lord God, I present my body a living sacrifice, holy, acceptable to God, which is my reasonable service. The love of Christ constrains me, because I judge thus: that if Jesus died for me, then I died; and He died for me, that I who live should live no longer for myself, but for Him who died for me and rose again. Whether I eat or drink, or whatever I do, I do all to Your glory, Lord God.

You are the Giver of all good gifts—and I can be so selfish,
withholding from those You want to bless through me and being
more concerned about my own glory than Yours.
Forgive me and transform me, Father God!

PROVERBS 3:9; 2 CORINTHIANS 9:6; 1 CORINTHIANS 16:2;
HEBREWS 6:10; ROMANS 12:1;
2 CORINTHIANS 5:14–15; 1 CORINTHIANS 10:31

My soul shall be satisfied as with marrow and fatness,
and my mouth shall praise You with joyful lips.
When I remember You on my bed,
I meditate on You in the night watches.

How precious are Your thoughts to me, O God! How great is the sum of them! If I should count them, they would be more in number than the sand; when I awake, I am still with You. How sweet are Your words to my taste, sweeter than honey to my mouth! Your love is better than wine.

Whom have I in heaven but You? And there is none upon earth that I desire besides You. You are fairer than the sons of men.

Like an apple tree among the trees of the woods, so are You, my Beloved among the sons. I sit down in Your shade with great delight, and Your fruit is sweet to my taste. You bring me to the banqueting house, and Your banner over me is love. Your countenance is like Lebanon, excellent as the cedars. Your mouth is most sweet . . . you are altogether lovely. You are my Beloved, and You are my friend.

Lord God, may I fall more in love with You today.

PSALM 63:5–6; PSALM 139:17–18; PSALM 119:103;
SONG OF SOLOMON 1:2; PSALM 73:25; PSALM 45:2;
SONG OF SOLOMON 2:3–4; SONG OF SOLOMON 5:15–16

Their Redeemer is strong.

You, Lord God, know my manifold transgressions and my mighty sins. You have given help to one who is mighty. You, Lord God, are my Savior, and my Redeemer, the Mighty One of Jacob. You are mighty to save . . . and able to keep me from stumbling. Where sin abounded, Your grace abounded much more.

Because I believe in Jesus I am not condemned; but he who does not believe is condemned already, because, Lord God, he has not believed in the name of Your only begotten Son. You are also able to save to the uttermost those like me who come to You through Jesus.

Is Your hand shortened at all that it cannot redeem?

Who shall separate me from the love of Christ? For I am persuaded that neither death nor life, nor angels nor principalities nor powers, nor things present nor things to come, nor height nor depth, nor any other created thing, shall be able to separate me from Your love, Father God, which is in Christ Jesus my Lord.

I praise You, Redeemer God, that no one
is ever beyond Your reach—and that once I am Yours,
nothing can separate me from Your love.

JEREMIAH 50:34; AMOS 5:12; PSALM 89:19; ISAIAH 49:26;
ISAIAH 63:1; JUDE 24; ROMANS 5:20; JOHN 3:18;
HEBREWS 7:25; ISAIAH 50:2; ROMANS 8:35, 38–39

I said in my haste, "I am cut off from before Your eyes";
nevertheless You heard the voice of my supplications
when I cried out to You.

Lord, I sink in deep mire, where there is no standing; I have come into deep waters where the floods overflow me. Waters flowed over my head; I said, "I am cut off!" I called on Your name, O Lord, from the lowest pit. You have heard my voice: "Do not hide Your ear from my sighing, from my cry for help." You drew near on the day I called on You, and said, "Do not fear!"

Lord, will You cast off forever? Will You be favorable no more? Has Your mercy ceased forever? Has Your promise failed forevermore? Have You, Lord God, forgotten to be gracious? Have You in anger shut up Your tender mercies? I said, "This is my anguish; but I will remember the years of the right hand of the Most High." I will remember Your works, Lord God; surely I will remember Your wonders of old. I would have lost heart, unless I had believed that I would see Your goodness, living God, in the land of the living.

Great is Your faithfulness, Lord! I will remember
Your works and Your tender mercies. Praise Your name!

PSALM 31:22; PSALM 69:2; LAMENTATIONS 3:54–57;
PSALM 77:7–11; PSALM 27:13

Whoever offers praise glorifies Me.

Lord God, may the word of Christ dwell in me richly in all wisdom, as I teach and admonish others in psalms and hymns and spiritual songs, singing with grace in my heart to You, Lord. And whatever I do in word or deed, may I do all in the name of my Lord Jesus, giving thanks to You, God the Father, through Him. May I glorify You, Lord God, in my body and in my spirit, which are Yours.

I am part of a royal priesthood called to proclaim Your praises, Almighty God, who called me out of darkness into Your marvelous light. As a living stone, I am being built up into a spiritual house, a holy priesthood, to offer up spiritual sacrifices acceptable to You, Holy God, through Jesus Christ. By Jesus let me continually offer the sacrifice of praise to You, God; the fruit of my lips, giving thanks to Your name.

My soul shall make its boast in You, gracious God; the humble shall hear of it and be glad. I call others to magnify You, Lord, with me, that we may exalt Your name together.

May I praise You, Lord, with my body,
my spirit, my words, my life!

PSALM 50:23; COLOSSIANS 3:16–17;
1 CORINTHIANS 6:20; 1 PETER 2:9;
1 PETER 2:5; HEBREWS 13:15; PSALM 34:2–3

*I will raise up for them a Prophet like you
from among their brethren.*

Lord God, Moses stood between You and Your people at that time, to declare to them Your word; for they were afraid. You are the one God, and there is one Mediator between You and men, the Man Christ Jesus.

Moses was very humble, more than all men who were on the face of the earth. Jesus, You invite me to take Your yoke upon myself and learn from You, for You are gentle and lowly in heart, and I find rest for my soul. May this mind be in me which was also in You, Christ Jesus, who, being in the form of God, did not consider it robbery to be equal with God, but made Yourself of no reputation, taking the form of a bondservant, and coming in the likeness of men.

Moses was faithful in all God's house as a servant, for a testimony of those things which would be spoken afterward, but You, Christ, are faithful as a Son over God's house, whose house I am part of if I hold fast the confidence and rejoicing of the hope firm to the end.

*Lord Jesus, enable me to follow Your example
of humble service.*

DEUTERONOMY 18:18; DEUTERONOMY 5:5;
1 TIMOTHY 2:5; NUMBERS 12:3; MATTHEW 11:29;
PHILIPPIANS 2:5–7; HEBREWS 3:5–6

Most assuredly, I say to you,
I am the door of the sheep.

L ord Jesus, the veil of the temple was torn in two from top to
bottom when You suffered once for sins, You the just, for me
the unjust, that You might bring me to God. The way
into the Holiest of All was not yet made manifest while the first
tabernacle was still standing.

You, Jesus, are the door. If I enter by You, I will be saved,
and will go in and out and find pasture.

I come to the Father only through You, Jesus. Through You
I have access by one Spirit to the Father. Therefore, I am no
longer a stranger and foreigner, but a fellow citizen with the
saints and members of the household of God. I have boldness to
enter the Holiest by Your blood, by a new, living way which You
consecrated for me, through the veil, . . . Your flesh. I have peace
with God through You, my Lord Jesus, through whom also I
have access by faith into Your grace in which I stand, and rejoice
in hope of the glory of God.

I praise You, Jesus, for through You
I have access to the Father!

JOHN 10:7; MATTHEW 27:51; 1 PETER 3:18; HEBREWS 9:8;
JOHN 10:9; JOHN 14:6; EPHESIANS 2:18–19;
HEBREWS 10:19–20; ROMANS 5:1–2

None of the accursed things shall remain in your hand.

Lord God, You call me to come out from among them and be separate, to not touch what is unclean. Your Word begs me as a sojourner and pilgrim, to abstain from fleshly lusts which war against my soul and to hate even the garment defiled by the flesh.

Now I am one of Your children, God; and it has not yet been revealed what I shall be, but I know that when Jesus is revealed, I shall be like Him, for I shall see Him as He is. And with this hope in Jesus I purify myself, just as He is pure. For Your grace, Lord God, that brings salvation has appeared to all men, teaching me that, denying ungodliness and worldly lusts, I should live soberly, righteously, and godly in the present age, looking for the blessed hope and glorious appearing of my great God and Savior Jesus Christ, who gave Himself for me, that He might redeem me from every lawless deed and purify for Himself His own special people, zealous for good works.

Lord God, please help me avoid what is unclean.
Empower me to live a godly and pure life.

DEUTERONOMY 13:17; 2 CORINTHIANS 6:17; 1 PETER 2:11;
JUDE 23; 1 JOHN 3:2–3; TITUS 2:11–14

Stand fast in the Lord.

My foot has held fast to Your steps, Lord. I have kept Your way and not turned aside.

You, Lord, love justice, and do not forsake Your saints. . . . Forever Lord, You shall preserve me from all evil; You shall preserve my soul.

The just live by faith; but if I draw back, Your soul has no pleasure in me. But I am not of those who draw back to perdition, but of those who believe to the saving of the soul. If others had been of us, they would have continued with us; but they went out that they might be made manifest, that none of them were of us.

If I abide in Your word, I am Your disciple. If I endure to the end I shall be saved. So enable me to watch, stand fast in the faith, be brave, be strong . . . to hold fast what I have, that no one may take my crown. If I overcome I shall be clothed in white garments, and You will not blot out my name from the Book of Life.

Thank You that, by Your grace, Your Word,
and Your Spirit, Lord, I will be able to stand fast!

———————

PHILIPPIANS 4:1; JOB 23:11; PSALM 37:28;
PSALM 121:7; HEBREWS 10:38–39; 1 JOHN 2:19; JOHN 8:31;
MATTHEW 24:13; 1 CORINTHIANS 16:13;
REVELATION 3:11; REVELATION 3:5

If his offering is a burnt sacrifice of the herd,
let him offer a male without blemish; he shall offer it
of his own free will.... Then he shall put his hand on the head of
the burnt offering, and it will be accepted on his behalf
to make atonement for him.

Lord Jesus, God promised to provide for Himself the lamb for a burnt offering. Indeed, You, Lord Jesus, are the Lamb of God who takes away the sin of the world! I have been sanctified through Your offering of Your body once for all ... a ransom for many.

No one takes Your life from You, but You lay it down of Yourself. You have power to lay it down, and You have power to take it again. Father God will love me freely. And You, Son of God, loved me and gave Yourself for me.

God made You who knew no sin to be sin for me, that I might become the righteousness of God in You. God made me accepted in You, the Beloved Son.

May I always be humbled and
awed by the gracious reality that You, Jesus,
died in my place.

LEVITICUS 1:3–4; GENESIS 22:8; JOHN 1:29; HEBREWS 10:10;
MATTHEW 20:28; JOHN 10:18; HOSEA 14:4;
GALATIANS 2:20; 2 CORINTHIANS 5:21; EPHESIANS 1:6

The Lord was my support.

Lord, truly, it is vain to hope for salvation from the hills, and from the multitude of mountains; for truly, in You, Lord God, is the salvation of Israel. You, Lord, are my rock and my fortress and my deliverer; my God, my strength, in whom I will trust; my shield and the horn of my salvation, my stronghold. I cry out and shout, as an inhabitant of Zion, for great is the Holy One of Israel in our midst!

Your angel, Lord God, encamps all around those who fear You, and delivers me. The righteous cry out, and You, Lord, hear, and deliver me out of all my troubles. Eternal God, You are my refuge, and underneath are the everlasting arms. So I boldly say: "The Lord is my helper; I will not fear. What can man do to me?" Who is God, except You, Lord? And who is a rock, except You, my God? It is You, Almighty God, who arms me with strength, and makes my way perfect.

By Your grace, Father God, I am what I am.

Lord God, may I always and only look to You,
my Shield, my Stronghold, my Helper.

PSALM 18:18; JEREMIAH 3:23; PSALM 18:2; ISAIAH 12:6;
PSALM 34:7, 17; DEUTERONOMY 33:27; HEBREWS 13:6;
PSALM 18:31–32; 1 CORINTHIANS 15:10

The Lord visited Sarah as He had said,
and the Lord did for Sarah as He had spoken.

I trust in You, Lord, at all times; I pour out my heart before You; God, You are a refuge for me. David strengthened himself in You, his God. You will surely visit me, and bring me . . . to the land of which You swore to Abraham, Isaac, and Jacob. You had certainly seen the oppression of Your people in Egypt; You heard their groaning and came down to deliver them. You brought them out, after You had shown wonders and signs in the land of Egypt, and in the Red Sea, and in the wilderness forty years. Not a word failed of any good thing which You, Lord God, had spoken to the house of Israel. All came to pass.

You who promised are faithful. Have You said, and will You not do it? Or have You spoken, and will You not make it good? Heaven and earth will pass away, but Your words will by no means pass away. The grass withers, the flower fades, but Your word, my God, stands forever.

You are Promise Maker and Promise Keeper.
Great is Your faithfulness, my God!

GENESIS 21:1; PSALM 62:8; 1 SAMUEL 30:6; GENESIS 50:24; ACTS 7:34, 36; JOSHUA 21:45; HEBREWS 10:23; NUMBERS 23:19; MATTHEW 24:35; ISAIAH 40:8

You shall call His name Jesus,
for He will save His people from their sins.

I know that You, Lord Jesus, were manifested to take away my sins . . . and that I, having died to sins, might live for righteousness. You are also able to save to the uttermost those like me who come to God through You.

You, Jesus, were wounded for my transgressions, You were bruised for my iniquities; the chastisement for my peace was upon You, and by Your stripes I am healed. My Lord God has laid my iniquity on You. Thus it was necessary for You, Lord Christ, to suffer so that repentance and remission of sins should be preached in Your name to all nations. You have appeared to put away sin by the sacrifice of Yourself.

God has exalted You to His right hand to be Prince and Savior, to give repentance. Through You, Jesus, is preached to me the forgiveness of sins; and by You, I believing, am justified from all things from which I could not be justified by the law of Moses. My sins are forgiven for Your name's sake.

Thank You, Jesus, for dying for my sins.
Teach me to live for righteousness!

MATTHEW 1:21; 1 JOHN 3:5; 1 PETER 2:24; HEBREWS 7:25;
ISAIAH 53:5–6; LUKE 24:46–47; HEBREWS 9:26;
ACTS 5:31; ACTS 13:38–39; 1 JOHN 2:12

His left hand is under my head,
and his right hand embraces me.

Underneath me, Lord God, are Your everlasting arms. When Peter saw that the wind was boisterous, he was afraid; and beginning to sink he cried out, saying, "Lord, save me!" And immediately Jesus stretched out His hand and caught him, and said to him, "O you of little faith, why did you doubt?" Lord, You order my steps and You delight in my way. Though I fall, I shall not be utterly cast down; for You, Lord, uphold me with Your hand.

As one beloved of the Lord, I shall dwell in safety by You, who shelters me all the day long; and I shall dwell between Your shoulders. I cast all my care upon You, for You care for me. He who touches me touches the apple of Your eye, Lord God.

I shall never perish; neither shall anyone snatch me out of Jesus' hand. You, Father, who have given me to Jesus, are greater than all.

My great and gracious God, thank You for caring for me,
protecting me, upholding me.

SONG OF SOLOMON 2:6; DEUTERONOMY 33:27;
MATTHEW 14:30–31; PSALM 37:23–24; DEUTERONOMY 33:12;
1 PETER 5:7; ZECHARIAH 2:8; JOHN 10:28–29

Brethren, the time is short.

Born of woman, I am of few days and full trouble. I come forth like a flower and fade away; I flee like a shadow and do not continue. The world is passing away, and the lust of it; but if I do Your will, God, I abide forever. As in Adam I die, in Christ I shall be made alive. Death is swallowed up in victory. For if I live, I live to the Lord; and if I die, I die to the Lord. Whether I live or die, I am the Lord's. To live is Christ, and to die is gain.

I do not cast away my confidence, a great reward. I have need of endurance, so that after I have done Your will, Lord God, I may receive the promise. For yet a little while, and You who is coming will come. The night is far spent, the day is at hand. Therefore I cast off the works of darkness, and I put on the armor of light. The end of all things is at hand; therefore I will be serious and watchful in my prayers.

Teach me to live, Lord, mindful that time is short.

---

1 CORINTHIANS 7:29; JOB 14:1–2; 1 JOHN 2:17;
1 CORINTHIANS 15:22, 54; ROMANS 14:8; PHILIPPIANS 1:21;
HEBREWS 10:35–37; ROMANS 13:12; 1 PETER 4:7

Behold! The Lamb of God.

Lord God, it is not possible that the blood of bulls and goats could take away sins. Therefore, when Your Son came into the world, He said to You: "Sacrifice and offering You did not desire, but a body You have prepared for Me. In burnt offerings and sacrifices for sin You had no pleasure. Then 'Behold, I have come—in the volume of the book it is written of Me—to do Your will, O God.'" Jesus was oppressed and afflicted, yet He opened not His mouth; He was led as a lamb to the slaughter, and as a sheep before its shearers is silent, so He opened not his mouth.

I was not redeemed with corruptible things, like silver or gold, but with the precious blood of Christ, as of a lamb without blemish and without spot. He was manifest in these last times for me who through Him believes in You, Lord God, that my faith and hope are in You.

Worthy is the Lamb who was slain to receive power and riches, wisdom, and strength and honor, glory and blessing!

May that song of the angels be my lifelong song, Lord!
All praise to You and to Your Son for
the sacrifice that saved my soul!

JOHN 1:29; HEBREWS 10:4–7; ISAIAH 53:7;
1 PETER 1:18–21; REVELATION 5:12

Consider what great things He has done for you.

Lord, my God, I shall remember that You have led me all the way these many years in the wilderness, to humble me and test me, to know what was in my heart, whether I would keep Your commandments or not. I should know in my heart that as a man chastens his son, so You, Lord God, chasten me.

I know, O Lord, that Your judgments are right, and that in faithfulness You have afflicted me. It is good for me that I have been afflicted, that I may learn Your statutes. Before I was afflicted I went astray, but now I keep Your word. You, Lord, have chastened me severely, but You have not given me over to death. You have not dealt with me according to my sins, nor punished me according to my iniquities. For as the heavens are high above the earth, so great is Your mercy toward those like me who fear You. You know my frame; You remember that I am dust.

Great are the things You have done for me—
even in the wilderness! I praise You, heavenly Father,
for Your love and faithfulness.

---

1 SAMUEL 12:24; DEUTERONOMY 8:2, 5; PSALM 119:75, 71, 67;
PSALM 118:18; PSALM 103:10–11, 14

*Whoever keeps His word,
truly the love of God is perfected in him.*

You, the God of peace who brought up my Lord Jesus from the dead, that great Shepherd of the sheep, through the blood of the everlasting covenant make me complete in every good work to do Your will, working in me what is well pleasing in Your sight, through Jesus Christ, to whom be glory forever and ever. Amen.

Now by this I know that I know You, if I keep Your commandments. If I love Jesus, I will keep His word; and You, my Father, will love me, and You and Your Son will come to me and make Your home with me. Whoever abides in Jesus does not sin. Whoever sins has neither seen Jesus nor known Him. So I let no one deceive me. I who practices righteousness am righteous, just as You are righteous. Love has been perfected in me in this: that I may have boldness in the day of judgment; because as You are, so am I in this world.

*Teach me to abide in Jesus that I might not sin,
that I might do Your will, keep Your Word,
and know Your fellowship and love.*

1 JOHN 2:5; HEBREWS 13:20–21; 1 JOHN 2:3;
JOHN 14:23; 1 JOHN 3:6–7; 1 JOHN 4:17

May

Surely the

Lord is in this place,

and

I did not know it.

The fruit of the Spirit is . . . peace.

To be spiritually minded, Lord God, is life and peace. You have called me to peace. Your Son leaves peace with me, His peace He gives to me; not as the world gives does He give to me. So I let not my heart be troubled, neither do I let it be afraid. You, the God of hope, fill me with all joy and peace in believing, that I may abound in hope by the power of Your Holy Spirit.

I know whom I have believed and am persuaded that You are able to keep what I have committed to You until that Day. You will keep me in perfect peace, when my mind is stayed on You, because I trust in You.

The work of righteousness will be peace, and the effect of righteousness, quietness and assurance forever. I will dwell in a peaceful habitation, in secure dwellings, and in quiet resting places. I listen to You and dwell safely, and am secure, without fear of evil.

Great peace have I who loves Your law.

Thank You for the gift of Your peace
and for the security and hope I find in You.

GALATIANS 5:22; ROMANS 8:6; 1 CORINTHIANS 7:15;
JOHN 14:27; ROMANS 15:13; 2 TIMOTHY 1:12; ISAIAH 26:3;
ISAIAH 32:17–18; PROVERBS 1:33; PSALM 119:165

Surely the Lord is in this place,
and I did not know it.

Lord God, where two or three are gathered together in Your name, You are there in our midst. You are with me always, even to the end of the age. Your Presence will go with me, and give me rest.

Where can I go from Your Spirit? Or flee from Your presence? If I ascend into heaven, You are there; if I make my bed in hell, behold, You are there. You are a God near at hand and not a God afar off. Can I hide myself in secret places, so You shall not see me? Do You not fill heaven and earth?

Even heaven and the heaven of heavens cannot contain You. How much less a temple I can be built! You are the High and Lofty One who inhabits eternity, whose name is Holy. You dwell in the high and holy place, with those like me who have a contrite and humble spirit, to revive the spirit of the humble, and to revive the heart of the contrite ones. I am a temple of You, O living God.

Thank You for being with me always, in all places.

GENESIS 28:16; MATTHEW 18:20; MATTHEW 28:20;
EXODUS 33:14; PSALM 139:7–8; JEREMIAH 23:23–24;
1 KINGS 8:27; ISAIAH 57:15; 2 CORINTHIANS 6:16

You shall be perfect,
just as your Father in heaven is perfect.

You are Almighty God; I walk before You and am blameless. I shall be holy to You, for You the Lord are holy, and have separated me from the peoples, that I should be Yours.

I was bought at a price; therefore I glorify You, my God, in my body and in my spirit, which are Yours.

I am complete in You, the head of all principality and power . . . who gave Yourself for me, that You might redeem me from every lawless deed. I will be diligent to be found by You in peace, without spot and blameless.

Blessed are the undefiled in the way, those who walk in Your law, Lord God! I look into the perfect law of liberty and continue in it, and am not a forgetful hearer but a doer of the work, I will be blessed in what I do. Search me, O God, and know my heart; try me, and know my anxieties; and see if there is any wicked way in me, and lead me in the way everlasting.

You call me to a holy life.
Empower me, Lord, to obey Your law and glorify You.

MATTHEW 5:48; GENESIS 17:1; LEVITICUS 20:26;
1 CORINTHIANS 6:20; COLOSSIANS 2:10; TITUS 2:14;
2 PETER 3:14; PSALM 119:1; JAMES 1:25; PSALM 139:23–24

Behold, the Lord's hand is not shortened, that it cannot save;
nor His ear heavy, that it cannot hear.

In the day when I cried out, You answered me, and made me bold with strength in my soul. As in answer to Daniel's prayer You sent Gabriel, swiftly, so Lord God, do not hide Your face from me; do not turn Your servant away in anger; You have been my help; do not leave me nor forsake me, O God of my salvation. But You, O Lord, do not be far from Me; O My Strength, hasten to help Me!

Ah, Lord God! Behold, You have made the heavens and the earth by Your great power and outstretched arm. There is nothing too hard for You. You delivered me from so great a death, and You do deliver me; in whom I trust that You will still deliver me. Shall You, Lord God, not avenge Your own elect—we who cry out day and night to You—though You bear long with us? Jesus tells me that You will avenge us speedily.

Lord God, there is nothing too hard for You!
Make me bold to seek Your face
and patient to wait for Your answer.

ISAIAH 59:1; PSALM 138:3; DANIEL 9:21;
PSALM 27:9; PSALM 22:19; JEREMIAH 32:17;
2 CORINTHIANS 1:10; LUKE 18:7–8

*Therefore do not worry, saying, "What shall we eat?" or
"What shall we drink?" or "What shall we wear?"
For your heavenly Father knows that you need all these things.*

Oh, as one of Your saints, I fear You, Lord! There is no want to those who fear You. The young lions lack and suffer hunger; but those who seek You, Lord, shall not lack any good thing. No good thing will You withhold from those who walk uprightly. O Lord of hosts, how blessed I am because I trust in You!

You want me to be without care...anxious for nothing, but in everything by prayer and supplication, with thanksgiving, to let my requests be made known to You, my God, my heavenly Father.

Are not two sparrows sold for a copper coin? And not one of them falls to the ground apart from Your will. But the very hairs of my head are all numbered. I do not fear therefore; I am of more value than many sparrows. Why am I so fearful? How is it that I have no faith? I will have faith in You, Lord God.

*Thank You that I can trust You completely to care for me
and provide for my needs.*

MATTHEW 6:31–32; PSALM 34:9–10; PSALM 84:11–12;
1 CORINTHIANS 7:32; PHILIPPIANS 4:6; MATTHEW 10:29–31;
MARK 4:40; MARK 11:22

Mercy and truth have met together;
righteousness and peace have kissed.

Almighty Lord, You are a just God and a Savior. You, Lord, are well pleased for Your righteousness' sake; You will exalt the law and make it honorable. Lord God, You were in Christ reconciling the world to Yourself, not imputing my trespasses to me. God, You set Jesus forth as a propitiation by His blood, through faith, to demonstrate Your righteousness, because in Your forbearance You had passed over the sins that I had previously committed, to demonstrate at the present time Your righteousness, that You might be just and the justifier of the one who has faith in Jesus. And He was wounded for my transgressions, He was bruised for my iniquities; the chastisement for our peace was upon Him, and by His stripes I am healed. Who shall bring a charge against me, Your elect? It is You, Lord God, who justifies. If I do not work but believe on You who justifies the ungodly, my faith is accounted for righteousness.

What a picture of grace: You are the Just and the Justifier!
I am thankful that righteousness and peace have kissed!

PSALM 85:10; ISAIAH 45:21; ISAIAH 42:21;
2 CORINTHIANS 5:19; ROMANS 3:25–26;
ISAIAH 53:5; ROMANS 8:33; ROMANS 4:5

You will hear of wars and rumors of wars.
See that you are not troubled.

L ord God, You are my refuge and strength, a very present help
in trouble. Therefore I will not fear, though the earth be
removed, and though the mountains be carried into
the midst of the sea; though its waters roar and be troubled,
though the mountains shake with its swelling. I will enter my
chambers, and shut my door behind me; hide myself, as it were,
for a little moment, until the indignation is past. For behold,
You, Lord, come out of Your place to punish the inhabitants of
the earth for their iniquity. In the shadow of Your wings I will
make my refuge, until these calamities have passed by. My life is
hidden with Christ in You, Lord God.

I will not be afraid of evil tidings; my heart is steadfast,
trusting in You, Lord.

Jesus has spoken to me, that in Him I may have peace. In
the world I will have tribulation; but I will be of good cheer, for
You have overcome the world.

You are my peace and hope, Lord God,
my Refuge and my Strength—and I praise You.

MATTHEW 24:6; PSALM 46:1–3; ISAIAH 26:20–21;
PSALM 57:1; COLOSSIANS 3:3; PSALM 112:7; JOHN 16:33

It pleased the Lord to bruise Him;
He has put Him to grief.

Lord Jesus, You prayed, "Now My soul is troubled, and what shall I say? 'Father, save Me from this hour'? For this purpose I came to this hour. Father, glorify Your name." Father answered, "I have glorified it and will glorify it again." You also prayed, "Father, if it is Your will, take this cup from Me; nevertheless not My will, but Yours, be done." An angel appeared to You from heaven, strengthening You. . . .

In appearance as a man, You humbled Yourself and became obedient to the point of death, even the death of the cross. Therefore Your Father loves You, because You lay down Your life that You may take it again. For You came down from heaven, not to do Your own will, but the will of Your Father who sent You. Shall You not drink the cup which Your Father has given You?

Your Father has not left You alone, for You always do those things that please Him. You are His beloved Son, in whom He is well pleased . . . His Elect One in whom His soul delights!

Jesus, enable me to follow
Your obedience, courage, and faith.

––––––––

ISAIAH 53:10; JOHN 12:27–28; LUKE 22:42–43;
PHILIPPIANS 2:8; JOHN 10:17; JOHN 6:38; JOHN 18:11;
JOHN 8:29; MATTHEW 3:17; ISAIAH 42:1

Faith is the substance of things hoped for,
the evidence of things not seen.

Lord God, if in this life only I have hope in Christ, I am of all men the most pitiable.

Eye has not seen, nor ear heard, nor have entered into the heart of man the things which You have prepared for those like me who love You. But You have revealed them to us through Your Spirit. After I believed, I was sealed with Your Holy Spirit of promise, who is the guarantee of my inheritance until the redemption of the purchased possession.

Jesus said to him, "Thomas, because you have seen Me, you have believed." I am blessed, for I have not seen and yet I have believed. I have not seen Jesus yet I love Him. Though now I do not see Him, yet believing, I rejoice with joy inexpressible and full of glory, receiving the end of my faith—the salvation of my soul.

I walk by faith, not by sight. I will not cast away my confidence, which has great reward.

What a privilege to be called to know Jesus,
believe in Him, and hope in Him!

HEBREWS 11:1; 1 CORINTHIANS 15:19; 1 CORINTHIANS 2:9–10;
EPHESIANS 1:13–14; JOHN 20:29; 1 PETER 1:8–9;
2 CORINTHIANS 5:7; HEBREWS 10:35

For this purpose the Son of God was manifested,
that He might destroy the works of the devil.

Lord God, I do not wrestle against flesh and blood, but against principalities, against powers, against the rulers of the darkness of this age, against spiritual hosts of wickedness in the heavenly places. Inasmuch as I have partaken of flesh and blood, Jesus Himself likewise shared in the same, that through death He might destroy him who had the power of death, that is, the devil. Having disarmed principalities and powers, Jesus made a public spectacle of them, triumphing over them in it. John the apostle heard a loud voice saying in heaven, "Now salvation, and strength, and the kingdom of our God, and the power of His Christ have come, for the accuser of our brethren, who accused them before our God day and night, has been cast down. And they overcame him by the blood of the Lamb and by the word of their testimony and they did not love their lives to the death."

Thanks be to You, Almighty God, who gives me the victory through my Lord Jesus Christ.

The battle is real, Lord, but the victory is sure—
and You give me strength in the meantime! I praise You!

---

1 JOHN 3:8; EPHESIANS 6:12; HEBREWS 2:14;
COLOSSIANS 2:15; REVELATION 12:10–11;
1 CORINTHIANS 15:57

Awake to righteousness,
and do not sin.

I am a son of light and of the day. Therefore I will not sleep, Lord God, as others do, but will watch and be sober. It is high time to awake out of sleep; for now my salvation is nearer than when I first believed. The night is far spent, the day is at hand. Therefore I cast off the works of darkness, and I put on the armor of light. I take up the whole armor of God, that I may be able to withstand in the evil day, and having done all, to stand. I cast away from myself all the transgressions which I have committed, and get myself a new heart and a new spirit. I lay aside all filthiness and overflow of wickedness, and receive with meekness the implanted word, which is able to save my soul. As a little child, I abide in Jesus, that when He appears, I may have confidence and not be ashamed before Him at His coming. If I know that He is righteous, I know that everyone who practices righteousness is born of Him.

Lord God, only in Your strength
can I live a righteous life that pleases You.
Please empower me!

---

1 CORINTHIANS 15:34; 1 THESSALONIANS 5:5–6;
ROMANS 13:11–12; EPHESIANS 6:13; EZEKIEL 18:31;
JAMES 1:21; 1 JOHN 2:28–29

*Beloved, let us love one another, for love is of God;
and everyone who loves is born of God and knows God.*

Father God, Your love has been poured out in my heart by Your Holy Spirit who was given to me. I did not receive the spirit of bondage again to fear, but I received the Spirit of adoption by whom I cry out, "Abba, Father."

The Spirit Himself bears witness with my spirit that I am Your child, Father God. I believe in Your Son and have the witness in myself.

In this the love of God was manifested toward me, that God has sent His only begotten Son into the world, that I might live through Him. In Him I have redemption through His blood, the forgiveness of sins, according to the riches of His grace. That in the ages to come You might show the exceeding riches of Your grace, Father, in Your kindness toward me in Christ Jesus.

Since, Lord God, You so loved me, I also ought to love others.

*You are love, God! It's Your very nature!
Fill me with that love, I ask, so that I might honor You
as I love people with Your love.*

---

1 JOHN 4:7; ROMANS 5:5; ROMANS 8:15–16; 1 JOHN 5:10;
1 JOHN 4:9; EPHESIANS 1:7; EPHESIANS 2:7; 1 JOHN 4:11

Pray everywhere, lifting up holy hands,
without wrath and doubting.

As a true worshiper, I will worship You, Father God, in spirit and truth; for You are seeking such to worship You. You are Spirit, and those of us who worship You must worship in spirit and truth. When I call . . . and when I cry, You will say, "Here I am." Whenever I stand praying, if I have anything against anyone, I will forgive him.

Without faith it is impossible to please You, Lord God, for I who come to You must believe that You are, and that You are a rewarder of those who diligently seek You. So I ask in faith, with no doubting, for if I doubt I am like a wave of the sea driven and tossed by the wind. For let me not then suppose that I will receive anything from You, Lord.

If I regard iniquity in my heart, You, Lord, will not hear me. These things were written to me, that I may not sin. And if I sin, I have an Advocate with the Father, Jesus Christ the righteous. And He Himself is the propitiation for my sins.

Lord God, to You I cry, keep me from sin and doubt.

---

1 TIMOTHY 2:8; JOHN 4:23–24; ISAIAH 58:9; MARK 11:25; HEBREWS 11:6; JAMES 1:6–7; PSALM 66:18; 1 JOHN 2:1–2

The fellowship of His sufferings.

Lord Jesus, it is enough for a disciple that he be like his teacher, and a servant like his master.

You, my Teacher and Master, were despised and rejected by men, a Man of sorrows and acquainted with grief. And we humans hid our faces from You; You were despised, and we did not esteem You. In the world I will have tribulation. Because I am not of the world, but You chose me out of the world, therefore the world hates me.

Jesus, You looked for someone to take pity, but there was none. So, too, at Paul's first defense no one stood with him, but all forsook him.

Foxes have holes and birds have nests, but You had nowhere to lay Your head. Here I have no continuing city, but I seek the one to come.

Let me run with endurance the race that is set before me, looking unto You, Jesus, the author and finisher of my faith, who for the joy that was set before You endured the cross, despising the shame, and have sat down at the right hand of the throne of God.

As I share in Your sufferings, Jesus, help me look to You!

PHILIPPIANS 3:10; MATTHEW 10:25; ISAIAH 53:3;
JOHN 16:33; JOHN 15:19; PSALM 69:20; 2 TIMOTHY 4:16;
MATTHEW 8:20; HEBREWS 13:14; HEBREWS 12:1–2

God will wipe away every tear . . . ; there shall be no more death,
nor sorrow, . . . for the former things have passed away.

Almighty God, You will swallow up death forever, and wipe away tears from my face; the rebuke of Your people You will take away from all the earth; for You, Lord God, have spoken. The sun shall no longer go down, nor shall the moon withdraw itself; for You, Lord, will be my everlasting light, and the days of my mourning shall be ended. Then I will not say, "I am sick"; I will dwell in it and be forgiven my iniquity. The voice of weeping shall no longer be heard in her, nor the voice of crying. Sorrow and sighing shall flee away.

You will ransom me from the power of the grave; You will redeem me from death. Death, God will be your plagues! Grave, He will be your destruction! The last enemy will be destroyed—death. Then it shall be brought to pass as written: "Death is swallowed up in victory."

The things which I cannot see are eternal.

No more death, weeping, tears, sorrow, or mourning.
Come quickly, almighty and victorious Lord!

REVELATION 21:4; ISAIAH 25:8; ISAIAH 60:20; ISAIAH 33:24;
ISAIAH 65:19; ISAIAH 35:10; HOSEA 13:14;
1 CORINTHIANS 15:26, 54; 2 CORINTHIANS 4:18

A bondservant of Jesus Christ.

I call You Teacher and Lord, and so You are. If I serve You, Lord Jesus, I will follow You; and where You are, there I, Your servant, will be also. If I serve You, Your Father will honor me. I take Your yoke and learn from You, for You are gentle and lowly in heart, and I find rest for my soul. Your yoke is easy and Your burden is light.

Things that were gain to me, these I count loss for You, Christ Jesus. Having been set free from sin, and become a slave of God, I have fruit to holiness, and the end, everlasting life.

You no longer call me servant, for a servant does not know what his master is doing; but You call me friend, for all that You heard from Your Father You have made known to me. I am no longer a slave but a son.

Therefore I stand fast in the liberty by which You, Jesus Christ, have made me free, and I will not be entangled again with a yoke of bondage. I have been called to liberty; I will not use liberty as an opportunity for the flesh.

As You lead, let me follow.

———————————

ROMANS 1:1; JOHN 13:13; JOHN 12:26;
MATTHEW 11:29–30; PHILIPPIANS 3:7; ROMANS 6:22;
JOHN 15:15; GALATIANS 4:7; GALATIANS 5:1, 13

I am the Lord your God: walk in My statutes,
keep My judgments, and do them.

Lord God, as You who called me are holy, I am also to be holy in all my conduct. If I say I abide in Jesus I ought to walk as He walked. If I know He is righteous, I know everyone who practices righteousness is born of Him. Circumcision and uncircumcision are nothing, but keeping Your commandments, God, is what matters. If I shall keep the whole law, and yet stumble in one point, I am guilty of all.

Not that I am sufficient of myself to think of anything as being from myself, but my sufficiency is from You, Lord God. So teach me, O Lord, the way of Your statutes.

I work out my own salvation with fear and trembling; for it is You who works in me both to will and to do for Your good pleasure. You are the God of peace and will make me complete in every good work to do Your will, working in me what is well pleasing in Your sight, through Jesus Christ.

Lord, may I know Your power
as I walk in Your ways and follow Christ's example.

EZEKIEL 20:19; 1 PETER 1:15; 1 JOHN 2:6, 29;
1 CORINTHIANS 7:19; JAMES 2:10; 2 CORINTHIANS 3:5;
PSALM 119:33; PHILIPPIANS 2:12–13; HEBREWS 13:20–21

As the Father has life in Himself,
so He has granted the Son to have life in Himself.

My Savior Jesus Christ has abolished death and brought life and immortality to light through the gospel. He is the resurrection and the life. Because He lives, I will live also. I have become a partaker of Christ . . . of the Holy Spirit . . . of the divine nature. The first Adam became a living being. The last Adam became a life-giving spirit. It is a mystery: we shall not all sleep, but we shall all be changed—in a moment, in the twinkling of an eye, at the last trumpet. For the trumpet will sound, and the dead will be raised incorruptible, and we shall be changed.

Holy, holy, holy, Lord God Almighty, who was and is and is to come! You live forever and ever. The blessed and only Potentate, the King of kings and Lord of lords, who alone has immortality. Now to the King eternal, immortal . . . be honor and glory forever and ever. Amen.

You alone are worthy of praise, Lord God!
I praise You for the gifts of life and life eternal!

JOHN 5:26; 2 TIMOTHY 1:10; JOHN 11:25; JOHN 14:19;
HEBREWS 3:14; HEBREWS 6:4; 2 PETER 1:4;
1 CORINTHIANS 15:45, 51–52; REVELATION 4:8–9;
1 TIMOTHY 6:15–16; 1 TIMOTHY 1:17

Wash me thoroughly from my iniquity.

Holy God, You will cleanse me from all my iniquity by which I have sinned against You, and You will pardon all my iniquities by which I have sinned and by which I have transgressed against You. Then You will sprinkle clean water on me, and I shall be clean; You will cleanse me from all my filthiness and from all my idols.

Unless I am born of water and the Spirit, I cannot enter Your kingdom, Lord God. If the blood of bulls and goats and the ashes of a heifer, sprinkling the unclean, sanctifies for the purifying of the flesh, how much more shall the blood of Christ, who through the eternal Spirit offered Himself without spot to God, cleanse my conscience from dead works to serve You, the living God?

You saved us for Your name's sake, that You might make Your mighty power known. Not unto me, O Lord, not unto me, but to Your name give glory, because of Your mercy, and because of Your truth.

Looking at You in all Your purity and holiness enables me
to see my sin more clearly, Lord God, and prompts me to praise You
for the forgiveness You graciously extend me.

PSALM 51:2; JEREMIAH 33:8; EZEKIEL 36:25; JOHN 3:5;
HEBREWS 9:13–14; PSALM 106:8; PSALM 115:1

Take heed to yourself.

Lord God, I know that everyone who competes for the prize is temperate in all things. Now they do it to obtain a perishable crown, but I for an imperishable crown. Therefore I run thus: not with uncertainty. Thus I fight: not as one who beats the air. But I discipline my body and bring it into subjection, lest, when I have preached to others, I myself should become disqualified. I put on the whole armor You provide, that I may be able to stand against the wiles of the devil. For I do not wrestle against flesh and blood, but against principalities, against powers, against the rulers of the darkness of this age, against spiritual hosts of wickedness in the heavenly places.

I who am Christ's have crucified the flesh with its passions and desires. If I live in the Spirit, I will also walk in the Spirit. For as many as are led by the Spirit of God, we are sons of God. I meditate on these things; I give myself entirely to them, that my progress may be evident to all.

Teach me, Lord, to walk in Your Spirit, exercise self-control, and stand against the devil.

1 TIMOTHY 4:16; 1 CORINTHIANS 9:25–27; EPHESIANS 6:11–12; GALATIANS 5:24–25; ROMANS 8:14; 1 TIMOTHY 4:15

*My brethren, be strong in the Lord and
in the power of His might.*

Lord God, Your grace is sufficient for me, for Your strength is made perfect in weakness. Therefore most gladly I will rather boast in my infirmities, that the power of Christ may rest upon me. Therefore I take pleasure in infirmities, in reproaches, in needs, in persecutions, in distresses, for Christ's sake. For when I am weak, then I am strong. I will go in Your strength, my Lord God; I will make mention of Your righteousness, of Yours only. The gospel of Christ is Your power of salvation.

I can do all things through Christ who strengthens me. I also labor, striving according to Jesus' working which works in me mightily. I have this treasure in earthen vessels, that the excellence of the power may be of You, Almighty God, and not of me. Your joy, Lord God, is my strength . . . and I am strengthened with all might, according to Your glorious power, for all patience and longsuffering with joy.

*Almighty God, I praise You for sharing Your strength—
through Christ—with me that I might glorify You with my life!*

EPHESIANS 6:10; 2 CORINTHIANS 12:9–10; PSALM 71:16;
ROMANS 1:16; PHILIPPIANS 4:13; COLOSSIANS 1:29;
2 CORINTHIANS 4:7; NEHEMIAH 8:10; COLOSSIANS 1:11

Peace I leave with you, My peace I give to you;
not as the world gives do I give to you.

Eternal God, the world is passing away, and the lust of it. Surely I walk about like a shadow; surely I busy myself in vain; I heap up riches, and do not know who will gather them. What fruit did I have then in the things of which I am now ashamed? For the end of those things is death.

Like Martha, I am worried and troubled about many things. But like Mary one thing is needed, and that good part will not be taken away. You want me to be without care.

These things You have spoken to me, that in You I may have peace. In the world I will have tribulation; but I can be of good cheer, You have overcome the world. You, the Lord of peace, give me peace always in every way. You, Lord, bless me and keep me; You make Your face shine upon me, and are gracious to me; You lift up Your countenance upon me, and give me peace.

May I focus on Jesus rather than on the fading things
and the tribulations of this world.

———————

JOHN 14:27; 1 JOHN 2:17; PSALM 39:6; ROMANS 6:21;
LUKE 10:41–42; 1 CORINTHIANS 7:32; JOHN 16:33;
2 THESSALONIANS 3:16; NUMBERS 6:24–26

You shall put the two stones on the shoulders
of the ephod as memorial stones for the sons of Israel.
So Aaron shall bear their names before the Lord.

Lord Jesus, because You continue forever, have an unchangeable priesthood. Therefore You are able to save to the uttermost those like me who come to God through You, since You always live to make intercession for us. You are able to keep me from stumbling, and to present me faultless before the presence of God's glory.

Seeing that I have in You, Jesus the Son of God, a great High Priest who has passed through the heavens, let me hold fast my confession. For I do not have a High Priest who cannot sympathize with my weaknesses, but was in all points tempted as I am, yet without sin. Let me therefore come boldly to the throne of grace.

Lord God, I who am among Your beloved, shall dwell in safety by You, who shelters me all the day long; and I shall dwell between Your shoulders.

Salvation from You, intercession from You, and righteousness in
You—I praise You, my Jesus, my High Priest and Savior!

EXODUS 28:12; HEBREWS 7:24–25; JUDE 24;
HEBREWS 4:14–16; DEUTERONOMY 33:12

Do not grieve the Holy Spirit of God,
by whom you were sealed for the day of redemption.

Lord God, You have given me the love of Your Holy Spirit . . . my Helper. In all my affliction You are afflicted, and the Angel of Your Presence saves me; in Your love and in Your pity You redeem, and You bear, and carry me. But I rebel and grieve Your Holy Spirit; so You turn Yourself against me as an enemy, and You fight against me.

I know that I abide in You, Lord God, and You in me, because You have given me of Your Spirit. Believing, I was sealed with the Holy Spirit of promise, the guarantee of my inheritance until the redemption of the purchased possession. So I will walk in the Spirit, and not fulfill the lust of the flesh. For the flesh lusts against the Spirit, and the Spirit against the flesh; and these are contrary to one another, so that I do not do the things that I wish.

Your Spirit also helps in my weaknesses.

> *Thank You, God, for the gift of the Holy Spirit,*
> *who is my Helper, my Strength, my Guide.*
> *May He enable me to live so that I honor You.*

───────────────

EPHESIANS 4:30; ROMANS 15:30; JOHN 14:26;
ISAIAH 63:9–10; 1 JOHN 4:13; EPHESIANS 1:13–14;
GALATIANS 5:16–17; ROMANS 8:26

How great is Your goodness,
which You have laid up for those who fear You.

Lord God, since the beginning of the world men have not heard nor perceived by the ear, nor has the eye seen any God besides You, who acts for me who waits for You. Eye has not seen, nor ear heard, nor have entered into my heart the things which You have prepared for those who love You. But You have revealed them through Your Spirit. You will show me the path of life; in Your presence is fullness of joy; at Your right hand are pleasures forevermore.

How precious is Your lovingkindness, O God! Therefore, as a child of man, I put my trust under the shadow of Your wings. I am abundantly satisfied with the fullness of Your house, and You give me drink from the river of Your pleasures. For with You is the fountain of life; in Your light I see light.

Godliness is profitable for all things, having promise of the life that now is and of that which is to come.

Lord God, may I live a godly life in Your light
and know Your joy and lovingkindness toward me.

PSALM 31:19; ISAIAH 64:4; 1 CORINTHIANS 2:9–10;
PSALM 16:11; PSALM 36:7–9; 1 TIMOTHY 4:8

Our Lord Jesus . . .
that great Shepherd of the sheep.

Jesus, my Chief Shepherd, You are the good shepherd; and You know Your sheep, and am known by Your own. Your sheep hear Your voice, and You know those who follow You. And You give me eternal life, and I shall never perish; neither shall anyone snatch me out of Your hand.

You, Lord, are my shepherd; I shall not want. You make me to lie down in green pastures; You lead me beside the still waters. You restore my soul, You lead me in the paths of righteousness for Your name's sake.

Like a sheep I have gone astray; turned to my own way; and the Lord God has laid on You my iniquity, the iniquity of us all. You are the good shepherd. The good shepherd gives His life for me. You will seek what was lost and bring back what was driven away, bind up the broken and strengthen what was sick. I was like a sheep going astray, but I have now returned to the Shepherd and Overseer of my soul.

You are the Good Shepherd, Jesus—and I, an often straying sheep, need You. I thank You for Your provision and protection.

HEBREWS 13:20; 1 PETER 5:4; JOHN 10:14, 27–28;
PSALM 23:1–3; ISAIAH 53:6; JOHN 10:11;
EZEKIEL 34:16; 1 PETER 2:25

The Lord is good, a stronghold in the day of trouble;
and He knows those who trust in Him.

I praise You, the Lord of hosts, for You, Lord, are good, for Your mercy endures forever. You, Lord God, are my refuge and strength, a very present help in trouble. I say of You, Lord, "You are my refuge and my fortress; my God, in You I will trust." Who is like me, one saved by You, Lord, the shield of my help and the sword of my majesty! As for You, God, Your way is perfect; Your word is proven; You are a shield to all who trust in You. For who is God, except You, Lord? And who is a rock, except You, my God?

If I love You, I am known by You. Your solid foundation stands sealed with: "You know those who are Yours" and "Let everyone who names the name of Christ depart from iniquity." You, Lord, know the way of the righteous, but the way of the ungodly shall perish. I have found grace in Your sight, and You know me by name.

What a privilege to be known by You, Lord God!
What a foundation for peace and hope!

NAHUM 1:7; JEREMIAH 33:11; PSALM 46:1; PSALM 91:2;
DEUTERONOMY 33:29; 2 SAMUEL 22:31–32; 1 CORINTHIANS 8:3;
2 TIMOTHY 2:19; PSALM 1:6; EXODUS 33:17

We also eagerly wait for the Savior.

Your grace, Lord God, that brings salvation has appeared to all men, teaching me that, denying ungodliness and worldly lusts, I should live soberly, righteously, and godly in the present age, looking for the blessed hope and glorious appearing of my great God and Savior Jesus Christ, who gave Himself for me, that He might redeem me from every lawless deed and purify for Himself His own special people, zealous for good works. I, according to Your promise, look for new heavens and a new earth in which righteousness dwells. Therefore, looking forward to these things, I will be diligent to be found by You in peace, without spot and blameless.

Christ was offered once to bear my sins. To those like me who eagerly wait for Him He will appear a second time, apart from sin, for salvation. And I will say in that day: "Behold, this is my God; I have waited for Him, and He will save me. This is the Lord; I have waited for Him; I will be glad and rejoice in His salvation."

I await Christ's coming!
He who is King of kings and Lord of Lords shall reign forever!
Hallelujah!

PHILIPPIANS 3:20; TITUS 2:11–14; 2 PETER 3:13–14;
HEBREWS 9:28; ISAIAH 25:9

The life of the flesh is in the blood, and I have given it to you
upon the altar to make atonement for your souls;
for it is the blood that makes atonement for the soul.

Lord God, indeed Your Lamb, Jesus, takes away the sin of the world . . . by His blood, the blood of the Lamb . . . the precious blood of Christ, as of a lamb without blemish and without spot. Without shedding of blood there is no remission. The blood of Jesus Christ Your Son cleanses me from all sin.

With His own blood He entered the Most Holy Place once for all, having obtained eternal redemption. Therefore, I have boldness to enter the Holiest by the blood of Jesus, by a new and living way which He consecrated for me, through the veil, that is, His flesh. So I draw near with a true heart in full assurance of faith.

I was bought at a price; therefore I glorify You, Lord God, in my body and in my spirit, which are Yours.

Lord God, You provided Your Son, the perfect Lamb,
sacrificed for sin once and for all!
May my life be an offering of thanksgiving!

LEVITICUS 17:11; JOHN 1:29; REVELATION 7:14;
I PETER 1:19; HEBREWS 9:22; I JOHN 1:7; HEBREWS 9:12;
HEBREWS 10:19–20, 22; I CORINTHIANS 6:20

Let us therefore be diligent to enter that rest.

Lord God, I enter by the narrow gate; for wide is the gate and broad is the way that leads to destruction. Narrow is the gate and difficult is the way which leads to life, and few find it. Your kingdom suffers violence, and the violent take it by force. I do not labor for the food which perishes, but for that which endures to everlasting life, which the Son of Man will give me. I will be even more diligent to make my calling and election sure, for so an entrance will be supplied to me abundantly into the everlasting kingdom of my Lord and Savior Jesus Christ. I will run in such a way that I may obtain it. Everyone who competes for the prize is temperate in all things. Now they do it to obtain a perishable crown, but I for an imperishable crown.

For I who have entered Your rest have myself also ceased from my works as You, God, did from Yours. You, Lord, will be to me an everlasting light, and You, God, my glory.

Help me, Lord God, live for You and
walk the narrow path so I may rest in You.

HEBREWS 4:11; MATTHEW 7:13–14; MATTHEW 11:12;
JOHN 6:27; 2 PETER 1:10–11; 1 CORINTHIANS 9:24–25;
HEBREWS 4:10; ISAIAH 60:19

Your name shall . . . be called . . . Israel;
for you have struggled with God and with men,
and have prevailed.

My Lord God, in his strength Jacob struggled with You. Yes he struggled with Your Angel and prevailed; he wept, and sought favor from You. Abraham did not waver at Your promise through unbelief, but was strengthened in faith, giving You glory.

I will have faith in You. For assuredly, Jesus taught, whoever says to this mountain, "Be removed and be cast into the sea," and does not doubt in his heart, but believes that those things he says will be done, he will have whatever he says. Therefore Jesus says to me, whatever things I ask when I pray, if I believe that I will receive them, I will have them. If I can believe, all things are possible to me who believes. I am blessed for I believe; there will be a fulfillment of those things which were told me from You, Lord.

Lord, increase my faith.

Yes, Lord, increase my faith so that I may see You more clearly,
love You more dearly, and follow You more nearly.

GENESIS 32:28; HOSEA 12:3–4; ROMANS 4:20;
MARK 11:22–24; MARK 9:23; LUKE 1:45; LUKE 17:5

June

In everything

by prayer and supplication,

with thanksgiving,

let your requests be made

known to God.

The fruit of the Spirit is love, joy, peace,
longsuffering, kindness, goodness, faithfulness.

You, Lord, the Lord God, are merciful and gracious, longsuffering, and abounding in goodness and truth. May I walk worthy of the calling with which I was called, with all lowliness and gentleness, with longsuffering, bearing with others in love. May I be kind to others, tenderhearted, forgiving others, even as You in Christ also forgave me. The wisdom that is from above is first pure, then peaceable, gentle, willing to yield, full of mercy and good fruits, without partiality and without hypocrisy. Love suffers long and is kind.

In due season I shall reap if I do not lose heart. Therefore I will be patient until the coming of the Lord Jesus. I see how the farmer waits for the precious fruit of the earth, waiting patiently for it until it receives the early and latter rain. I will also be patient. I will establish my heart, for the coming of the Lord is at hand.

Lord, teach me to live so that Your Holy Spirit's presence
in me bears fruit that blesses others and honors You.

GALATIANS 5:22; EXODUS 34:6; EPHESIANS 4:1–2;
EPHESIANS 4:32; JAMES 3:17; 1 CORINTHIANS 13:4;
GALATIANS 6:9; JAMES 5:7–8

Thus you shall eat it: with a belt on your waist. . . .
So you shall eat it in haste. It is the Lord's Passover.

I will arise and depart, for this is not my rest. Here I have no continuing city, but I seek the one to come. There remains therefore a rest for me who am one of Yours, Lord God.

I will let my waist be girded and my lamps burn; and I myself will be like one who waits for the master, when he will return from the wedding, that when he comes and knocks I may open to him immediately. Blessed are those servants whom the master, when he comes, will find watching. I gird up the loins of my mind, I will be sober, and I will rest my hope fully upon the grace that is to be brought to me at the revelation of Jesus Christ. One thing I do, forgetting those things which are behind . . . I press toward the goal for the prize of the upward call of God in Christ Jesus. Therefore if I am mature, this should be my mind-set.

May I be ever watching and
ready for the return of Your victorious Son.

EXODUS 12:11; MICAH 2:10; HEBREWS 13:14; HEBREWS 4:9;
LUKE 12:35–37; 1 PETER 1:13; PHILIPPIANS 3:13–15

Watch therefore, for you know neither the day nor the hour in which the Son of Man is coming.

I take heed to myself, lest my heart be weighed down with carousing, drunkenness, and cares of this life, and that Day come on me unexpectedly. For it will come as a snare on all those who dwell on the face of the whole earth. I watch therefore, and pray always that I may be counted worthy to escape all these things that will come to pass, and to stand before the Son of Man.

The day of the Lord so comes as a thief in the night. For when they say, "Peace and safety!" then sudden destruction comes upon them, as labor pains upon a pregnant woman. And they shall not escape. But I am not in darkness, so that this Day should overtake me as a thief. I am a son of light and son of the day. I am not of the night nor of darkness. Therefore let me not sleep, as others do, but let me watch and be sober.

I look forward to Your return, Lord Jesus!
Keep me ready and watching, I pray!

MATTHEW 25:13; LUKE 21:34–36; 1 THESSALONIANS 5:2–6

The glory of this latter temple shall be greater than the former, . . . and in this place I will give peace.

Lord God, the house to be built for You, must be exceedingly magnificent, famous and glorious throughout all countries. And Your glory did fill Your house.

Yet Your Son Jesus said, "Destroy this temple, and in three days I will raise it up." He was speaking of the temple of His body. What was made glorious had no glory, because of the glory that excels. The Word became flesh and dwelt among us, and we beheld His glory, the glory as of Your only begotten, full of grace and truth. God, You have in these last days spoken to us by Your Son, whom You have appointed heir of all things, through whom also You made the worlds.

Glory to You, Lord God in the highest, and on earth peace, goodwill toward men! Praise to Jesus, Prince of Peace, Himself my peace. Your peace, Lord God, which surpasses all understanding, will guard my heart and mind through Christ Jesus.

Lord God, the glorious temple of Your Son's resurrected body is key to my peace with You. I praise You!

HAGGAI 2:9; 1 CHRONICLES 22:5; 2 CHRONICLES 7:2; JOHN 2:19, 21; 2 CORINTHIANS 3:10; JOHN 1:14; HEBREWS 1:1–2; LUKE 2:14; ISAIAH 9:6; EPHESIANS 2:14; PHILIPPIANS 4:7

*When you have done all those things which you are commanded,
say, "We are unprofitable servants."*

Lord, where is my boasting then? It is excluded. By what law?
Of works? No; by the law of faith. What do I have, Lord
God, that I did not receive? If I did indeed receive it,
why do I boast as if I had not received it? By grace I have been
saved through faith, that not of myself; it is Your gift to me,
O God, not of works, lest I should boast. For I am Your
workmanship, created in Christ Jesus for good works, which You
prepared beforehand that I should walk in them.

By Your grace, Lord God, I am what I am, and Your grace
toward me was not in vain; but if I labor more abundantly than
others, it is not I, but Your grace with me. For of You, Almighty
God, and through You and to You are all things. All things come
from You; of Your own I have given You.

Do not enter into judgment with me, Your servant, for in
Your sight, Lord God, no one living is righteous.

*This unprofitable servant thanks You for
countless ways You pour Your grace into my life!*

LUKE 17:10; ROMANS 3:27; 1 CORINTHIANS 4:7;
EPHESIANS 2:8–10; 1 CORINTHIANS 15:10; ROMANS 11:36;
1 CHRONICLES 29:14; PSALM 143:2

He will quiet you with His love.

Lord God, as with Israel, You did not set Your love on me nor choose me because I was more in number than any other people, for I was among the least of all peoples; but because You love me. I love You because You first loved me. You have reconciled me in the body of Jesus' flesh through death, to present me holy, and blameless, and above reproach in Your sight.

In this is love, not that I loved You, but that You loved me and sent Your Son to be the propitiation for my sins. You demonstrate Your own love toward me, in that while I was still a sinner, Your Son died for me.

Suddenly, at Jesus' baptism, Your voice came from heaven, saying, "This is My beloved Son, in whom I am well pleased." You love Him, because He lay down His life that He may take it again. Your Son, being the brightness of Your glory and the express image of Your person, and upholding all things by the word of Your power, when He had by Himself purged my sins, sat down at the right hand of Your Majesty on high.

Great is Your love, Lord God! All praise to You!

Zephaniah 3:17; Deuteronomy 7:7–8; 1 John 4:19; Colossians 1:22; 1 John 4:10; Romans 5:8; Matthew 3:17; John 10:17; Hebrews 1:2–3

*Men always ought to pray
and not lose heart.*

Lord God, if I have a friend, and go to him at midnight and say to him, "Friend, lend me three loaves; for a friend of mine has come to me on his journey, and I have nothing to set before him"; and he will answer from within and say, "Do not trouble me; the door is now shut, and my children are with me in bed; I cannot rise and give to you". Jesus taught that, though he will not rise and give to me because I am his friend, yet because of my persistence he will rise and give me as many as I need. So I will pray always with all prayer and supplication in the Spirit, being watchful to this end with all perseverance and supplication for all the saints.

As Jacob, I say, "I will not let You go unless You bless me!" Answer me the same way: "You have struggled with God and with men, and have prevailed." I will continue earnestly in prayer, being vigilant in it with thanksgiving. . . .

Vigilant like Jesus who went out to the mountain to pray, and continued all night in prayer to You, Lord God.

*Thank You, Lord, for calling me
and enabling me to persist in prayer to You.*

LUKE 18:1; LUKE 11:5–8; EPHESIANS 6:18;
GENESIS 32:26, 28; COLOSSIANS 4:2; LUKE 6:12

*The Lord made all he did
to prosper in his hand.*

Father, I am blessed for I fear You, and walk in Your ways. When I eat the labor of my hands, I shall be happy, and it shall be well with me. I trust in You, Lord, and do good; I dwell in the land, and I feed on Your faithfulness. I delight myself also in You, Lord, and You shall give me the desires of my heart. I will not be afraid, nor dismayed, for You, the Lord my God, are with me wherever I go.

I seek first Your kingdom and Your righteousness, and all these things shall be added to me.

As long as I seek You, Lord, You make me prosper. I stay aware not to forget You, Lord God, by not keeping Your commandments, Your judgments, and Your statutes which You command me today. May I never say in my heart, "My power and the might of my hand have gained me this wealth."

Are not You, the Lord my God, with me? And have You not given me rest on every side?

*Great is Your faithfulness—
and countless are Your blessings in my life!
I praise You, Lord!*

GENESIS 39:3; PSALM 128:1–2; PSALM 37:3–4; JOSHUA 1:9;
MATTHEW 6:33; 2 CHRONICLES 26:5;
DEUTERONOMY 8:11, 17; 1 CHRONICLES 22:18

No man ever spoke like this Man!

Y ou are fairer than the sons of men, Lord Jesus; grace is poured upon Your lips; therefore God has blessed You forever. The Lord God has given You the tongue of the learned, that You should know how to speak a word in season to me when I am weary. Your mouth is most sweet, yes, You are altogether lovely. You are my Beloved, and You are my friend.

All bore witness to You, and marveled at the gracious words which proceeded out of Your mouth. You taught as one having authority, and not as the scribes.

So I let Your word, Jesus, dwell in me richly in all wisdom. The sword of the Spirit is the word of God, which is living and powerful, and sharper than any two-edged sword. The weapons of my warfare are not carnal but mighty in God for pulling down strongholds, casting down arguments and every high thing that exalts itself against the knowledge of God, bringing every thought into captivity in obedience to You, Christ Jesus.

May I feed on all of God's Word, Lord Jesus,
for it holds the words of life!

JOHN 7:46; PSALM 45:2; ISAIAH 50:4; SONG OF SOLOMON 5:16;
LUKE 4:22; MATTHEW 7:29; COLOSSIANS 3:16;
EPHESIANS 6:17; HEBREWS 4:12; 2 CORINTHIANS 10:4–5

The younger son . . . journeyed to a far country,
and there wasted his possessions with prodigal living.

My gracious God, such a sinner I once was! But I was washed, I was sanctified, I was justified in the name of the Lord Jesus and by Your Holy Spirit. I was by nature a child of wrath, just as the others. But You, Lord God, who are rich in mercy, because of Your great love with which You loved me, even when I was dead in trespasses, made me alive with Christ (by grace I have been saved), and raised me up, and made me sit in the heavenly places in Christ Jesus.

In this is love, not that I loved You, Lord God, but that You loved me and sent Your Son to be the propitiation for my sins.

Father God, You demonstrated Your own love toward me, in that while I was still a sinner, Christ died for me. If when I was Your enemy I was reconciled to You through the death of Your Son, much more, having been reconciled, I shall be saved by Your life.

Mercy, grace, love, forgiveness, cleansing, life eternal—
all this and more You give,
Lord God, to sinners like me. Thank You!

LUKE 15:13; 1 CORINTHIANS 6:11; EPHESIANS 2:3–6;
1 JOHN 4:10; ROMANS 5:8, 10

He arose and came to his father.
But when he was still a great way off,
his father saw him and had compassion, and ran
and fell on his neck and kissed him.

Merciful and gracious Lord, slow to anger, and abounding in mercy. You will not always strive with me, nor will You keep Your anger forever. You have not dealt with me according to my sins, nor punished me according to my iniquities. For as the heavens are high above the earth, so great is Your mercy toward those who fear You; as far as the east is from the west, so far have You removed my transgressions from me. As a father pities his children, so You, Lord, pity those who fear You.

I received the Spirit of adoption by whom I cry out, "Abba, Father." The Spirit Himself bears witness with my spirit that I am Your child, dear God. I who once was far off have been made near by the blood of Christ. Now, therefore, I am no longer a stranger and a foreigner, but a fellow citizen with the saints and members of the household of God.

May I, Your child and a citizen in Your kingdom,
honor You with my life!

LUKE 15:20; PSALM 103:8–13; ROMANS 8:15–16;
EPHESIANS 2:13, 19

Everything that can endure fire,
you shall put through the fire,
and it shall be clean.

You, Lord God, are testing me to know whether I love You, my God, with all my heart and with all my soul. You will sit as a refiner and a purifier of silver; as You will purify the sons of Levi, so purify and purge me as gold and silver, that I may offer to You an offering in righteousness. My work will become clear; for the Day will declare it, because it will be revealed by fire; and the fire will test my work, of what sort it is.

You will turn Your hand against me, and thoroughly purge away my dross, and take away all my alloy. You will refine me and try me.

You, O God, have tested me; You have refined me as silver is refined. I went through fire and through water; but You brought me out to rich fulfillment.

When I walk through the fire, I shall not be burned, nor shall the flame scorch me.

May I trust Your refining process in my life, Lord God,
and Your sustaining power when the fire rages.

NUMBERS 31:23; DEUTERONOMY 13:3;
MALACHI 3:3; 1 CORINTHIANS 3:13; ISAIAH 1:25;
JEREMIAH 9:7; PSALM 66:10, 12; ISAIAH 43:2

Abide in Me, and I in you.

Lord Jesus, I have been crucified with You, it is no longer I who live, but You live in me; and the life which I now live in the flesh I live by faith in You, Son of God, who loved me and gave Yourself for me.

For I know that in me (that is, in my flesh) nothing good dwells; for to will is present with me, but how to perform what is good I do not find. O wretched man that I am! Who will deliver me from this body of death? I thank God through You, Jesus Christ my Lord! If You, Christ, are in me, my body is dead because of sin, but the Spirit is life because of righteousness. So I continue in the faith, grounded and steadfast, and am not moved away from the hope of the gospel which I heard.

As if a little child, I abide in You, that when You appear, I may have confidence and not be ashamed before You at Your coming. I who say I abide in You ought also to walk just as You walked.

As I abide in You, Lord Jesus, and You in me,
may my life reflect more clearly Your love and Your likeness.

JOHN 15:4; GALATIANS 2:20; ROMANS 7:18, 24–25;
ROMANS 8:10; COLOSSIANS 1:23; 1 JOHN 2:28; 1 JOHN 2:6

*As the sufferings of Christ abound in us,
so our consolation also abounds through Christ.*

Lord God, what a privilege to enter the fellowship of Your Son's sufferings. I rejoice to the extent that I partake of Christ's sufferings, that when His glory is revealed, I may also be glad with exceeding joy. For if I died with Him, I shall also live with Him. If a child, then an heir—Your heir, Lord God, and a joint heir with Christ, if indeed I suffer with Him, that I may also be glorified with Him.

Lord God, determining to show more abundantly to the heirs of promise the immutability of Your counsel, You confirmed it by an oath, that by two immutable things, in which it is impossible for God to lie, I might have strong consolation, who have fled for refuge to lay hold of the hope set before me. My Lord Jesus Christ Himself, and You, my God and Father, who have loved me and given me everlasting consolation and good hope by grace, comfort my heart and establish me in every good word and work.

*May I welcome participation in Jesus' sufferings, Lord God,
and joyfully anticipate the glory to come.*

2 CORINTHIANS 1:5; PHILIPPIANS 3:10; 1 PETER 4:13;
2 TIMOTHY 2:11; ROMANS 8:17; HEBREWS 6:17–18;
2 THESSALONIANS 2:16–17

The secret things belong to the Lord our God,
but those things which are revealed belong to us.

Lord God, my heart is not haughty, nor my eyes lofty. Neither do I concern myself with great matters, nor with things too profound for me. Surely I have calmed and quieted my soul, like a weaned child with his mother; like a weaned child is my soul within me.

Your secret, Lord, is with those who fear You, and You will show me Your covenant. You are the God in heaven who reveals secrets. Indeed these are the mere edges of Your ways, and how small a whisper I hear of You!

Jesus no longer calls me a servant, for a servant does not know what his master is doing; but He has called me friend, for all things that He heard from You, Father, He has made known to me. If I love Jesus, I will keep His commandments. And He will pray to You, Father, and You will give me another Helper, that He may abide with me forever—the Spirit of truth.

Thank You for sharing Your salvation secret,
Lord God, and for choosing me to be saved! What a privilege
to be called Your friend and given Your Spirit!

DEUTERONOMY 29:29; PSALM 131:1–2; PSALM 25:14;
DANIEL 2:28; JOB 26:14; JOHN 15:15; JOHN 14:15–17

See then that you walk circumspectly,
not as fools but as wise, redeeming the time,
because the days are evil.

My Lord God, I take careful heed, to do the commandment and the law, to love You, to walk in all Your ways, to keep Your commandments, to hold fast to You, and to serve You with all my heart and with all my soul. I walk in wisdom toward those who are outside, redeeming the time. I let my speech always be with grace, seasoned with salt, that I may know how I ought to answer each one. I abstain from every form of evil.

While the bridegroom was delayed, the foolish maids all slumbered and slept. And at midnight a cry was heard: "Behold, the bridegroom is coming; go out to meet him!" I watch therefore, for I know neither the day nor the hour in which the Son of Man is coming.

I will be even more diligent to make my call and election sure, for if I do these things I will never stumble. Blessed are those servants whom the master, when he comes, will find watching.

In these evil days may I serve You with all my heart
as I walk in wisdom and watch for Jesus' return.

EPHESIANS 5:15–16; JOSHUA 22:5; COLOSSIANS 4:5–6;
1 THESSALONIANS 5:22; MATTHEW 25:5–6, 13;
2 PETER 1:10; LUKE 12:37

*In everything by prayer and supplication, with thanksgiving,
let your requests be made known to God.*

I love You, Lord, because You have heard my voice and my supplications. Because You have inclined Your ear to me, therefore I will call upon You as long as I live.

When I pray, I do not use vain repetitions as the heathen do. For they think that they will be heard for their many words. The Spirit helps in my weaknesses. For I do not know what I should pray for as I ought, but the Spirit Himself makes intercession for me with groanings which cannot be uttered.

I desire therefore that the men pray everywhere, lifting up holy hands, without wrath and doubting. I pray always with all prayer and supplication in the Spirit, being watchful to this end with all perseverance and supplication for all the saints.

If two of us agree on earth concerning anything that we ask, it will be done for us by You, my Father in heaven.

*May I never take for granted the privilege of prayer.
May I never underestimate its effect.
And may I never grow weary in that divine work!*

PHILIPPIANS 4:6; PSALM 116:1–2; MATTHEW 6:7;
ROMANS 8:26; I TIMOTHY 2:8; EPHESIANS 6:18; MATTHEW 18:19

You shall put the mercy seat on top of the ark, . . .
and there I will meet with you.

Lord God, the way into the Holiest of All was not yet made manifest. Then Your Son Jesus cried out again with a loud voice, and yielded up His spirit. Then, behold, the veil of the temple was torn in two from top to bottom.

So having boldness to enter the Holiest by the blood of Jesus, by a new and living way which He consecrated for me, through the veil, that is, His flesh, I draw near to You, Lord God, with a true heart in full assurance of faith, having my heart sprinkled from an evil conscience and my body washed with pure water. I come boldly to the throne of grace, that I may obtain mercy and find grace to help in time of need.

Christ Jesus, whom You set forth to be a propitiation by His blood, through faith, to demonstrate Your righteousness, because in Your forbearance You had passed over the sins that were previously committed—through Him I have access by one Spirit to You, Father God.

Holy God, my salvation—my access to Your throne—cost You dearly.
May I never take for granted the grace of Your forgiveness.

EXODUS 25:21–22; HEBREWS 9:8; MATTHEW 27:50–51;
HEBREWS 10:19–20, 22; HEBREWS 4:16;
ROMANS 3:24–25; EPHESIANS 2:18

Holiness, without which no one will see the Lord.

Father God, unless I am born again, I cannot see Your kingdom. There shall by no means enter it anything that defiles. There is no spot in me.

I shall be holy, for You, the Lord my God, are holy. As an obedient child, not conforming myself to the former lusts, as in my ignorance; but as You who called me are holy, I am also to be holy in all my conduct, because it is written, "Be holy, for I am holy." And if I call on You, Father God, who without partiality judges according to each one's work, I will conduct myself throughout the time of my stay here in fear. I put off, concerning my former conduct, the old man which grows corrupt according to the deceitful lusts, and am renewed in the spirit of my mind, and I put on the new man which You created, Lord God, in true righteousness and holiness. You chose me in Jesus before the foundation of the world, that I should be holy and without blame before You in love.

I can only live the life I just prayed about in Your power, Lord! Help me!

HEBREWS 12:14; JOHN 3:3; REVELATION 21:27;
SONG OF SOLOMON 4:7; LEVITICUS 19:2; 1 PETER 1:14–17;
EPHESIANS 4:22–24; EPHESIANS 1:4

Take this child away and nurse him for me,
and I will give you your wages.

Lord Jesus, I go into Your vineyard, and I know that whatever is right You will give me. Whoever gives me a cup of water to drink in Your name, because I belong to You, assuredly he will by no means lose his reward. The generous soul will be made rich, and he who waters will also be watered himself. Father God is not unjust to forget my work and labor of love in that I have ministered to the saints, and do minister.

I will receive my own reward according to my own labor.

Jesus, even the righteous wonder: "Lord, when did we see You hungry and feed You, or thirsty and give You drink? When did we see You a stranger and take You in, or naked and clothe You?" And God the King will answer and say to them, "Inasmuch as you did it to one of the least of these My brethren, you did it to Me." So, blessed of God the Father, I will inherit the kingdom prepared for me from the foundation of the world.

May I obediently do all things as unto You, Jesus,
that needs may be met and
You may be glorified.

EXODUS 2:9; MATTHEW 20:4; MARK 9:41;
PROVERBS 11:25; HEBREWS 6:10; 1 CORINTHIANS 3:8;
MATTHEW 25:37–38, 40, 34

*Christ also suffered for us, leaving us an example,
that you should follow His steps.*

Y ou, Lord Jesus, the Son of Man, did not come to be served, but to serve. And You taught, if I desire to be first I shall be slave of all.

Jesus of Nazareth, You went about doing good. Likewise, I am to bear others' burdens, and so fulfill Your law.

With Your meekness and gentleness, Jesus . . . and in lowliness of mind, may I esteem others better than myself.

You prayed, "Father, forgive them, for they do not know what they do." May I be kind to others, tenderhearted, forgiving others, just as God in You, Jesus, also forgave me.

If I say I abide in You I ought myself also to walk just as You walked. I look unto You, Jesus, the author and finisher of my faith, who for the joy that was set before You endured the cross, despising the shame, and have sat down at the right hand of the throne of God.

*Lord, may I serve as You served:
with meekness, gentleness, love, and joy.*

---

1 PETER 2:21; MARK 10:45; MARK 10:44; ACTS 10:38;
GALATIANS 6:2; 2 CORINTHIANS 10:1; PHILIPPIANS 2:3;
LUKE 23:34; EPHESIANS 4:32; 1 JOHN 2:6; HEBREWS 12:2

You died, and your life
is hidden with Christ in God.

Lord God, how shall I who died to sin live any longer in it? I have been crucified with Christ; it is no longer I who live, but Christ lives in me; the life which I now live in the flesh I live by faith in the Son of God, who loved me and gave Himself for me. He died for me, that I who live should live no longer for myself, but for Him who died for me and rose again. If I am in Christ, I am a new creation; old things have passed away; all things have become new.

I am in You who are true, in Your Son Jesus Christ. As You, Father, are in Jesus, and He in You; that all believers also may be one in You, I am part of the body of Christ, and a member individually. Because Jesus lives, I will live also.

I am dead to sin and alive in Christ!
I praise You, Lord God, that I am a new creation
for now and for eternity.

———

COLOSSIANS 3:3; ROMANS 6:2; GALATIANS 2:20;
2 CORINTHIANS 5:15; 2 CORINTHIANS 5:17;
1 JOHN 5:20; JOHN 17:21; 1 CORINTHIANS 12:27;
JOHN 14:19; REVELATION 2:17

I will pray the Father,
and He will give you another Helper, . . .
the Spirit of truth.

J esus, You taught that it is to my advantage that You go away; for if You did not go away, the Helper would not come to me; but if You departed, You would send Him to me.

Your Spirit bears witness with my spirit that I am a child of God. I did not receive the spirit of bondage again to fear, but I received the Spirit of adoption by whom I cry out, "Abba, Father." The Spirit helps in my weaknesses. For I do not know what I should pray for as I ought, but the Spirit Himself makes intercession for me with groanings which cannot be uttered.

The God of hope fills me with all joy and peace in believing, that I may abound in hope by the power of the Holy Spirit. Hope does not disappoint, because the love of God has been poured out in my heart by the Holy Spirit who was given to me.

By this I know that I abide in God, and He in me, because He has given me of His Spirit.

Your Spirit, Jesus, is an amazing gift!
May His presence in my life bring glory to God!

JOHN 14:16–17; JOHN 16:7; ROMANS 8:16; ROMANS 8:15;
ROMANS 8:26; ROMANS 15:13; ROMANS 5:5; 1 JOHN 4:13

The ark of the covenant of the Lord went before them . . .
to search out a resting place for them.

My times are in Your hand, mighty God. You will choose my inheritance for me. Lead me, O Lord, in Your righteousness. Make Your way straight before my face.

I commit my way to You, Lord, I trust also in You, and You shall bring it to pass. In all my ways I will acknowledge You, and You shall direct my paths. My ears shall hear a word behind me, saying, "This is the way, walk in it," whenever I turn to the right hand or whenever I turn to the left.

You, Lord, are my shepherd; I shall not want. You make me to lie down in green pastures; You lead me beside the still waters. As a father pities his children, so You, Lord, pity those who fear You. For You know my frame; You remember that I am dust. You, my heavenly Father, know that I need all these things. I cast all my care upon You, for You care for me.

Thank You, Good Shepherd, that You guide and protect me,
provide for me and care for me, day by day!

NUMBERS 10:33; PSALM 31:15; PSALM 47:4; PSALM 5:8;
PSALM 37:5; PROVERBS 3:6; ISAIAH 30:21; PSALM 23:1–2;
PSALM 103:13–14; MATTHEW 6:32; 1 PETER 5:7

When He is revealed, we shall be like Him,
for we shall see Him as He is.

Lord God, as many as received Jesus, to each of us He gave the right to become Your children, to those who believe in His name. You have given me exceedingly great and precious promises, that through these I may be a partaker of the divine nature, having escaped the corruption that is in the world through lust.

Since the beginning of the world men have not heard nor perceived by the ear, nor has the eye seen any God besides You, who acts for the one who waits for You. Now I see in a mirror, dimly, but then face to face. Now I know in part, but then I shall know just as I also am known. Jesus Christ will transform my lowly body that it may be conformed to His glorious body, according to the working by which He is able even to subdue all things to Himself. As for me, Lord God, I will see Your face in righteousness; I shall be satisfied when I awake in Your likeness.

To see You, Lord; to be made like Christ;
to be loved as Your child—
I praise You for these wonderful
and trustworthy promises!

1 JOHN 3:2; JOHN 1:12; 2 PETER 1:4; ISAIAH 64:4;
1 CORINTHIANS 13:12; PHILIPPIANS 3:20–21; PSALM 17:15

"Oh, that You would bless me indeed, . . . and that
You would keep me from evil." . . .
So God granted him what he requested.

Your blessing, Lord, makes me rich, and You add no sorrow with it. When You give quietness, who then can make trouble? And when You hide Your face, who then can see You?

Salvation belongs to You, Lord God. Your blessing is upon Your people. How great is Your goodness, which You have laid up for those who fear You, which You have prepared for those who trust in You in the presence of the sons of men! Jesus did not pray that You should take me out of the world, but that You should keep me from the evil one.

I ask, and it will be given to me; I seek, and I will find; I knock, and it will be opened to me. For everyone who asks receives, and seeks finds, and to him who knocks it will be opened. You, Lord, redeem the soul of Your servants, and if I trust in You I shall not be condemned.

I praise You for Your immeasurable goodness, Lord!
May I always trust in You who is faithful and kind,
all-wise, all-powerful, and all-loving.

---

1 CHRONICLES 4:10; PROVERBS 10:22; JOB 34:29;
PSALM 3:8; PSALM 31:19; JOHN 17:15;
MATTHEW 7:7–8; PSALM 34:22

Who is able to stand?

Lord God, who can endure the day of Jesus' coming? And who can stand when He appears? For He is like a refiner's fire and like launderers' soap.

The apostle John was permitted to see the future when a great multitude which no one could number, of all nations, tribes, peoples, and tongues, standing before the throne and before the Lamb, clothed with white robes, with palm branches in their hands. These are the ones who come out of the great tribulation, and washed their robes and made them white in the blood of the Lamb. They shall neither hunger anymore nor thirst anymore; the sun shall not strike them nor any heat; for the Lamb who is in the midst of the throne will shepherd them and lead them to living fountains of waters. And God will wipe away every tear from their eyes.

There is no condemnation to those of us who are in Christ Jesus, who do not walk according to the flesh, but according to the Spirit. I stand fast therefore in the liberty by which Christ has made me free.

Lord God, enable me to walk according to Your guiding Spirit and to stand fast in the freedom of Your forgiveness.

REVELATION 6:17; MALACHI 3:2; REVELATION 7:9, 14–17; ROMANS 8:1; GALATIANS 5:1

I know that my Redeemer lives.

Father God, if when I was Your enemy, I was reconciled to You through the death of Your Son, much more, having been reconciled, I shall be saved by His life. Jesus, because He continues forever, has an unchangeable priesthood. Therefore He is also able to save to the uttermost those who come to You, Lord God, through Him, since He ever lives to make intercession for us.

Because Jesus lives, I will live also. If in this life only I have hope in Christ, I am of all men the most pitiable. But now Christ is risen from the dead, and has become the firstfruits of those who have fallen asleep

Lord, You say, "The Redeemer will come to Zion, and to those who turn from transgression in Jacob." I now have redemption through His blood, the forgiveness of sins, according to the riches of His grace. I was not redeemed with corruptible things, like silver or gold, from my aimless conduct received by tradition from my fathers, but with the precious blood of Christ, as of a lamb without blemish and without spot.

Thank You, God, that Your Son—my Redeemer—lives!
And thank You, Jesus, that You intercede for me.

JOB 19:25; ROMANS 5:10; HEBREWS 7:24–25;
JOHN 14:19; 1 CORINTHIANS 15:19–20; ISAIAH 59:20;
EPHESIANS 1:7; 1 PETER 1:18–19

His commandments are not burdensome.

Father God, who sent Jesus, it is Your will that everyone who sees the Son and believes in Him may have everlasting life. Whatever I ask I receive from You, because I keep Your commandments and do those things that are pleasing in Your sight.

Jesus' yoke is easy and His burden is light. If I love Him, I will keep His commandments. I have His commandments and keep them, and I love Jesus. And if I love Him I will be loved by You, Father, and Jesus will love me and manifest Himself to me.

I am happy—I have found wisdom, and gained understanding. Wisdom's ways are ways of pleasantness, and all her paths are peace. Great peace have those who love Your law, and nothing causes me to stumble. I delight in Your law, Lord God, according to the inward man.

This is Your commandment: that I should believe on the name of Your Son Jesus Christ and love others. Love does no harm to a neighbor; therefore love is the fulfillment of the law.

When You call, Almighty God, You empower.
Empower me, I ask, to obey Your commandments.

---

1 JOHN 5:3; JOHN 6:40; 1 JOHN 3:22; MATTHEW 11:30;
JOHN 14:15, 21; PROVERBS 3:13, 17; PSALM 119:165;
ROMANS 7:22; 1 JOHN 3:23; ROMANS 13:10

*As many as I love,
I rebuke and chasten.*

Lord God, may I not despise Your chastening, nor be discouraged when I am rebuked by You; for whom You love, Lord, You chasten, and scourge every son whom You receive . . . just as a father the son in whom he delights. You bruise, but You bind up; You wound, but Your hands make whole. So I humble myself under Your mighty hand, Lord God, that You may exalt me in due time. You have tested me in the furnace of affliction.

You do not afflict willingly, nor grieve the children of men. You have not dealt with me according to my sins, nor punished me according to my iniquities. For as the heavens are high above the earth, so great is Your mercy toward those who fear You; as far as the east is from the west, so far have You removed my transgressions from me. As a father pities his children, so You, Lord God, pity those who fear You. For You know my frame; You remember that I am dust.

*Thank You, Lord, for loving me
with Your correcting, forgiving, and merciful love.*

REVELATION 3:19; HEBREWS 12:5–6; PROVERBS 3:12;
JOB 5:18; 1 PETER 5:6; ISAIAH 48:10;
LAMENTATIONS 3:33; PSALM 103:10–14

July

You are a gracious

and merciful God,

slow to anger and

abundant in lovingkindness,

One who relents from

doing harm.

The fruit of the Spirit is . . . goodness.

May I imitate You, Lord God, as a dear child. Enable me to love my enemies, bless those who curse me, do good to those who hate me, and pray for those who spitefully use me and persecute me, that, heavenly Father, I may be Your child; for You make Your sun rise on the evil and on the good, and send rain on the just and on the unjust. Enable me to be merciful, just as You, Father God, also are merciful.

The fruit of the Spirit is in all goodness, righteousness, and truth.

When Your kindness and love toward us appeared, not by works of righteousness which I have done, but according to Your mercy You saved me, through the washing of regeneration and renewing of the Holy Spirit, whom You poured out on me abundantly through Jesus Christ my Savior. You, Lord, are good to all, and Your tender mercies are over all Your works. You who did not spare Your own Son, but delivered Him up for me, how shall You not with Him also freely give me all things?

May the fruit of Your Spirit be obvious in my life,
my good and gracious God.

GALATIANS 5:22; EPHESIANS 5:1; MATTHEW 5:44–45;
LUKE 6:36; EPHESIANS 5:9; TITUS 3:4–6;
PSALM 145:9; ROMANS 8:32

This is the ordinance of the Passover:
No foreigner shall eat it.

Father, in Christ I have an altar from which those who serve the tabernacle have no right to eat. Unless I am born again, I cannot see Your kingdom, Lord God. At that time I was without Christ, being an alien from the commonwealth of Israel and a stranger from the covenants of promise. But now in Christ Jesus I who once was far off have been brought near by the blood of Christ.

For Jesus Himself is my peace, who has made both Jews and Gentiles one, having abolished in His flesh the enmity, that is, the law of commandments contained in ordinances, so as to create in Himself one new man from the two, thus making peace.

Now, therefore, I am no longer a stranger and a foreigner, but a fellow citizen with the saints and members of Your household, Lord God.

If I hear Jesus' voice and open the door, He will come in to me and dine with me, and I with Him.

What a privilege to be a member of Your household,
a citizen of Your kingdom,
Lord God. May my life reflect that status.

EXODUS 12:43; HEBREWS 13:10; JOHN 3:3; EPHESIANS 2:12–13;
EPHESIANS 2:14–15; EPHESIANS 2:19; REVELATION 3:20

If children, then heirs—
heirs of God and joint heirs with Christ.

Heavenly Father, if I am Christ's, then I am Abraham's seed, and heirs according to the promise.

Behold what manner of love You, Father God, have bestowed on me, that I should be called Your child! Therefore I am no longer a slave but a son, and if a son, then Your heir through Christ. You, Lord God, predestined me to adoption as a son by Jesus Christ to Yourself, according to the good pleasure of Your will.

Father, Jesus desired that we whom You gave Him may be with Him where He is, that we may behold His glory which You have given Him.

If I overcome, and keep Jesus' works until the end, to me He will give power over the nations. If I overcome, Jesus will grant to me to sit with Him on His throne, as He also overcame and sat down with You, Father God, on Your throne.

What a glorious future You have for Your heirs, Father God!
Thank You that I am numbered among them!

ROMANS 8:17; GALATIANS 3:29; 1 JOHN 3:1;
GALATIANS 4:7; EPHESIANS 1:5; JOHN 17:24;
REVELATION 2:26; REVELATION 3:21

Leaning on Jesus' bosom.

Lord God, as one whom his mother comforts, so You will comfort me. They brought little children to Jesus, that He might touch them. And He took them up in His arms, laid His hands on them, and blessed them. Jesus called His disciples to Himself and said, "I have compassion on the multitude, because they have now continued with Me three days and have nothing to eat. And I do not want to send them away hungry, lest they faint on the way." Jesus is a High Priest who sympathizes with my weaknesses. In His love and in His pity He redeemed me.

Jesus will not leave me an orphan; He will come to me. Can a woman forget her nursing child, and not have compassion on the son of her womb? Surely they may forget, yet You, Lord God, will not forget me.

The Lamb who is in the midst of the throne will shepherd me and lead me to living fountains of waters. And You, Lord God, will wipe away every tear from my eyes.

May I lean on Your bosom, Lord God,
knowing that I find in You compassion, sympathy,
redemption, and faithful love.

JOHN 13:23; ISAIAH 66:13; MARK 10:13, 16;
MATTHEW 15:32; HEBREWS 4:15; ISAIAH 63:9; JOHN 14:18;
ISAIAH 49:15; REVELATION 21:4

We have known and
believed the love that God has for us.

Lord God, You who are rich in mercy, because of Your great love with which You loved me, even when I was dead in trespasses, made me alive with Christ (by grace I have been saved), and raised me up and made me sit in the heavenly places in Christ Jesus, that in the ages to come You might show the exceeding riches of Your grace in Your kindness toward me in Christ Jesus.

You, Lord God, so loved the world that You gave Your only begotten Son, that whoever believes in Him should not perish but have everlasting life. You who did not spare Your own Son, but delivered Him up for me, how shall You not with Him also freely give me all things? You, Lord, are good to all, and Your tender mercies are over all Your works.

I love You because You first loved me.

Blessed am I who believed, for there will be a fulfillment of those things which You told me, Lord God.

Your amazing love and grace truly defy description, Lord God.
Thank You for loving me.

1 JOHN 4:16; EPHESIANS 2:4–7; JOHN 3:16; ROMANS 8:32;
PSALM 145:9; 1 JOHN 4:19; LUKE 1:45

Let your speech always be with grace.

Lord God, You say that a word fitly spoken is like apples of gold in settings of silver. Like an earring of gold and an ornament of fine gold is a wise rebuker to an obedient ear. So let no corrupt word proceed out of my mouth, but what is good for necessary edification, that it may impart grace to the hearers. A good man out of the good treasure of his heart brings forth good things, and an evil man out of the evil treasure brings forth evil things. By my words I will be justified. The tongue of the wise promotes health.

Once, those who feared You, Lord, spoke to one another, and You listened and heard them; so a book of remembrance was written before You for those who fear You and who meditate on Your name.

If I take out the precious from the vile, I shall be as Your mouth. But as I abound in everything—in faith, in speech, in knowledge, in all diligence—I seek to abound in this grace also.

Lord God, only in Your power will I be
able to control my tongue.
Teach me to speak words of grace always.

COLOSSIANS 4:6; PROVERBS 25:11–12; EPHESIANS 4:29;
MATTHEW 12:35, 37; PROVERBS 12:18; MALACHI 3:16;
JEREMIAH 15:19; 2 CORINTHIANS 8:7

*Then Jesus was led up
by the Spirit into the wilderness
to be tempted by the devil.*

Lord God, in the days of His flesh, when Jesus had offered up prayers and supplications, with vehement cries and tears to You who was able to save Him from death, and was heard because of His godly fear, though He was a Son, yet He learned obedience by the things which He suffered. And having been perfected, He became the author of eternal salvation to all who obey Him. I do not have a High Priest who cannot sympathize with my weaknesses, but was in all points tempted as I am, yet without sin.

No temptation has overtaken me except such as is common to man; but You, Lord God, are faithful, who will not allow me to be tempted beyond what I am able, but with the temptation will also make the way of escape, that I may be able to bear it. Your grace is sufficient for me, for Your strength is made perfect in weakness.

*When I face temptation, Lord God, prompt me to remember
Your all-sufficient grace and turn to You for strength.*

MATTHEW 4:1; HEBREWS 5:7–9; HEBREWS 4:15;
1 CORINTHIANS 10:13; 2 CORINTHIANS 12:9

If we confess our sins,
He is faithful and just to forgive us our sins
and to cleanse us from all unrighteousness.

Father, I acknowledge my transgressions, and my sin is always before me. Against You, You only, have I sinned, and done this evil in Your sight.

The prodigal arose and came to his father. But when he was still a great way off, his father saw him and had compassion, and ran and fell on his neck and kissed him. So You have blotted out, like a thick cloud, my transgressions, and like a cloud, my sins. I return to You, for You have redeemed me. My sins are forgiven me for Your name's sake. In Christ You forgave me . . . that You might be just and the justifier of the one who, like me, has faith in Jesus.

Then Jesus will sprinkle clean water on me, and I shall be clean. May I walk with You in white, may I be worthy.

This is He who came by water and blood—Jesus Christ; not only by water, but by water and blood.

May I always be awed by
Your gracious plan of forgiveness, Lord God.
You have redeemed me by the blood of Your Son—
and I praise You!

---

1 JOHN 1:9; PSALM 51:3–4; LUKE 15:20; ISAIAH 44:22;
1 JOHN 2:12; EPHESIANS 4:32; ROMANS 3:26; EZEKIEL 36:25;
REVELATION 3:4; 1 JOHN 5:6

I have removed your iniquity from you,
and I will clothe you with rich robes.

Father, how blessed I am, for my transgression is forgiven, my sin is covered. I am like an unclean thing. I know that in me (that is, in my flesh) nothing good dwells; for to will is present with me, but how to perform what is good I do not find.

Having been baptized into Christ I have put on Christ. I have put off the old man with his deeds, and have put on the new man who is renewed in knowledge according to the image of You who created me. Not having my own righteousness, which is from the law, but the righteousness which is from You, Lord God, by faith.

You bring out the best robe and put it on me. The fine linen is the righteous acts of the saints. I will greatly rejoice in You, Lord, my soul shall be joyful in You, my God; for You have clothed me with the garments of salvation, He has covered me with the robe of righteousness.

You not only forgive my sins, Lord God,
but You make me a new person
and clothe me in the righteousness of Christ.
What cause for unending joy!

ZECHARIAH 3:4; PSALM 32:1; ISAIAH 64:6; ROMANS 7:18;
GALATIANS 3:27; COLOSSIANS 3:9–10; PHILIPPIANS 3:9;
LUKE 15:22; REVELATION 19:8; ISAIAH 61:10

A disciple is not above his teacher.

Lord Jesus, I call You Teacher and Lord, and I say well, for so You are.

It is enough for a disciple that he be like his teacher, and a servant like his master. If they persecuted You, they will also persecute me. You say that if they kept Your word, they will keep my word also. Jesus, You have given me God's word; and the world has hated me because I am not of the world, just as You are not of the world.

I consider You who endured such hostility from sinners against Yourself, lest I become weary and discouraged in my soul. I have not yet resisted to bloodshed, striving against sin.

Enable me to run with endurance the race that is set before me, looking unto You, Lord Jesus, the author and finisher of my faith, who for the joy that was set before You endured the cross, despising the shame, and sat down at the right hand of the throne of God. Therefore, since You, Jesus Christ, suffered for me in the flesh, I arm myself also with the same mind.

Jesus, make me a faithful disciple,
willing to speak boldly and able to stand
any persecution that comes my way.

MATTHEW 10:24; JOHN 13:13; MATTHEW 10:25;
JOHN 15:20; JOHN 17:14; HEBREWS 12:3–4;
HEBREWS 12:1–2; 1 PETER 4:1

I am with you to save you.

Lord God, shall the prey be taken from the mighty, or the captives of the righteous be delivered? You say even the captives of the mighty shall be taken away, and the prey of the terrible be delivered; for You will contend with him who contends with me. All flesh shall know that You, the Lord, are my Savior, and my Redeemer, the Mighty One of Jacob. So I fear not, for You are with me; I will not be dismayed, for You are my God. You will strengthen me, yes, You will help me, You will uphold me with Your righteous right hand.

I do not have a High Priest who cannot sympathize with my weaknesses, but was in all points tempted as I am, yet without sin. In that He Himself has suffered, being tempted, He is able to aid me when I am tempted. Lord God, You order my steps as of a good man, and You delight in my way. Though I fall, I shall not be utterly cast down; for You, Lord, uphold me with Your hand.

Lord God, thank You that Jesus helps me
when I am tempted and thank You for upholding me
with Your powerful right hand.

JEREMIAH 15:20; ISAIAH 49:24–26; ISAIAH 41:10;
HEBREWS 4:15; HEBREWS 2:18; PSALM 37:23–24

My Presence will go with you,
and I will give you rest.

Lord God, enable me to be strong and of good courage, may I not fear nor be afraid; for You, Lord God, are the One who goes with me. You will not leave me nor forsake me. You, Lord, are the One who goes before me. You will be with me; so I do not fear nor am dismayed. Have You not commanded me? So I will be strong and of good courage; I will not be afraid, nor be dismayed, for You, Lord God, are with me wherever I go. In all my ways I acknowledge You, and You shall direct my paths.

You have said, "I will never leave you nor forsake you." So I boldly say: "The Lord is my helper; I will not fear. What can man do to me?" My sufficiency is from You, Lord God.

I pray, "Do not lead me into temptation." O Lord, I know the way of man is not in himself; it is not in me who walks to direct my own steps. My times are in Your hand.

In Your presence I know Your power, peace, guidance,
protection, and love. Thank You, God!

EXODUS 33:14; DEUTERONOMY 31:6, 8; JOSHUA 1:9;
PROVERBS 3:6; HEBREWS 13:5–6; 2 CORINTHIANS 3:5;
MATTHEW 6:13; JEREMIAH 10:23; PSALM 31:15

*I am my beloved's,
and his desire is toward me.*

Father, I know whom I have believed and am persuaded that You are able to keep what I have committed to You until that Day. I am persuaded that neither death nor life, nor angels nor principalities nor powers, nor things present nor things to come, nor height nor depth, nor any other created thing, shall be able to separate me from Your love, Lord God, which is in Christ Jesus. Those whom You gave Jesus He has kept; and none is lost.

You, Lord God, take pleasure in Your people. Your delight was with the sons of men . . . and You loved me with Your great love. Greater love has no one than this, than to lay down one's life for his friends.

I was bought at a price; therefore I glorify You in my body and in my spirit, which are Yours. If I live, I live to You, Lord God; and if I die, I die to You. Therefore, whether I live or die, I am Yours, Lord God.

*Lord God, thank You for Your love,
demonstrated in Your Son's death on the cross
and promised to me for eternity!*

SONG OF SOLOMON 7:10; 2 TIMOTHY 1:12; ROMANS 8:38–39;
JOHN 17:12; PSALM 149:4; PROVERBS 8:31; EPHESIANS 2:4;
JOHN 15:13; 1 CORINTHIANS 6:20; ROMANS 14:8

*Out of the abundance of the heart
the mouth speaks.*

May the word of Christ dwell in me richly in all wisdom. I will keep my heart with all diligence, for out of it spring the issues of life. Death and life are in the power of my tongue. As the mouth of the righteous speaks wisdom, and his tongue talks of justice, and Your law, Lord God, is in his heart; none of his steps shall slide. So help me let no corrupt word proceed out of my mouth, but what is good for necessary edification, that it may impart grace to the hearers.

Lord, I can only speak the things which I have seen and heard in Your Word. I believe, therefore I speak.

If I confess Jesus before men, He will also confess me before You, my Father who is in heaven. With the heart I believe unto righteousness, and with the mouth confession is made unto salvation.

*May my heart of love and my knowledge of You,
Lord God, overflow in words of praise and truth especially
to those who don't yet know You.*

MATTHEW 12:34; COLOSSIANS 3:16; PROVERBS 4:23;
PROVERBS 18:21; PSALM 37:30–31; EPHESIANS 4:29;
ACTS 4:20; PSALM 116:10; MATTHEW 10:32; ROMANS 10:10

Your will be done on earth as it is in heaven.

I bless You, Lord, as Your angels, who excel in strength, who do Your word, heeding the voice of Your word. Bless the Lord, all you His hosts, you ministers of His, who do His pleasure.

Jesus came from heaven, not to do His own will, but Your will, Lord God. I delight to do Your will, O my God, and Your law is within my heart. Like Jesus, may I say, "My Father, if this cup cannot pass away from me unless I drink it, Your will be done."

Not everyone who says to Jesus, "Lord, Lord," shall enter His kingdom, but he who does the will of His Father in heaven. Not the hearers of the law are just in Your sight, Lord God, but the doers of the law will be justified. If I know these things, I am blessed if I do them. If I know to do good and do not do it, to me it is sin.

I am not to be conformed to this world, but be transformed by the renewing of my mind.

May I do what I know of Your law, Lord—
and may I keep learning more.

MATTHEW 6:10; PSALM 103:20–21; JOHN 6:38; PSALM 40:8;
MATTHEW 26:42; MATTHEW 7:21; ROMANS 2:13;
JOHN 13:17; JAMES 4:17; ROMANS 12:2

*You shall be to Me a kingdom of priests
and a holy nation.*

You, Lord Jesus, were slain, and have redeemed us to God by Your blood out of every tribe and tongue and people and nation, and have made us kings and priests to our God. I am part of a chosen generation, a royal priesthood, a holy nation, God's own special people, that I may proclaim the praises of Him who called me out of darkness into His marvelous light.

I shall be named a priest of the Lord, they shall call me a servant of God . . . a priest of God and of Christ.

Therefore, as a partaker of the heavenly calling, I consider the Apostle and High Priest of my confession, Christ Jesus. By Him may I continually offer the sacrifice of praise to God, that is, the fruit of my lips, giving thanks to His name.

For I am His workmanship, created in You, Christ Jesus, for good works, which God prepared beforehand that I should walk in them. The temple of God is holy, which temple I am.

*God's workmanship, His chosen people, a royal priesthood,
a holy nation—enable me, Lord Jesus, to live up to this high calling,
to proclaim Your praises, and to do good works.*

EXODUS 19:6; REVELATION 5:9–10; 1 PETER 2:9;
ISAIAH 61:6; REVELATION 20:6; HEBREWS 3:1; HEBREWS 13:15;
EPHESIANS 2:10; 1 CORINTHIANS 3:17

You are a gracious and merciful God,
slow to anger and abundant in lovingkindness,
One who relents from doing harm.

Lord, I pray, let Your power be great as You have spoken: You, Lord, are longsuffering and abundant in mercy, forgiving iniquity and transgression; but You by no means clear the guilty, visiting the iniquity of the fathers on the children to the third and fourth generation.

Oh, do not remember former iniquities against me! Let Your tender mercies come speedily to meet me. Help me, O God of my salvation, for the glory of Your name; and deliver me, and provide atonement for my sins, for Your name's sake! O Lord, though my iniquities testify against me, do it for Your name's sake; for my backslidings are many; I have sinned against You. I acknowledge, O Lord, my wickedness and the iniquity of my fathers, for we have sinned against You.

O Lord, if You should mark iniquities, who could stand? But I have forgiveness with You, so I fear You.

Thank You for forgiving my sins—
my sins against You!—rather than keeping a record of them.
I praise You, merciful God, that You are
slow to anger and abounding in lovingkindness.

JONAH 4:2; NUMBERS 14:17–18; PSALM 79:8–9;
JEREMIAH 14:7, 20; PSALM 130:3–4

He calls his own sheep
by name and leads them out.

Lord God, Your solid foundation stands, having this seal: "The Lord knows those who are His," and, "Let everyone who names the name of Christ depart from iniquity." Many will say to Jesus in that day, "Lord, Lord, have we not prophesied in Your name, cast out demons in Your name, and done many wonders in Your name?" And then He will declare to them, "I never knew you; depart from Me, you who practice lawlessness!" You, Lord God, know the way of the righteous, but the way of the ungodly shall perish.

Jesus has inscribed me on the palms of His hands; my walls are continually before Him. Set me as a seal upon Your heart, Lord God, as a seal upon Your arm. You, Almighty God, are good, a stronghold in the day of trouble; and You know those who trust in You.

Jesus goes to prepare a place for me. And if He goes and prepares a place for me, He will come again and receive me to Himself; that where He is, there I may be also.

What a privilege to know You, Lord God—
and to have You know me by name.

JOHN 10:3; 2 TIMOTHY 2:19; MATTHEW 7:22–23;
PSALM 1:6; ISAIAH 49:16; SONG OF SOLOMON 8:6;
NAHUM 1:7; JOHN 14:2–3

He who is mighty has done great things for me,
and holy is His name.

Who is like You, O Lord, among the gods? Who is like You, glorious in holiness, fearful in praises, doing wonders? Among the gods there is none like You, O Lord; nor are there any works like Your works. Who shall not fear You, O Lord, and glorify Your name? For You alone are holy. Hallowed be Your name.

Blessed are You, the Lord God of Israel, for You have visited and redeemed Your people.

Who is this who comes from Edom, with dyed garments from Bozrah, this One who is glorious in His apparel, traveling in the greatness of His strength? It is You, God, who speaks in righteousness, mighty to save. Lord God, You have given help to one who is mighty; You have exalted one chosen from the people.

Now to Him who is able to do exceedingly abundantly above all that I ask or think, according to the power that works in me . . . be glory.

It is good to praise Your name,
Lord for You alone are worthy of praise!
You are mighty, righteous, holy,
and able to do far greater things
than any human can ask or imagine!

LUKE 1:49; EXODUS 15:11; PSALM 86:8; REVELATION 15:4;
MATTHEW 6:9; LUKE 1:68; ISAIAH 63:1; PSALM 89:19;
EPHESIANS 3:20–21

They are not of the world,
just as I am not of the world.

Jesus, You were despised and rejected by men, a Man of sorrows and acquainted with grief. In the world I will have tribulation; but I can be of good cheer, You have overcome the world.

Such a High Priest was fitting for me, Jesus who is holy, harmless, undefiled, separate from sinners . . . so that I may become blameless and harmless, a child of God without fault in the midst of a crooked and perverse generation.

Jesus of Nazareth, You went about doing good and healing all who were oppressed by the devil, for God was with You. Therefore, as I have opportunity, may I do good to all, especially to those who are of the household of faith.

Jesus, You were the true Light which gives light to every man coming into the world. As one of God's children, I am the light of the world. A city that is set on a hill cannot be hidden. May I let my light so shine before men, that they may see my good works and glorify my Father in heaven.

Lord, Jesus, show me the good works
You would have me do
and use me to be Your light.

JOHN 17:16; ISAIAH 53:3; JOHN 16:33; HEBREWS 7:26;
PHILIPPIANS 2:15; ACTS 10:38; GALATIANS 6:10;
JOHN 1:9; MATTHEW 5:14, 16

What is the profit of circumcision?

Lord, to You there is much in every way! So I circumcise myself to You, Lord, and take away the foreskin of my heart. If my uncircumcised heart is humbled, and I accept my guilt—then You, Lord God, will remember Your covenant with Jacob, and Your covenant with Isaac and Your covenant with Abraham You will remember.

Jesus Christ has become a servant to the circumcision for Your truth, Lord God, to confirm the promises made to the fathers. In Him I was circumcised with the circumcision made without hands, by putting off the body of the sins of the flesh, by the circumcision of Christ. I, being dead in my trespasses and the uncircumcision of my flesh, God has made alive together with Him, having forgiven me all trespasses.

I put off, concerning my former conduct, the old man which grows corrupt according to the deceitful lusts, and I am renewed in the spirit of my mind, and I put on the new man which You created, Lord God, in true righteousness and holiness.

Lord God, thank You for sending Jesus
who circumcised my heart and made me new in Him.

ROMANS 3:1; ROMANS 3:2; JEREMIAH 4:4;
LEVITICUS 26:41–42; ROMANS 15:8; COLOSSIANS 2:11;
COLOSSIANS 2:13; EPHESIANS 4:22–24

For the death that He died, He died to sin once for all;
but the life that He lives, He lives to God.

Y ou, Lord Jesus, were numbered with the transgressors.
You were offered once to bear the sins of many. Jesus, You
bore my sins in Your own body on the tree, that I, having
died to sins, might live for righteousness—by Your stripes I was
healed. By one offering You have perfected forever those who are
being sanctified.

But Jesus, because You continue forever, You have an
unchangeable priesthood. Therefore You are able to save to the
uttermost those who come to God through You, since You always
live to make intercession for me. While I was still a sinner, You
died for me. Much more then, having now been justified by
Your blood, I shall be saved from wrath through You.

Therefore, since You suffered for me in the flesh, I arm
myself also with the same mind, for if I have suffered in the flesh
I have ceased from sin, that I no longer should live the rest of my
time in the flesh for the lusts of men, but for the will of God.

Your death gave me life, Jesus.
Thank You.

———————————

ROMANS 6:10; ISAIAH 53:12; HEBREWS 9:28;
1 PETER 2:24; HEBREWS 10:14; HEBREWS 7:24–25;
ROMANS 5:8–9; 1 PETER 4:1–2

Then comes the end.

Lord Jesus. of that day and hour no one knows, not even the angels in heaven, nor You, the Son of God, but only the Father. So I take heed, watch and pray; for I do not know when the time is. And what You say to me, Jesus, You say to all: Watch! You, Lord Jesus, are not slack concerning Your promise, as some count slackness, but is longsuffering toward us, not willing that any should perish but that all should come to repentance. Your coming, Lord Jesus, is at hand. The Judge is standing at the door! Surely You are coming quickly.

Therefore, since all these things will be dissolved, what manner of persons ought I to be in holy conduct and godliness?

The end of all things is at hand; therefore I will be serious and watchful in my prayers. My waist will be girded and my lamps burning; and I myself will be like men who wait for their master, when he will return from the wedding, that when he comes and knocks they may open to him immediately.

May I be ready to open the door to You, Lord Jesus!
Come quickly, Lord!

---

1 CORINTHIANS 15:24; MARK 13:32–33, 37; 2 PETER 3:9;
JAMES 5:8–9; REVELATION 22:20; 2 PETER 3:11;
1 PETER 4:7; LUKE 12:35–36

[Be] patient in tribulation.

I t is You, Lord. Do what seems good to You." "For if I were righteous, I could not answer You; I would beg mercy of my Judge. . . . You, Lord God, gave, and You, Lord, have taken away; blessed be the name of the Lord. . . . Shall I indeed accept good from God, and shall I not accept adversity?"

My Jesus wept. He was a Man of sorrows and acquainted with grief. Surely He has borne my griefs and carried my sorrows.

Lord, those You love You chasten, and scourge every son whom You receive. Now no chastening seems to be joyful for the present, but painful; nevertheless, afterward it yields the peaceable fruit of righteousness to those who have been trained by it. May I be strengthened with all might, according to Your glorious power, for all patience and longsuffering with joy. In the world I will have tribulation; but I can be of good cheer; Jesus, has overcome the world.

May the reality of Your sovereignty
and of Your love for me, Father,
enable me to be patient, open to Your training,
and even cheerful during trials and tribulation.

ROMANS 12:12; 1 SAMUEL 3:18; JOB 9:15; JOB 1:21;
JOB 2:10; JOHN 11:35; ISAIAH 53:3–4; HEBREWS 12:6, 11;
COLOSSIANS 1:11; JOHN 16:33

We know that we have passed from death to life.

Loving God, My Savior said, "He who hears My word and believes in Him who sent Me has everlasting life, and shall not come into judgment, but has passed from death into life." I who have Your Son, Lord God, have life; he who does not have the Son of God does not have life.

God, You establish me in Christ and anoint me; You also have sealed me and given me Your Spirit in my heart as a guarantee. By this I know that I am of the truth, and shall assure my heart before You, God. If my heart does not condemn me, I have confidence toward You. I know that I am of You, Lord God, and the whole world lies under the sway of the wicked one.

I am one Jesus made alive, who was dead in trespasses and sins. Lord God, You made me alive together with Christ. You have delivered me from the power of darkness and conveyed me into the kingdom of the Son of Your love.

I praise You, merciful God, for You have
enabled me to pass from death to life,
from separation from You to relationship with You.

---

1 JOHN 3:14; JOHN 5:24; 1 JOHN 5:12;
2 CORINTHIANS 1:21–22; 1 JOHN 3:19, 21; 1 JOHN 5:19;
EPHESIANS 2:1, 5; COLOSSIANS 1:13

By faith Abraham obeyed
when he was called to go out
to the place which he would receive
as an inheritance.

You, Lord God, will choose my inheritance for me. You encircle me, You instruct me, You keep as the apple of Your eye. As an eagle stirs up its nest, hovers over its young, spreading out its wings, taking them up, carrying them on its wings, so You, Lord God, lead me, and there is no foreign god with me.

You are the Lord my God, who teaches me to profit, who leads me by the way I should go. Who teaches like You?

I walk by faith, not by sight. Here I have no continuing city, but I seek the one to come. As a sojourner and pilgrim, I abstain from fleshly lusts which war against the soul. I arise and depart, for this is not my rest; because it is defiled, it shall destroy me, yes, with utter destruction.

Lord God, may I have faith
like Abraham's as I follow You
and journey through life.

HEBREWS 11:8; PSALM 47:4; DEUTERONOMY 32:10–12;
ISAIAH 48:17; JOB 36:22; 2 CORINTHIANS 5:7;
HEBREWS 13:14; 1 PETER 2:11; MICAH 2:10

Christ, who is the image of God.

Your glory, Lord God, shall be revealed, and all flesh shall see it together. No one has seen You at any time. The only begotten Son, who is in Your bosom, Father God, has declared You. And the Word became flesh and dwelt among us, and we beheld His glory, the glory as of the only begotten of the Father, full of grace and truth. Those who saw Jesus have seen You, Father God . . . for He is the brightness of Your glory and the express image of Your person. You, Lord God, were manifested in the flesh.

In Jesus I have redemption through His blood, the forgiveness of sins. He is Your image, invisible God, the firstborn over all creation. Whom You foreknew, Lord God, You also predestined to be conformed to the image of Your Son, that He might be the firstborn among many brethren.

As I have borne the image of the man of dust, I shall also bear the image of Jesus, the heavenly Man.

Thank You, Lord God,
that I shall one day bear the image of Christ,
who bears Your image.

———————

2 Corinthians 4:4; Isaiah 40:5; John 1:18, 14;
John 14:9; Hebrews 1:3; 1 Timothy 3:16;
Colossians 1:14–15; Romans 8:29; 1 Corinthians 15:49

Walk in love.

Loving Father, a new commandment Jesus gives me, that I love others; as He has loved me, that I also love others. Above all things I am to have fervent love for others, for love will cover a multitude of sins. Love covers all sins.

Whenever I stand praying, if I have anything against anyone, I am to forgive him, that You, my Father in heaven, may also forgive me my trespasses. Enable me, Lord, to love my enemies, do good, and lend, hoping for nothing in return. May I not rejoice when my enemy falls, nor let my heart be glad when he stumbles. May I not return evil for evil or reviling for reviling, but on the contrary blessing, knowing that I was called to this, that I may inherit a blessing. As much as depends on me, I will live peaceably with all men. I will be kind to others, tenderhearted, forgiving others, even as You, Lord God, in Christ forgave me.

May I not love in word or in tongue, but in deed and in truth.

Only by Your grace is it possible for me
to love in deed and truth.
Fill me with Your grace, I pray.

EPHESIANS 5:2; JOHN 13:34; 1 PETER 4:8; PROVERBS 10:12;
MARK 11:25; LUKE 6:35; PROVERBS 24:17; 1 PETER 3:9;
ROMANS 12:18; EPHESIANS 4:32; 1 JOHN 3:18

Oh, that You would rend the heavens!
That You would come down!

Make haste, Lord Jesus, and be like a gazelle or a young stag on the mountains of spices. I groan within myself, eagerly waiting for the adoption, the redemption of my body. Bow down Your heavens, O Lord, and come down; touch the mountains, and they shall smoke.

Jesus, You were taken up from earth into heaven, and You will come in like manner as the apostles saw You go into heaven. To those who eagerly wait for You, You will appear a second time, apart from sin, for salvation. It will be said in that day: "Behold, this is our God; we have waited for Him, and He will save us. This is the Lord; we have waited for Him; we will be glad and rejoice in His salvation."

You say, "Surely I am coming quickly." Amen. Even so, come, Lord Jesus! I look forward to the blessed hope and glorious appearing of my great God and Savior Jesus Christ. My citizenship is in heaven.

With the saints of the ages,
I look forward to Your second coming,
my Savior and my King! Come, Lord Jesus!

ISAIAH 64:1; SONG OF SOLOMON 8:14; ROMANS 8:23;
PSALM 144:5; ACTS 1:11; HEBREWS 9:28; ISAIAH 25:9;
REVELATION 22:20; TITUS 2:13; PHILIPPIANS 3:20

Seek those things which are above, where Christ is,
sitting at the right hand of God.

Father, I seek to get wisdom! I seek to get understanding!
I seek the wisdom that is from above. The deep says,
"It is not in me"; and the sea says, "It is not with me."
I was buried with Jesus through baptism into death, that just as
He was raised from the dead by Your glory, Father God, I also
should walk in newness of life. For if I have been united in the
likeness of Jesus' death, certainly I also shall be in the likeness of
His resurrection.

So I lay aside every weight, and the sin which so easily
ensnares me, and I run with endurance the race that is set before
me. You, Lord God, made me alive with Christ and raised me
up, and made me sit in the heavenly places in Christ Jesus.

When I say such things I declare plainly that I seek a
homeland. So I seek You, Lord God, with all the meek of the
earth, who have upheld Your justice. I seek righteousness, I seek
humility.

Thank You for showing me the wisdom
of seeking after things eternal—
Your kingdom, Your righteousness,
Your wisdom, Your love.

COLOSSIANS 3:1; PROVERBS 4:5; JAMES 3:17; JOB 28:14;
ROMANS 6:4–5; HEBREWS 12:1; EPHESIANS 2:4–6;
HEBREWS 11:14; EPHESIANS 2:3

Endure hardship as a good soldier of Jesus Christ.

Lord God, You have given Jesus as a witness to the people, a leader and commander for the people. It was fitting for You, for whom are all things and by whom are all things, in bringing many sons to glory, to make the captain of our salvation perfect through sufferings. I must enter Your kingdom through many tribulations, Lord God.

I do not wrestle against flesh and blood, but against principalities, against powers, against the rulers of the darkness of this age, against spiritual hosts of wickedness in the heavenly places. Therefore I take up the whole armor that You provide, God. I do not war according to the flesh. For the weapons of my warfare are not carnal but mighty in Your power for pulling down strongholds.

May You, the God of all grace, who called me to Your eternal glory by Christ Jesus, after I have suffered a while, perfect, establish, strengthen, and settle me.

Lord God, thank You for providing me,
Your humble soldier,
with battle armor and Your constant presence.

2 TIMOTHY 2:3; ISAIAH 55:4; HEBREWS 2:10; ACTS 14:22;
EPHESIANS 6:12–13; 2 CORINTHIANS 10:3–4; 1 PETER 5:1

August

Your word

is a lamp to my feet

and a

light to my path.

The fruit of the Spirit is . . . faithfulness.

By grace I have been saved through faith, and that not of myself; it is Your gift, O God. Without faith it is impossible to please You. I believe in Jesus; I am not condemned; but he who does not believe is condemned already, because he has not believed in the name of the only begotten Son of God. Lord, I believe; help my unbelief!

When I keep Your word, Lord God, truly Your love is perfected in me. Faith working through love—for faith without works is dead.

I walk by faith, not by sight. I have been crucified with Christ; it is no longer I who live, but Christ lives in me; and the life which I now live in the flesh I live by faith in the Son of God, who loved me and gave Himself for me. Although I have not seen Jesus, I love Him. Though now I do not see Jesus, yet believing, I rejoice with joy inexpressible and full of glory, receiving the end of my faith—the salvation of my soul.

May my faithfulness to You, my ever-faithful God,
be obvious in my love, my obedience, and my joy.

GALATIANS 5:22; EPHESIANS 2:8; HEBREWS 11:6; JOHN 3:18;
MARK 9:24; 1 JOHN 2:5; GALATIANS 5:6; JAMES 2:20;
2 CORINTHIANS 5:7; GALATIANS 2:20; 1 PETER 1:8–9

The Lamb slain from the foundation of the world.

Lord God, You commanded that the Passover lamb shall be
without blemish. Then the whole assembly of the
congregation of Israel should kill it at twilight.
And they should take some of the blood and put it on the two
doorposts and on the lintel of the houses where they eat it.
You promised that when You saw the blood, You would pass over
those homes. Jesus' blood of sprinkling was spilled, and Christ,
my Passover, was sacrificed for me. Thus He was delivered by
Your determined purpose and foreknowledge, Lord God . . . and
according to Your own purpose and grace which was given to us
in Christ Jesus before time began.

I have redemption through Jesus' blood, the forgiveness
of sins.

Therefore, since Christ suffered for me in the flesh, I arm
myself also with the same mind, for I have suffered in the flesh
and have ceased from sin, that I no longer should live the rest of
my time in the flesh for the lusts of men, but for the will of God.

*May I honor Jesus, who made the ultimate sacrifice
on behalf of my sin, by dying to myself and living for Your will,
my gracious and merciful God.*

REVELATION 13:8; EXODUS 12:5–7, 13; HEBREWS 12:24;
1 CORINTHIANS 5:7; ACTS 2:23; 2 TIMOTHY 1:9;
EPHESIANS 1:7; 1 PETER 4:1–2

His mercy is on those who fear Him.

Oh, how great is Your goodness, Lord God, which You have laid up for those who fear You, which You have prepared for those who trust in You in the presence of men! You shall hide me in the secret place of Your presence from the plots of man; You shall keep me secretly in a pavilion from the strife of tongues.

If I call on You, Father, who without partiality judges according to each one's work, I will conduct myself throughout the time of my stay here in fear. You, Lord God, are near to all who call upon You in truth. You will fulfill the desire of those who fear You; You also will hear my cry and save me.

Because my heart was tender, and I humbled myself before You, Lord, and because I tore my clothes and wept before You, You have heard me. On me will You look: on me, for I am poor and of a contrite spirit, and I tremble at Your word. You, Lord God, are near to those who have a broken heart, and You save such as have a contrite spirit.

Holy God, keep me aware of my sin,
humble, contrite, and rooted in Your love.

LUKE 1:50; PSALM 31:19–20; 1 PETER 1:17;
PSALM 145:18–19; 2 KINGS 22:19; ISAIAH 66:2; PSALM 34:18

"It is finished!"
And bowing His head, He gave up His spirit.

Jesus, You are the author and finisher of my faith. You glorified God on the earth. You finished the work which He gave You to do. I have been sanctified through the offering of Your body, Jesus Christ, once for all. And every priest stands ministering daily and offering repeatedly the same sacrifices, which can never take away sins. But Jesus, after You had offered one sacrifice for sins forever, sat down at the right hand of God, from that time waiting till Your enemies are made Your footstool. For by one offering You have perfected forever those who are being sanctified. You have wiped out the handwriting of requirements that was against me, which was contrary to me. And You have taken it out of the way, having nailed it to the cross.

You lay down Your life that You may take it again. No one took it from You, but You lay it down of Yourself. You have power to lay it down, and You have power to take it again. Greater love has no one than this, than to lay down one's life for his friends.

You laid down Your life for me, Lord Jesus.
In gratitude may I lay down my life in love.

JOHN 19:30; HEBREWS 12:2; JOHN 17:4;
HEBREWS 10:10–14; COLOSSIANS 2:14; JOHN 10:17–18;
JOHN 15:13

Walk in newness of life.

As I presented my members as slaves of uncleanness, and of lawlessness leading to more lawlessness, so I now present my members as a slave of righteousness for holiness. By Your mercies, Lord God, I present my body a living sacrifice, holy, acceptable to You, which is my reasonable service. And I will not be conformed to this world, but I will be transformed by the renewing of my mind.

Since I am in Christ, I am a new creation; old things have passed away; all things have become new. In Christ Jesus, neither circumcision nor uncircumcision avails anything, but a new creation. And as I walk according to this rule, peace and mercy be upon me. Therefore I should no longer walk as the rest of the Gentiles walk, in the futility of their mind. I have not so learned Christ, if indeed I have heard Him and have been taught by Him, as the truth is in Jesus. I put on the new man who was created according to Your instruction, God, in righteousness and true holiness.

Teach me, Lord God, to walk in the newness of life in Christ Jesus and make me a slave to righteousness.

ROMANS 6:4; ROMANS 6:19; ROMANS 12:1–2;
2 CORINTHIANS 5:17; GALATIANS 6:15–16;
EPHESIANS 4:17, 20–21, 24

Whom the Lord loves He corrects.

I confess, Lord God, that You, even You, are He, and there is no God besides You; You kill and You make alive; You wound and You heal; nor is there any who can deliver from Your hand. The thoughts that You think toward me, Lord God, are thoughts of peace and not of evil, to give me a future and a hope. And You say, "My thoughts are not your thoughts, nor are your ways My ways."

You will allure me, will bring me into the wilderness, and speak comfort to me. As a man chastens his son, so You, Lord God, chasten me. Now no chastening seems to be joyful for the present, but painful; nevertheless, afterward it yields the peaceable fruit of righteousness to those who have been trained by it. I humble myself under Your mighty hand, Lord God, that You may exalt me in due time.

I know, O Lord, that Your judgments are right, and that in faithfulness You have afflicted me.

Heavenly Father, You love me enough to chasten me.
May I humble myself under Your chastening hand,
confident of Your love,
and anticipating the fulfillment
of the good plans You have for me.

PROVERBS 3:12; DEUTERONOMY 32:39; JEREMIAH 29:11;
ISAIAH 55:8; HOSEA 2:14; DEUTERONOMY 8:5; HEBREWS 12:11;
1 PETER 5:6; PSALM 119:75

The Helper, the Holy Spirit,
whom the Father will send in My name.

If the woman knew the gift of God, and who it was who said to her, "Give Me a drink," she would have asked Jesus, and He would have given her living water. If I, being evil, know how to give good gifts to my children, how much more will You, my heavenly Father, give the Holy Spirit to those who ask You! Most assuredly, Jesus says to me, whatever I ask You, Father God, in His name You will give me. Until now I have asked nothing in Jesus' name. If I ask, I will receive, that my joy may be full. I do not have because I do not ask.

Lord God, Your Spirit of truth has come, and He guides me into all truth; for He does not speak on His own authority, but whatever He hears He will speak; and He tells me things to come. He glorifies Jesus, for He takes of what is His and declares it to me.

When I rebel I grieve Your Holy Spirit; so You, Lord God, turn Yourself against me as an enemy, and You fight against me.

Lord God, teach me to live in Your truth
and not to grieve Your Spirit.

JOHN 14:26; JOHN 4:10; LUKE 11:13; JOHN 16:23–24;
JAMES 4:2; JOHN 16:13–14; ISAIAH 63:10

The path of the just is like the shining sun,
that shines ever brighter unto the perfect day.

Father, not having already attained, or being already perfected; I press on, that I may lay hold of that for which Christ Jesus has also laid hold of me. Let me know, and pursue knowledge of You, Lord God.

I, made righteous in Christ, will shine forth as the sun in Your kingdom, Father God. I, with unveiled face, beholding as in a mirror Your glory, Lord God, am being transformed into the same image from glory to glory, by Your Spirit. When that which is perfect has come, that which is in part will be done away. Now I see in a mirror, dimly, but then face to face. Now I know in part, but then I shall know just as I also am known. Now I am a child of God; and it has not yet been revealed what I shall be, but I know that when Jesus is revealed, I shall be like Him, for I shall see Him as He is. With this hope in Him I purify myself, just as He is pure.

Freed from sin, knowing You fully,
shining forth in Your righteousness—Lord,
I thank You for this solid hope!

PROVERBS 4:18; PHILIPPIANS 3:12; HOSEA 6:3;
MATTHEW 13:43; 2 CORINTHIANS 3:18;
1 CORINTHIANS 13:10, 12; 1 JOHN 3:2–3

You are all fair, my love,
and there is no spot in you.

Father, the description: The whole head is sick, and the whole heart faints. From the sole of the foot even to the head, there is no soundness in it, but wounds and bruises and putrefying sores; they have not been closed or bound up, or soothed with ointment, fits me. I am like an unclean thing, and all my righteousness is like filthy rags. I know that in me (that is, in my flesh) nothing good dwells.

I was washed, I was sanctified, and I was justified in the name of the Lord Jesus and by Your Spirit, Lord God. The royal child is all glorious within. Lord God, my beauty was perfect through Your splendor which You had bestowed on me.

May Your beauty, Lord, be upon me.

These are the ones who washed their robes and made them white in the blood of the Lamb. Jesus will present to You, Lord God, a glorious church, not having spot or wrinkle or any such thing, but holy and without blemish. I am complete in You.

You've changed me from unclean and filthy to cleansed
and glorified through Jesus' blood. Thank You, Lord God.

Song of Solomon 4:7; Isaiah 1:5–6; Isaiah 64:6;
Romans 7:18; 1 Corinthians 6:11; Psalm 45:13;
Ezekiel 16:14; Psalm 90:17; Revelation 7:14;
Ephesians 5:27; Colossians 2:10

I do not pray that You should take them out of the world,
but that You should keep them from the evil one.

Lord God, make me blameless and harmless, Your child without fault in the midst of a crooked and perverse generation, among whom I shine as a light in the world. I am the salt of the earth and the light of the world. May my light so shine before men, that they may see my good works and glorify You, my Father in heaven.

Keep me from sinning against You.

Lord God, You are faithful, who will establish me and guard me from the evil one. I do not do wrong, because of my fear of You, Lord God. Jesus gave Himself for my sins, that He might deliver me from this present evil age, according to Your will, my God and Father. Now to Jesus who is able to keep me from stumbling, and to present me faultless before the presence of Your glory with exceeding joy, to God my Savior, who alone is wise, be glory and majesty, dominion and power, both now and forever. Amen.

All praise to You, O God!
You alone can make me Your light
and keep me from sinning.
Do so, I ask!

JOHN 17:15; PHILIPPIANS 2:15; MATTHEW 5:13–14, 16;
GENESIS 20:6; 2 THESSALONIANS 3:3; NEHEMIAH 5:15;
GALATIANS 1:4; JUDE 24–25

That through death He might destroy him
who had the power of death.

Father, my Savior Jesus Christ has abolished death and brought life and immortality to light through the gospel. Lord God, You will swallow up death forever, and You will wipe away tears from all faces; the rebuke of Your people—my rebuke—You will take away from all the earth; for You, Lord God, have spoken. When this corruptible has put on incorruption, and this mortal has put on immortality, then shall be brought to pass the saying that is written: "Death is swallowed up in victory." "O Death, where is your sting? O Hades, where is your victory?" The sting of death is sin, and the strength of sin is the law. But I give thanks to You, Lord, who gives me the victory through my Lord Jesus Christ.

You, Father God, have not given me a spirit of fear, but of power and of love and of a sound mind. Yea, though I walk through the valley of the shadow of death, I will fear no evil; for You are with me; Your rod and Your staff, they comfort me.

I rejoice in Your victory over death, Lord God,
and the gifts of life and immortality You give Your people!

HEBREWS 2:14; 2 TIMOTHY 1:10; ISAIAH 25:8;
1 CORINTHIANS 15:54–57; 2 TIMOTHY 1:7; PSALM 23:4

The Lord will not cast off forever.
Though He causes grief, yet He will show compassion.

You say to me, Lord God, "Do not fear for I am with you; I will not make a complete end of you. I will rightly correct you." My Lord and my Redeemer, You say that for a mere moment You have forsaken me, but with great mercies You will gather me. With a little wrath You hid Your face from me for a moment; but with everlasting kindness You will have mercy on me. Lord God and the One who has mercy on me, You say that, while the mountains shall depart and the hills be removed, but Your kindness shall not depart from me, nor shall Your covenant of peace be removed. Though I am afflicted, tossed with tempest, and not comforted, You say You will lay my stones with colorful gems, and lay my foundations with sapphires.

I will bear Your indignation, Lord God, because I have sinned against You, until You plead my case and execute justice for me. You will bring me forth to the light; I will see Your righteousness.

Thank You for this big-picture reminder
that You will not cast me off
or cause me grief forever. I praise You,
my Redeemer God,
for Your everlasting mercy, kindness,
compassion, and love.

LAMENTATIONS 3:31–32; JEREMIAH 46:28;
ISAIAH 54:7–8, 10–11; MICAH 7:9

He has prepared a city for them.

L ord Jesus, You, have gone to prepare a place for me, and will come again and receive me to Yourself; that where You are, there I may be also. An inheritance incorruptible and undefiled and that does not fade away is reserved in heaven for me. Here I have no continuing city, but I seek the one to come.

Jesus, You were taken up from earth into heaven, and You will so come in like manner as the apostles saw You go into heaven. Therefore I will be patient until Your coming. The farmer waits for the precious fruit of the earth, waiting patiently for it until it receives the early and latter rain. I also will be patient. I will establish my heart, for Your coming, my Lord, is at hand. Yet a little while, and You who are coming will come and will not tarry.

Those who are alive and remain shall be caught up together in the clouds with the dead in Christ, to meet You, Lord Jesus, in the air. And thus I shall always be with You, Lord. We comfort one another with these words.

Thank You, Jesus, for preparing an eternal home in Your glorious presence.

HEBREWS 11:16; JOHN 14:3; 1 PETER 1:4; HEBREWS 13:14;
ACTS 1:11; JAMES 5:7–8; HEBREWS 10:37;
1 THESSALONIANS 4:17–18

The joy of the Lord is your strength.

Sing, O heavens! Be joyful, O earth! And break out in singing, O mountains! For my Lord God has comforted us, His people, and He will have mercy on His afflicted. Lord God, You are my salvation, I will trust and not be afraid; for You, Lord, are my strength and my song; You also have become my salvation. You, Lord, are my strength and my shield; my heart trusted in You, and I am helped; therefore my heart greatly rejoices, and with my song I will praise You. My soul shall be joyful in You, my God; for You have clothed me with the garments of salvation, You have covered me with the robe of righteousness, as a bridegroom decks himself with ornaments, and as a bride adorns herself with her jewels.

Therefore I have reason to glory in Christ Jesus in the things which pertain to You, Lord God. I rejoice in You, God, through my Lord Jesus Christ, through whom I have now received the reconciliation. I will joy in You, the God of my salvation.

All praise to You, almighty and merciful God.
I do indeed find in You countless reasons for joy!

NEHEMIAH 8:10; ISAIAH 49:13; ISAIAH 12:2; PSALM 28:7;
ISAIAH 61:10; ROMANS 15:17; ROMANS 5:11; HABAKKUK 3:18

The God of peace . . . make you complete
in every good work to do His will.

You call me to be complete, be of good comfort, be of one mind, to live in peace; and You, the God of love and peace, are with me.

By grace I have been saved through faith, and that not of myself; it is Your gift to me, Lord God, not of works, lest I should boast. Every good gift and every perfect gift is from above, and comes down from You who are the Father of lights, with whom there is no variation or shadow of turning.

I work out my own salvation with fear and trembling; for it is You, Lord God, who works in me both to will and to do for Your good pleasure. I can be transformed by the renewing of my mind, that I may prove what is Your good and acceptable and perfect will. May I be filled with the fruits of righteousness which are by Jesus Christ, to Your glory and praise, Lord God.

Not that I am sufficient of myself to think of anything as being from me, but my sufficiency is from God.

Lord, fill me with Your grace
so You can use me in Your kingdom.

HEBREWS 13:20–21; 2 CORINTHIANS 13:11; EPHESIANS 2:8–9;
JAMES 1:17; PHILIPPIANS 2:12–13; ROMANS 12:2;
PHILIPPIANS 1:11; 2 CORINTHIANS 3:5

The house to be built for the Lord
must be exceedingly magnificent.

Lord, as a living stone, I am being built up into a spiritual house. I am Your temple, Lord God, and Your Spirit dwells in me. If I defile Your temple, You will destroy me. For Your temple is holy, which temple I am. My body is the temple of the Holy Spirit who is in me, whom I have from You, Lord God, and I am not my own. For I was bought at a price; therefore I am to glorify You in my body spirit, which are Yours. What agreement has Your temple, Lord God, with idols? I am a temple of the living God. As You have said, You will dwell in me and walk among me. You will be my God, and I shall be Yours. I have been built on the foundation of the apostles and prophets, Jesus Christ Himself being the chief cornerstone, in whom the whole building, being fitted together, grows into a holy temple in You, Lord God, in whom I am being built together for a dwelling place for You in the Spirit.

May the truth that Your Spirit dwells within me
guide my words and deeds.

---

1 CHRONICLES 22:5; 1 PETER 2:5; 1 CORINTHIANS 3:16–17;
1 CORINTHIANS 6:19–20; 2 CORINTHIANS 6:16;
EPHESIANS 2:19–22

Pray for one another, that you may be healed.

Abraham answered and said, "Indeed now, I who am but dust and ashes have taken it upon myself to speak to the Lord: Suppose there were five less than the fifty righteous; would You destroy all of the city for lack of five?" So You said, "If I find there forty-five, I will not destroy it."

Jesus said, "Father, forgive them, for they do not know what they do." I am to pray for those who spitefully use me and persecute me.

Jesus prays for us. He does not pray for the world but for us whom You have given Him, for we are Yours. Jesus, do not pray for us alone, but also for those who will believe in Him through our word. We are to bear one another's burdens, and so fulfill the law of Christ.

The effective, fervent prayer of a righteous man avails much. Elijah was a man with a nature like ours, and he prayed earnestly that it would not rain; and it did not rain on the land for three years and six months.

*Thank You for teaching me to pray
and for providing the examples of Abraham,
Jesus, and Elijah. May I put into practice what I've learned!*

JAMES 5:16; GENESIS 18:27–28; LUKE 23:34;
MATTHEW 5:44; JOHN 17:9, 20; GALATIANS 6:2;
JAMES 5:16–17

What god is there in heaven or on earth
who can do anything like Your works and Your mighty deeds?

O Lord, who in the heavens can be compared to You? Who among the sons of the mighty can be likened to You, Lord? O Lord God of hosts, who is mighty like You? Your faithfulness also surrounds You. Among the gods there is none like You, O Lord; nor are there any works like Your works. For Your word's sake, and according to Your own heart, You have done all these great things, to make me, Your servant, know them. You are great, O Lord God. There is none like You, nor is there any God besides You, according to all that I have heard with my ears.

Eye has not seen, nor ear heard, nor have entered into the heart of man the things which You have prepared for those who love You. But You have revealed them to me through Your Spirit. The secret things belong to You, Lord God, but those things which are revealed belong to us and to our children.

Great is Your faithfulness, Almighty God.
Infinite is Your mercy! Immeasurable is Your grace!
You alone are worthy of praise!

DEUTERONOMY 3:24; PSALM 89:6, 8; PSALM 86:8;
2 SAMUEL 7:21–22; I CORINTHIANS 2:9–10;
DEUTERONOMY 29:29

As He who called you is holy,
you also be holy in all your conduct.

Lord God, in Your Word I am exhorted and charged to walk worthy of You who calls me into Your own kingdom and glory. May I proclaim Your praises, Lord God, for You called me out of darkness into Your marvelous light.

I was once darkness, but now I am light in You, Lord. Enable me to walk as a child of light (for the fruit of the Spirit is in all goodness, righteousness, and truth), finding out what is acceptable to You, Lord God. I will have no fellowship with the unfruitful works of darkness, but rather expose them. I will be filled with the fruits of righteousness which are by Jesus Christ, to Your glory and praise.

May my light so shine before men, that they may see my good works and glorify You, my Father in heaven. Therefore, whether I eat or drink, or whatever I do, may I do all to Your glory, Lord God.

Only with Your help, Lord, will I be able to live a life
of holiness and glorify You in all I say, do, and think.
Help me!

1 PETER 1:15; 1 THESSALONIANS 2:11–12;
1 PETER 2:9; EPHESIANS 5:8–11; PHILIPPIANS 1:11;
MATTHEW 5:16; 1 CORINTHIANS 10:31

God is not a man, that He should lie,
nor a son of man, that He should repent.

Lord God, You are the Father of lights, with whom there is no
variation or shadow of turning. Jesus Christ is the same
yesterday, today, and forever.

Your truth, God, shall be my shield and buckler.

You, Lord, determining to show more abundantly to the
heirs of promise the immutability of Your counsel, confirmed it
by an oath, that by two immutable things, in which it is
impossible for You to lie, I might have strong consolation, who
have fled for refuge to lay hold of the hope set before me.

You, faithful God, keep covenant and mercy for a thousand
generations with those who love You and keep Your
commandments. All Your paths, Lord God, are mercy and truth,
to me if I keep Your covenant and Your testimonies. I am happy
for I have You, the God of Jacob, for my help, whose hope is in
You, the Lord my God, who keeps truth forever.

Almighty God, You do not change—nor does Your truth.
Great is Your faithfulness, and great is my love for You,
my Fortress, my Shield, my Rock.

NUMBERS 23:19; JAMES 1:17; HEBREWS 13:8;
PSALM 91:4; HEBREWS 6:17–18; DEUTERONOMY 7:9;
PSALM 25:10; PSALM 146:5–6

You are my portion, O Lord.

Lord, In Christ all things are mine. I am Christ's, and Christ is Yours. My Savior Jesus Christ gave Himself for me. You gave Christ to be head over all things to the church. Christ loved the church and gave Himself for me, that He might present me to Himself, a part of the glorious church, not having spot or wrinkle or any such thing, but that I should be holy and without blemish.

My soul shall make its boast in You, Lord God. I will greatly rejoice in You, my soul shall be joyful in You, my God; for You have clothed me with the garments of salvation, You have covered me with the robe of righteousness.

Whom have I in heaven but You, Lord God? There is none upon earth that I desire besides You. My flesh and my heart fail; but You are the strength of my heart and my portion forever. My soul has said, "You are my Lord." You are the portion of my inheritance and my cup; You maintain my lot. The lines have fallen to me in pleasant places; yes, I have a good inheritance.

Lord, I have an amazing inheritance in You.
All praise to You!

PSALM 119:57; 1 CORINTHIANS 3:21, 23; TITUS 2:13–14;
EPHESIANS 1:22; EPHESIANS 5:25, 27; PSALM 34:2;
ISAIAH 61:10; PSALM 73:25–26; PSALM 16:2, 5–6

None of us lives to himself,
and no one dies to himself.

Lord, if I live, I live to You, and if I die, I die to You, Lord. Whether I live or die, I am Yours. Let me not seek my own, but the other's well-being. I was bought at a price; therefore I glorify God in my body and spirit, which are Yours.

Christ will be magnified in my body, whether by life or by death. For to me, to live is Christ, and to die is gain. But if I live on in the flesh, this will mean fruit from my labor; yet what I shall choose I cannot tell. For I am hard-pressed between the two, having a desire to depart and be with Christ, which is far better.

I through the law died to the law that I might live to You, Lord God. I have been crucified with Christ; it is no longer I who live, but Christ lives in me; and the life which I now live in the flesh I live by faith in the Son of God, who loved me and gave Himself for me.

I don't die to myself; may I not live to myself.
May I—as Jesus did—
seek the other's well-being and serve with love.

ROMANS 14:7; ROMANS 14:8; 1 CORINTHIANS 10:24;
1 CORINTHIANS 6:20; PHILIPPIANS 1:20–23;
GALATIANS 2:19–20

I have loved you with an everlasting love;
therefore with lovingkindness I have drawn you.

Lord, I, too, am bound to give You praise, always, for my brethren beloved by You, because from the beginning You chose us for salvation through sanctification by the Spirit and belief in the truth, to which You called me by the gospel, for the obtaining of the glory of my Lord Jesus Christ. You, Lord God, have saved me and called me with a holy calling, not according to my works, but according to Your own purpose and grace which was given to me in Christ Jesus before time began. Your eyes saw my substance, being yet unformed. And in Your book they all were written, the days fashioned for me, when as yet there were none of them.

God, You so loved the world that You gave Your only begotten Son, that whoever believes in Him should not perish but have everlasting life.

In this is love, not that I loved You, Lord God, but that You loved me and sent Your Son to be the propitiation for my sins.

What amazing and immeasurable love!
May I love others as graciously
as You have loved and continue to love me!

JEREMIAH 31:3; 2 THESSALONIANS 2:13–14; 2 TIMOTHY 1:9;
PSALM 139:16; JOHN 3:16; 1 JOHN 4:10

I know their sorrows.

Father, Jesus Christ was a Man of sorrows and acquainted with grief. He can sympathize with my weaknesses.

He Himself took my infirmities and bore my sicknesses. Jesus, once being wearied from His journey, sat by the well.

When Jesus saw her weeping, and the Jews who came with her weeping, He groaned in the spirit and was troubled. Jesus wept. In that Jesus Himself has suffered, being tempted, He is able to aid those who are tempted.

Lord God, You looked down from the height of Your sanctuary; from heaven You viewed the earth, to hear the groaning of the prisoner, to release those appointed to death. You know the way that I take; when You have tested me, I shall come forth as gold. When my spirit was overwhelmed within me, You knew my path.

Anyone who touches me touches the apple of Your eye, Lord God. In all Your people's affliction You were afflicted, and the Angel of Your Presence saved us.

You know me and my sorrows,
my compassionate and gracious God.
You comfort me and rescue me, and I praise You!

Exodus 3:7; Isaiah 53:3; Hebrews 4:15; Matthew 8:17;
John 4:6; John 11:33; John 11:35; Hebrews 2:18;
Psalm 102:19–20; Job 23:10; Psalm 142:3;
Zechariah 2:8; Isaiah 63:9

Look to the rock from which you were hewn,
and to the hole of the pit from which you were dug.

Indeed, Lord, I was brought forth in iniquity. No eye pitied me, but I was thrown out into the open field, when I was loathed on the day I was born. And when You passed by me, Lord God, and saw me struggling in my own blood, You said to me, "Live!"

You also brought me up out of a horrible pit, out of the miry clay, and set my feet upon a rock, and established my steps You have put a new song in my mouth—praise to You, my God.

When I was still without strength, in due time Christ died for the ungodly me. Scarcely for a righteous man will one die; perhaps for a good man someone would even dare to die. But You, Lord God, demonstrate Your own love toward me, in that while I was still a sinner, Christ died for me. You, who are rich in mercy, because of Your great love with which You loved me, even when I was dead in trespasses, You made me alive with Christ.

Thank You, God, for Your mercy, Your forgiveness,
Your deliverance, and Your love.

ISAIAH 51:1; PSALM 51:5; EZEKIEL 16:5–6; PSALM 40:2–3;
ROMANS 5:6–8; EPHESIANS 2:4–5

*You shall also make a plate of pure gold and engrave on it,
like the engraving of a signet: Holiness To The Lord.*

Lord God, help me to pursue holiness, without which I will
not see You. You are Spirit, and those who worship You must
worship in spirit and truth. I am like an unclean
thing, and all my righteousnesses are like filthy rags. By those
who come near You, Lord God, You must be regarded as holy;
and before all the people You must be glorified.

This is the law of the temple: The whole area surrounding
the mountaintop is most holy. Holiness adorns Your house,
O Lord, forever.

For my sake, Jesus sanctifies Himself, that I also may be
sanctified by the truth. Seeing that I have a great High Priest
who has passed through the heavens, Jesus the Son of God,
I come boldly to Your throne of grace, that I may obtain mercy
and find grace to help in time of need.

*Thank You for cleansing me by the blood of Your Son.
Thank You, Holy God, for welcoming me to Your throne of grace
and being the Source of help whatever my needs—
spiritual, physical, emotional.*

EXODUS 28:36; HEBREWS 12:14; JOHN 4:24; ISAIAH 64:6;
LEVITICUS 10:3; EZEKIEL 43:12; PSALM 93:5;
JOHN 17:19; HEBREWS 4:14, 16

*Your word is a lamp to my feet
and a light to my path.*

Lord God, by Your word, I have kept away from the paths of the destroyer. Uphold my steps in Your paths, that my footsteps may not slip. When I roam, Your commands will lead me; when I sleep, they will keep me; and when I awake, they will speak with me. For Your commandment is a lamp, and Your law a light. My ears shall hear a word behind me, saying, "This is the way, walk in it," whenever I turn to the right hand or whenever I turn to the left.

Jesus is the light of the world. When I follow Him I do not walk in darkness, but have the light of life. I also have the prophetic word confirmed, which I heed as a light that shines in a dark place. Now I see in a mirror, dimly, but then face to face. Now I know in part, but then I shall know just as I also am known. In heaven I will need no lamp nor sunlight, for You, Lord God, give light. And I shall reign forever and ever.

*Thank You for providing
light in this dark and lost world.*

PSALM 119:105; PSALM 17:4–5;
PROVERBS 6:22–23; ISAIAH 30:21; JOHN 8:12; 2 PETER 1:19;
1 CORINTHIANS 13:12; REVELATION 22:5

The accuser of our brethren, who accused them before our God day and night, has been cast down.

Lord God, I can overcome Satan by the blood of the Lamb and by the word of my testimony. Who shall bring a charge against me, Your elect, Lord God? It is You who justify. Who is He who condemns? It is Christ who died, and furthermore is also risen, who is even at Your right hand, who also makes intercession for me.

Having disarmed principalities and powers, Jesus made a public spectacle of them. Through death Jesus destroyed him who had the power of death, that is, the devil, and released me who through fear of death was all my lifetime subject to bondage. In all these things I am more than a conqueror through Jesus who loved me. I put on the whole of Your armor, Lord God, that I may be able to stand against the wiles of the devil. And I take the sword of the Spirit, which is Your Word. Thanks be to You, Almighty God, who gives me the victory through my Lord Jesus Christ.

Lord God, victory over the devil,
sin, and death is mine through Your Son.
All praise to You!

REVELATION 12:10; REVELATION 12:11; ROMANS 8:33–34; COLOSSIANS 2:15; HEBREWS 2:14–15; ROMANS 8:37; EPHESIANS 6:11, 17; 1 CORINTHIANS 15:57

Whoever trusts in the Lord, happy is he.

Lord God, like Abraham may I not waver at Your promise through unbelief, but be strengthened in faith, giving You glory, and being fully convinced that what You had promised You were also able to perform. The children of Judah prevailed, because they relied on You, the God of their fathers.

You are my refuge and strength, a very present help in trouble. Therefore I will not fear, even though the earth be removed, and though the mountains be carried into the midst of the sea. It is better to trust in You, Lord, than to put confidence in man. It is better to trust in You than to put confidence in princes. Lord, You order my steps as of a good man, and You delight in my way. Though I fall, I shall not be utterly cast down; for You, Lord, uphold me with Your hand.

Lord, I've tasted and seen that You are good; I am blessed when I trust in You! Oh, I fear You, Lord. There is no want to me when I fear You.

Lord, may I trust in Your promises
and Your ability and willingness to keep them.
Then I will know Your blessings.

PROVERBS 16:20; ROMANS 4:20–21; 2 CHRONICLES 13:18;
PSALM 46:1–2; PSALM 118:8–9; PSALM 37:23–24;
PSALM 34:8–9

The king held out . . . the golden scepter . . .
Then Esther went near and touched the top of the scepter.

Mighty God, when I cry to You, Lord God, You will hear, for You are gracious.

I have known and believed the love that You have for me. You are love, and when I abide in love I abide in You, and You in me. Love has been perfected in this: that I may have boldness in the day of judgment; because as You are, so am I in this world. There is no fear in love; but perfect love casts out fear, because fear involves torment. But if I fear I have not been made perfect in love. I love You, God, because You first loved me.

I draw near with a true heart in full assurance of faith, having my heart sprinkled from an evil conscience and my body washed with pure water. Through Jesus I have access by one Spirit to You, my heavenly Father. I have boldness and access with confidence through faith in Jesus. I therefore come boldly to the throne of grace, that I may obtain mercy and find grace to help in time of need.

The earthly king extended temporary access.
You, my heavenly King,
extend eternal access to Your throne.

ESTHER 5:2; EXODUS 22:27; 1 JOHN 4:16–19;
HEBREWS 10:22; EPHESIANS 2:18;
EPHESIANS 3:12; HEBREWS 4:16

*The free gift which came from many offenses
resulted in justification.*

Loving Father, though my sins are like scarlet, they shall be as white as snow; though they are red like crimson, they shall be as wool. You, Lord God, are He who blots out my transgressions for Your own sake; and You will not remember my sins. So I put You in remembrance; let us contend together; I state my case, that I may be acquitted. You have blotted out, like a thick cloud, my transgressions, and like a cloud, my sins. I return to You, for You have redeemed me.

God, You so loved the world that You gave Your only begotten Son, that whoever believes in Him should not perish but have everlasting life. But the free gift is not like the offense. For if by the one man's offense many died, much more Your grace and the gift by the grace of the one Man, Jesus Christ, abounded to many. I was washed, I was sanctified, I was justified in the name of the Lord Jesus and by Your Spirit, Lord God.

*From now through eternity I will be praising You for the gift—
the grace—of justification and cleansing from my sins.
Thank You, Lord God!*

Romans 5:16; Isaiah 1:18; Isaiah 43:25–26; Isaiah 44:22;
John 3:16; Romans 5:15; 1 Corinthians 6:11

September

Open my eyes,

that I may see

wondrous things from

Your law.

The fruit of the Spirit is . . . kindness.

The humble shall increase their joy in You, Lord, and the poor among men shall rejoice in You, the Holy One of Israel. Unless I am converted and become as a little child, I will by no means enter the kingdom of heaven.

Therefore whoever humbles himself as a little child is the greatest in the kingdom of heaven. The incorruptible beauty of a gentle and quiet spirit is very precious in Your sight, Lord God. Love does not parade itself, is not puffed up.

So I will pursue gentleness. I will take Jesus' yoke upon me and learn from Him, for He is gentle and lowly in heart. He was oppressed and afflicted, yet He opened not His mouth; He was led as a lamb to the slaughter, and as a sheep before its shearers is silent, so He opened not His mouth. Christ suffered for me, leaving me an example, that I should follow His steps: "Who committed no sin, nor was deceit found in His mouth"; who, when He was reviled, did not revile in return; but committed Himself to Him who judges righteously.

Lord God, teach me to follow Jesus'
example of humility.

GALATIANS 5:22; ISAIAH 29:19; MATTHEW 18:3–4;
1 PETER 3:4; 1 CORINTHIANS 13:4; 1 TIMOTHY 6:11;
MATTHEW 11:29; ISAIAH 53:7; 1 PETER 2:21–23

Wait on the Lord; be of good courage,
and He shall strengthen your heart.

Lord God, I have heard, and I know: You, the everlasting God, the Creator of the ends of the earth, neither faint nor are weary. You give power to the weak, and to those of us who have no might You increase strength. I will not fear, for You are with me; I will not be dismayed, for You are my God.

You will strengthen me, yes, You will help me, You will uphold me with Your righteous right hand. You have been a strength to the poor, a strength to the needy in his distress, a refuge from the storm, a shade from the heat; for the blast of the terrible ones is as a storm against the wall.

The testing of my faith produces patience. So let patience have its perfect work, that I may be perfect and complete, lacking nothing. I do not cast away my confidence, which has great reward. For I have need of endurance, so that after I have done Your will, Lord God, I may receive the promise.

Teach me to wait on You, to know Your presence with me,
to find strength in You, and to persevere in my faith.

PSALM 27:14; ISAIAH 40:28–29; ISAIAH 41:10; ISAIAH 25:4;
JAMES 1:3–4; HEBREWS 10:35–36

Nor shall leaven be seen among you in all your quarters.

Lord God, to fear You is to hate evil. I abhor what is evil. I will abstain from every form of evil. I will look carefully lest I fall short of Your grace; lest any root of bitterness springing up cause trouble, and by this many become defiled.

If I regard iniquity in my heart, You, my Lord, will not hear.

A little leaven leavens the whole lump. Therefore I will purge out the old leaven, that I may be a new lump, since I truly am unleavened. For indeed Christ, my Passover, was sacrificed for me. Therefore let me keep the feast, not with old leaven, nor with the leaven of malice and wickedness, but with the unleavened bread of sincerity and truth. Let me examine myself, and so let me eat of that bread and drink of that cup.

May I—and everyone—who names the name of Christ depart from iniquity. Such a High Priest was fitting for us, who is holy, harmless, undefiled, separate from sinners. In Him there is no sin.

Remove, Holy God, the leaven of sin from my life.
May I flee from evil.

———————

EXODUS 13:7; PROVERBS 8:13; ROMANS 12:9;
1 THESSALONIANS 5:22; HEBREWS 12:15; PSALM 66:18;
1 CORINTHIANS 5:6–8; 1 CORINTHIANS 11:28;
2 TIMOTHY 2:19; HEBREWS 7:26; 1 JOHN 3:5

Sit still, my daughter.

I will take heed, and be quiet; I will not fear or be fainthearted. I will be still, and know that You are God. Lord, did You not say to me that if I would believe I would see Your glory? The loftiness of man shall be bowed down, and the haughtiness of men shall be brought low; You alone, Lord God, will be exalted in that day.

Mary sat at Jesus' feet and heard His word. Mary chose that good part, which will not be taken away from her. In returning and rest I shall be saved; in quietness and confidence shall be my strength. So I will meditate within my heart on my bed, and be still.

I rest in You, Lord, and wait patiently for You; I do not fret because of him who prospers in his way, because of the man who brings wicked schemes to pass.

I will not be afraid of evil tidings; my heart is steadfast, trusting in You, Lord. My heart is established.

Whoever believes will not act hastily.

Sitting still, Lord God, is so countercultural
and so against my nature. Help me to sit still and
wait on You to speak and to guide.

RUTH 3:18; ISAIAH 7:4; PSALM 46:10; JOHN 11:40;
ISAIAH 2:17; LUKE 10:39, 42; ISAIAH 30:15; PSALM 4:4;
PSALM 37:7; PSALM 112:7–8; ISAIAH 28:16

As the body is one and has many members,
. . . so also is Christ.

Jesus is the head of the body, the church. He is head over all things to the church, which is His body, the fullness of Him who fills all in all. I am a member of His body, of His flesh and of His bones.

As You prepared a body for Christ, so, Lord God, Your eyes saw my substance, being yet unformed. And in Your book they all were written, the days fashioned for me, when as yet there were none of them.

I was Yours, Lord, and You gave me to Jesus. You chose me in Jesus before the foundation of the world. You foreknew me, and You also predestined me to be conformed to the image of Your Son.

Help me grow up in all things into Him who is the head— Christ—from whom the whole body, joined and knit together by what every joint supplies, causes growth of the body for the edifying of itself in love.

By Your grace, may I who call You "Lord"
know the unity and love of Your body, the church.

---

1 CORINTHIANS 12:12; COLOSSIANS 1:18; EPHESIANS 1:22–23;
EPHESIANS 5:30; HEBREWS 10:5; PSALM 139:16;
JOHN 17:6; EPHESIANS 1:4;
ROMANS 8:29; EPHESIANS 4:15–16

Let us lift our hearts and hands to God in heaven.

O Lord my God, who is like You, who dwells on high, who humbles Yourself to behold the things that are in the heavens and in the earth? To You, O Lord, I lift up my soul. I spread out my hands to You; my soul longs for You like a thirsty land. Do not hide Your face from me, lest I be like those who go down into the pit. Cause me to hear Your lovingkindness in the morning, for in You do I trust; cause me to know the way in which I should walk, for I lift up my soul to You.

Because Your lovingkindness is better than life, my lips shall praise You. Thus I will bless You while I live; I will lift up my hands in Your name. O Lord, rejoice Your servant's soul, for to You I lift up my soul. For You, Lord, are good, and ready to forgive, and abundant in mercy to all those of us who call upon You.

Whatever I ask in Jesus' name, that He will do.

I lift my heart and my soul to You, Lord—
to You whose lovingkindness is better than life—
and I praise You!

LAMENTATIONS 3:41; PSALM 113:5–6;
PSALM 25:1; PSALM 143:6–8;
PSALM 63:3–4; PSALM 86:4–5; JOHN 14:13

Rejoicing in hope.

Lord God, I have hope which You laid up for me in heaven. If in this life only I have hope in Christ, I am of all men the most pitiable. I must, through many tribulations, enter Your kingdom, Lord God. Whoever does not bear Your cross and come after You cannot be Your disciple. I should not be shaken by afflictions; for I know that I am appointed to this.

So I will rejoice in the Lord always. Again I will rejoice! You, God of hope, fill me with all joy and peace in believing, that I may abound in hope by the power of the Holy Spirit. God and Father of my Lord Jesus Christ, I bless You who according to Your abundant mercy have begotten me to a living hope through the resurrection of Jesus Christ from the dead. Having not seen Jesus, yet I love Him. Though now I do not see Him, yet believing, I rejoice with joy inexpressible and full of glory. Through Him I have access by faith into this grace in which I stand, I rejoice in hope of Your glory, Lord God.

Lord God, thank You for the gift of hope
that brings joy inexpressible!

ROMANS 12:12; COLOSSIANS 1:5; 1 CORINTHIANS 15:19;
ACTS 14:22; LUKE 14:27; 1 THESSALONIANS 3:3;
PHILIPPIANS 4:4; ROMANS 15:13;
1 PETER 1:3; 1 PETER 1:8; ROMANS 5:2

You have been weighed in the balances,
and found wanting.

You, Lord, are the God of knowledge; and by You actions are weighed. What is highly esteemed among men is an abomination in Your sight, Holy God. You do not see as man sees; for man looks at the outward appearance, but You look at the heart. I will not be deceived, You are not mocked; for whatever I sow, that I will also reap. For if I sow to my flesh I will of my flesh reap corruption, but if I sow to the Spirit I will of the Spirit reap everlasting life.

What profit is it to me if gain the whole world, and lose my own soul? Or what will a man give in exchange for his soul? What things were gain to me, these I have counted loss for Christ.

Behold, You desire truth in the inward parts. You have tested my heart; You have visited me in the night; You have tried me and have found nothing.

Holy God, though You can see into my heart,
You can also cleanse it from the sin You find there!

DANIEL 5:27; 1 SAMUEL 2:3; LUKE 16:15; 1 SAMUEL 16:7;
GALATIANS 6:7–8; MATTHEW 16:26; PHILIPPIANS 3:7;
PSALM 51:6; PSALM 17:3

He has filled the hungry with good things,
and the rich He has sent away empty.

Father, too easily I say, "I am rich, have become wealthy, and need of nothing"—and do not know that I am wretched, miserable, poor, blind, and naked—You counsel me to buy from You gold refined in the fire, that I may be rich. As many as You love, You rebuke and chasten. Therefore I will be zealous and repent.

Blessed am I when I hunger and thirst for righteousness, for I shall be filled. The poor and needy seek water, but there is none, their tongues fail for thirst. You, Lord God, will hear them; You, the God of Israel, will not forsake them. You are the Lord my God, I open my mouth wide, You will fill it.

Why do I spend money for what is not bread, and my wages for what does not satisfy? May I listen carefully to Jesus, and eat what is good, and let my soul delight itself in abundance. You are the bread of life. I come to You and shall never hunger, and I believe in You and shall never thirst.

Thank You, Father God, for providing the food of Your truth and
Your presence, food that truly nourishes and sustains.

LUKE 1:53; REVELATION 3:17–19; MATTHEW 5:6;
ISAIAH 41:17; PSALM 81:10; ISAIAH 55:2; JOHN 6:35

I will give them one heart and one way,
that they may fear Me forever,
for the good of them and their children after them.

Lord, You will give me a new heart and put a new spirit within me. Good and upright are You, Lord; therefore You teach sinners in the way. The humble You guide in justice, and the humble You teach Your way. All Your paths, Lord God, are mercy and truth, to me if I keep Your covenant and Your testimonies.

Jesus prayed that believers may be one, as You, Father, are in Him, and He in You; that we also may be one in You and Jesus, that the world may believe that You sent Him.

I will walk worthy of the calling with which I was called, with all lowliness and gentleness, endeavoring to keep the unity of the Spirit in the bond of peace. There is one body and one Spirit, just as I was called in one hope of your calling; one Lord, one faith, one baptism; one God and Father of all, who is above all, and through all, and in us all.

Lord God, may Your unity, love,
and joy characterize Your people. May Your Spirit in us
make us Your light in this world.

JEREMIAH 32:39; EZEKIEL 36:26; PSALM 25:8–10;
JOHN 17:21; EPHESIANS 4:1–6

Do not be conformed to this world,
but be transformed by the renewing of your mind.

Lord, I endeavor not to follow a crowd to do evil. I know that friendship with the world is enmity with You, Lord God. If I want to be a friend of the world I make myself Your enemy.

What fellowship has righteousness with lawlessness? What communion has light with darkness? What accord has Christ with Belial? What part have I, a believer, with an unbeliever? What agreement has the temple of God with idols? I will not love the world or the things in the world. If I love the world, Your love, Father God, is not in me. The world is passing away, and the lust of it; but if I do Your I will abide forever.

I once walked according to the course of this world, according to the prince of the power of the air, the spirit who now works in the sons of disobedience. I have not learned greedy uncleanness in Christ . . . for the truth is in Jesus.

The world is tangible and its temptations, powerful.
Lord, keep my eyes fixed on You and my heart rooted in Your
truth so I love and serve You, not the world.

ROMANS 12:2; EXODUS 23:2; JAMES 4:4;
2 CORINTHIANS 6:14–16; 1 JOHN 2:15, 17;
EPHESIANS 2:2; EPHESIANS 4:20–21

I have seen his ways, and will heal him.

Lord, You are the One who heals me.

You, Lord God, have searched me and known me. You know my sitting down and my rising up; You understand my thought afar off. You comprehend my path and my lying down, and are acquainted with all my ways. You have set my iniquities before You, my secret sins in the light of Your countenance. All things are naked and open to the eyes of Him to whom I must give account.

Lord God, You say, "Come now, and let us reason together." Though my sins are like scarlet, they shall be as white as snow; though they are red like crimson, they shall be as wool. God, You are gracious to me, and say, "Deliver him from going down to the Pit; I have found a ransom." Jesus was wounded for my transgressions, He was bruised for my iniquities; the chastisement for my peace was upon Him, and by His stripes I am healed. Lord God, You sent Jesus to heal the brokenhearted. My faith has made me well. I go in peace, healed of my affliction.

You provided healing for my sin on the cross,
and I humbly thank You.

———————

ISAIAH 57:18; EXODUS 15:26; PSALM 139:1–3; PSALM 90:8;
HEBREWS 4:13; ISAIAH 1:18; JOB 33:24; ISAIAH 53:5;
ISAIAH 61:1; MARK 5:34

If anyone thirsts, let him come to Me and drink.

My soul longs, and, even faints for Your courts, O Lord; my heart and my flesh cry out for You, living God. You are my God; early will I seek You; my soul thirsts for You; my flesh longs for You in a dry and thirsty land where there is no water. So I have looked for You in the sanctuary, to see Your power and Your glory.

You invite everyone who thirsts to come to the waters; and those who have no money, to come, buy and eat, to come, buy wine and milk without money and without price. The Spirit and the bride say, "Come!" Let me who hears say, "Come!" And he who thirsts come. If I desire, I may take the water of life freely. I drink of the water You give and will never thirst. The water You give will become in me a fountain of water springing up into everlasting life. As Your beloved friend I will eat and drink deeply.

Lord Jesus, Your precious blood is drink for my sin-sick soul.
Nothing else can satisfy.

JOHN 7:37; PSALM 84:2; PSALM 63:1–2;
ISAIAH 55:1; REVELATION 22:17; JOHN 4:14;
SONG OF SOLOMON 5:1; JOHN 6:55

I, even I, am He who comforts you.

I praise You, God and Father of my Lord Jesus Christ, Father of mercies and God of all comfort, who comforts me in all my tribulation, that I may be able to comfort those who are in any trouble, with the comfort with which I myself am comforted by You, Lord God. As a father pities his children, so You, Lord, pity those of us who fear You. For You know my frame; You remember that I am dust. As one whom his mother comforts, so You will comfort me. So I cast all my care upon You, for You care for me.

You, O Lord, are a God full of compassion, and gracious, longsuffering and abundant in mercy and truth.

Lord, You give me another Helper, the Spirit of truth... who helps in my weaknesses.

You, Lord God, will wipe away every tear from my eyes; there shall be no more death, nor sorrow, nor crying. There shall be no more pain, for the former things have passed away.

I thank You, my compassionate and gracious,
patient and kind God, for comfort now and for the
promise of comfort for eternity.

ISAIAH 51:12; 2 CORINTHIANS 1:3–4; PSALM 103:13–14;
ISAIAH 66:13; 1 PETER 5:7; PSALM 86:15;
JOHN 14:16–17; ROMANS 8:26; REVELATION 21:4

*Sin shall not have dominion over you,
for you are not under law but under grace.*

Father, what then? Shall I sin because I am not under law but under grace? Certainly not! I have become dead to the law through the body of Christ, that I may be married to another—to Jesus who was raised from the dead, that I should bear fruit to God. I am not without Your law, Father, for, I am under Christ's law. The sting of death is sin, and the strength of sin is the law. But I thank You, Lord God, who gives me the victory through my Lord Jesus Christ.

The law of the Spirit of life in Christ Jesus has made me free from the law of sin and death. Whoever commits sin is a slave of sin. If the Son makes me free, I shall be free indeed.

Therefore, I will stand fast in the liberty by which Christ has made me free, and not be entangled again with a yoke of bondage to sin.

*May I never cheapen Your costly grace, Lord,
by sinning intentionally knowing that You will forgive me.
Instead, enable me to avoid sin and glorify You.*

ROMANS 6:14; ROMANS 6:15; ROMANS 7:4;
1 CORINTHIANS 9:21; 1 CORINTHIANS 15:56–57;
ROMANS 8:2; JOHN 8:34, 36; GALATIANS 5:1

The Lord weighs the hearts.

You, Lord, know the way of the righteous, but the way of the ungodly shall perish. You will show who is Yours and who is holy. You, Father God, who see in secret will reward me openly.

Search me, O God, and know my heart; try me, and know my anxieties; and see if there is any wicked way in me, and lead me in the way everlasting. There is no fear in love; but perfect love casts out fear.

Lord, all my desire is before You; and my sighing is not hidden from You. When my spirit was overwhelmed within me, then You knew my path. Lord God, You who search my heart know what the mind of the Spirit is, because He makes intercession for me according to Your will.

Your solid foundation stands, having this seal: "The Lord knows those who are His," and, "Let everyone who names the name of Christ depart from iniquity."

Thank You that You know those of us who are Yours.
I'm glad that You know my heart yet love me anyway.
May I depart from iniquity and
lead a life that honors and glorifies You.

PROVERBS 21:2; PSALM 1:6; NUMBERS 16:5; MATTHEW 6:4;
PSALM 139:23–24; 1 JOHN 4:18; PSALM 38:9;
PSALM 142:3; ROMANS 8:27; 2 TIMOTHY 2:19

A bruised reed He will not break.

Lord God, the sacrifices You welcome are a broken spirit, a broken and a contrite heart—these, O God, You will not despise. You heal my broken heart and bind up my wounds. You are the High and Lofty One who inhabits eternity, whose name is Holy. You dwell in the high and holy place and with those who have a contrite and humble spirit, to revive the spirit of the humble, and to revive the heart of the contrite ones. You will not contend forever, nor will You always be angry; for my spirit would fail before You, as would my soul which You have made.

You will seek what was lost and bring back what was driven away, bind up the broken and strengthen what was sick. Therefore strengthen my hands which hang down, and my feeble knees, and make straight paths for my feet, so that what is lame may not be dislocated, but rather be healed. You, my God, will come and save me.

Almighty God, I praise You for seeking sinners, strengthening those who are bruised reeds, and saving those who offer the sacrifice of a contrite heart.

MATTHEW 12:20; PSALM 51:17;
PSALM 147:3; ISAIAH 57:15–16; EZEKIEL 34:16;
HEBREWS 12:12–13; ISAIAH 35:4

*Open my eyes, that I may see
wondrous things from Your law.*

Father God, You opened my understanding, that I might comprehend Your Scriptures. It has been given to me to know the mysteries of the kingdom of heaven, but to others it has not been given. I thank You, Father, Lord of heaven and earth, because You have hidden these things from the wise and prudent and have revealed them to babes. Father, for it seemed good in Your sight. I have not received the spirit of the world, but Your Spirit Lord God, that I might know the things that You have freely given to us. How precious also are Your thoughts to me, O God! How great is the sum of them! If I should count them, they would be more in number than the sand. Oh, the depth of the riches both of the wisdom and knowledge of You, Lord God! How unsearchable are Your judgments and Your ways past finding out! For who has known Your mind, O Lord? Or who has become Your counselor? For of You and through You and to You are all things, to whom be glory forever. Amen.

*Thank You, Lord, for revealing
the mysteries of Your salvation plan, Your love,
and Your life-changing truths.*

PSALM 119:18; LUKE 24:45; MATTHEW 13:11;
MATTHEW 11:25–26; 1 CORINTHIANS 2:12; PSALM 139:17–18;
ROMANS 11:33–34, 36

The God of all grace.

Yου will proclaim Your name before me, Lord God, You will be gracious to whom You will be gracious. You are gracious to me, and say, "Deliver him from going down to the Pit; I have found a ransom." I have been justified freely by Your grace through the redemption that is in Christ Jesus, whom You set forth as a propitiation by His blood, through faith, to demonstrate Your righteousness, because in Your forbearance You had passed over sins that were previously committed. Grace and truth came through Jesus Christ.

By grace I have been saved through faith, and that not of myself; it is Your gift to me, O God. I receive grace, mercy, and peace from You, Father God, and from Jesus Christ my Lord. Grace was given to me according to the measure of Christ's gift. As I have received a gift, I minister to others, as a good steward of Your manifold grace, Lord God. You give more grace.

May I grow in the grace and knowledge of my Lord and Savior Jesus Christ. To You be the glory both now and forever.

Thank You, Lord God, for Your indescribable grace.

---

1 PETER 5:10; EXODUS 33:19; JOB 33:24; ROMANS 3:24–25; JOHN 1:17; EPHESIANS 2:8; 1 TIMOTHY 1:2; EPHESIANS 4:7; 1 PETER 4:10; JAMES 4:6; 2 PETER 3:18

Happy is the man who finds wisdom,
and the man who gains understanding.

Whoever finds wisdom, Lord God, finds life, and obtains Your favor.

Yet, Lord, You caution me, "Let not the wise man glory in his wisdom, let not the mighty man glory in his might, but let him who glories glory in this, that he understands and knows Me, that I am the Lord." The fear of You, Lord God, is the beginning of wisdom.

What things were gain to me, these I have counted loss for Christ. Yet indeed I also count all things loss for the excellence of the knowledge of Christ Jesus my Lord, for whom I have suffered the loss of all things, and count them as rubbish, that I may gain Christ. In Jesus are hidden all the treasures of wisdom and knowledge. Your wisdom says: Counsel is mine, and sound wisdom; I am understanding, I have strength.

Christ Jesus became for us wisdom and righteousness and sanctification and redemption.

He who wins souls is wise.

Lord, thank You for setting me on the lifelong path
of growing in wisdom. Thank You for calling me to know Jesus
as both my Savior and the Source of all wisdom.

PROVERBS 3:13; PROVERBS 8:35; JEREMIAH 9:23–24;
PROVERBS 9:10; PHILIPPIANS 3:7–8; COLOSSIANS 2:3;
PROVERBS 8:14; 1 CORINTHIANS 1:30; PROVERBS 11:30

*We know that all things work together for good
to those who love God.*

Father God, surely the wrath of man shall praise You, with the remainder of wrath You shall gird Yourself. People mean evil against me; but You, Lord God, mean it for good.

All things are mine: whether the world or life or death, or things present or things to come—all are mine. And I am Christ's, and Christ is Yours, Lord God. All things are for my sake, that grace, having spread through the many, may cause thanksgiving to abound to Your glory. Therefore I do not lose heart. Even though my outward man is perishing, yet the inward man is being renewed day by day. For my light affliction, which is but for a moment, is working for me a far more exceeding and eternal weight of glory.

So I count it all joy when I fall into various trials, knowing that the testing of my faith produces patience. I let patience have its perfect work, that I may be perfect and complete, lacking nothing.

*Thank You for the peace, hope, security, confidence,
and patience that come with my knowing that You, heavenly Father,
are absolutely sovereign!*

ROMANS 8:28; PSALM 76:10; GENESIS 50:20;
1 CORINTHIANS 3:21–23; 2 CORINTHIANS 4:15–17; JAMES 1:2–4

May my meditation be sweet to Him;
I will be glad in the Lord.

Like an apple tree among the trees of the woods, so is my Beloved among the sons. In His shade is great delight, and His fruit is sweet. For who in the heavens can be compared to You, Lord God? Who among the sons of the mighty can be likened to You?

The beloved of the Song is white and ruddy, chief among ten thousand. My Jesus is one pearl of great price . . . the ruler over the kings of the earth.

His head is like the finest gold; his locks are wavy, and black as a raven. Jesus is head over all things . . . the head of the body, the church.

His cheeks are like a bed of spices, banks of scented herbs. Jesus could not be hidden.

His lips are lilies, dripping liquid myrrh. No man ever spoke like Jesus!

His countenance is like Lebanon, excellent as the cedars. Lord God, make Your face shine upon me, Your servant. Lift up the light of Your countenance upon me.

Lord, receive my praises as I receive Your blessings!

PSALM 104:34; SONG OF SOLOMON 2:3; PSALM 89:6;
SONG OF SOLOMON 5:10; MATTHEW 13:46; REVELATION 1:5;
SONG OF SOLOMON 5:11; EPHESIANS 1:22; COLOSSIANS 1:18;
SONG OF SOLOMON 5:13; MARK 7:24; SONG OF SOLOMON 5:13;
JOHN 7:46; SONG OF SOLOMON 5:15; PSALM 31:16; PSALM 4:6

Our God did not forsake us.

Father, help me concerning the fiery trial which is to try me, not to think as though some strange thing were happening. Lord God, if I endure chastening, You deal with me as with a son; for what son is there whom a father does not chasten? But if I am without chastening, of which all have become partakers, then I am illegitimate and not a son.

You, my God, are testing me to know whether I love You with all my heart and with all my soul.

You, Lord God, will not forsake Your people, for Your great name's sake, because it has pleased You to make me Yours. Can a woman forget her nursing child, and not have compassion on the son of her womb? Surely they may forget, yet You will not forget me. I am happy to have the God of Jacob for my help; my hope is in You, the Lord my God.

Shall You not avenge me Your own elect who cries out day and night to You, though You bear long with me? You will avenge me speedily.

You love me with a perfect Father's love that
disciplines and never forsakes.
Thank You for choosing to love me.

EZRA 9:9; 1 PETER 4:12; HEBREWS 12:7–8;
DEUTERONOMY 13:3; 1 SAMUEL 12:22; ISAIAH 49:15;
PSALM 146:5; LUKE 18:7–8

It is good for me to draw near to God.

Lord God, I have loved the habitation of Your house, and the place where Your glory dwells. A day in Your courts is better than a thousand. I would rather be a doorkeeper in Your house, my God, than dwell in the tents of wickedness. Blessed am I whom You choose, and cause to approach You, that I may dwell in Your courts. I shall be satisfied with the goodness of Your house, of Your holy temple.

You, Lord, are good to those who wait for You, to the soul who seeks You. You, Lord, will wait, that You may be gracious to me; and therefore You will be exalted, that You may have mercy on me. For You are a God of justice; blessed are all who wait for You.

Therefore, having boldness to enter the Holiest by the blood of Jesus, by a new and living way which He consecrated for me, I draw near with a true heart in full assurance of faith, having my heart sprinkled from an evil conscience.

It is good to be near You, God.
Thank You for graciously providing a way that I may
dwell in Your courts now and forever.

PSALM 73:28; PSALM 26:8; PSALM 84:10; PSALM 65:4;
LAMENTATIONS 3:25; ISAIAH 30:18; HEBREWS 10:19–20, 22

Let patience have its perfect work,
that you may be perfect and complete, lacking nothing.

Now for a little while, if need be, I have been grieved by various trials, that the genuineness of my faith, being much more precious than gold that perishes, though it is tested by fire, may be found to praise, honor, and glory at the revelation of Jesus Christ. I glory in tribulations, knowing that tribulation produces perseverance; and perseverance, character; and character, hope.

It is good that I should hope and wait quietly for Your salvation, Lord God. I have a better and an enduring possession for myself in heaven. So I do not cast away my confidence, which has great reward. For I have need of endurance, so that after I have done Your will, Lord God, I may receive the promise. My Lord Jesus Christ Himself, and You, my God and Father, who has loved me and given me everlasting consolation and good hope by grace, comfort my heart.

Thank You for reminding me that You,
Almighty God, are in charge, that trials are not pointless,
and that eternal rewards await.

JAMES 1:4; I PETER 1:6–7; ROMANS 5:3–4;
LAMENTATIONS 3:26; HEBREWS 10:34–36;
2 THESSALONIANS 2:16–17

A God of truth and without injustice;
righteous and upright is He.

Lord God, You are the One who judges righteously. I must appear before the judgment seat of Christ, that I may receive the things done in the body, according to what I have done, whether good or bad. I shall give account of myself to You, O God. The soul who sins shall die.

You, the Lord of hosts, say, "Awake, O sword, against My Shepherd, against the Man who is My Companion. Strike the Shepherd." So You, Lord God, have laid on Jesus, the Good Shepherd, my iniquity. Mercy and truth have met together; righteousness and peace have kissed. Mercy triumphs over judgment. The wages of sin is death, but Your gift, Lord God, is eternal life in Christ Jesus my Lord.

You are a just God and a Savior; there is none besides You . . . who are both just and the justifier of the person like me who has faith in Jesus. I am justified freely by Your grace through the redemption that is in Christ Jesus.

All praise to You, Lord God, the Just and the Justifier,
for Your eternal plan of salvation.

DEUTERONOMY 32:4; 1 PETER 2:23; 2 CORINTHIANS 5:10;
ROMANS 14:12; EZEKIEL 18:4; ZECHARIAH 13:7; ISAIAH 53:6;
PSALM 85:10; JAMES 2:13; ROMANS 6:23; ISAIAH 45:21;
ROMANS 3:26; ROMANS 3:24

*Humble yourselves under the mighty hand of God,
that He may exalt you in due time.*

Lord, everyone proud in heart is an abomination to You. Though they join forces, none will go unpunished. Lord, You are my Father; I am the clay, and You my potter; and I am the work of Your hand. Do not be furious, O Lord, nor remember iniquity forever; indeed, please look—I am one of Your people! You have chastised me, and I was chastised, like an untrained bull; restore me, and I will return, for You are the Lord my God. Surely, after my turning, I repented; and after I was instructed, I struck myself on the thigh; I was ashamed, yes, even humiliated, because I bore the reproach of my youth. It is good for me to bear the yoke in my youth.

Affliction does not come from the dust, nor does trouble spring from the ground; yet I, a human being, am born to trouble, as the sparks fly upward.

*That final truth is humbling, Lord: I am born to trouble.
Thank You that You remember I am dust and forgive my sins.
Keep me mindful of my sins and therefore humble, I pray.*

1 PETER 5:6; PROVERBS 16:5; ISAIAH 64:8–9;
JEREMIAH 31:18–19; LAMENTATIONS 3:27; JOB 5:6–7

They shall put My name on the children of Israel,
and I will bless them.

O Lord my God, masters besides You have had dominion over me; but by You only I make mention of Your name. I have become like those of old, over whom You never ruled, those who were never called by Your name.

But now all peoples of the earth shall see that I am called by Your name, Lord God, and they shall be afraid of me. You, Lord, will not forsake me, for Your great name's sake, because it has pleased You to make me Yours.

O Lord, hear! O Lord, forgive! O Lord, listen and act! Do not delay for Your own sake, my God, for Your city and Your people are called by Your name. Help me, O God of my salvation, for the glory of Your name; and deliver me, and provide atonement for my sins, for Your name's sake! Why should the nations say, "Where is their God?" Your name, Lord God, is a strong tower; we who are righteous in Christ run to it and are safe.

Thank You, Almighty God, that You won't forsake me,
You forgive my sins, and You act on behalf of Your children.

NUMBERS 6:27; ISAIAH 26:13; ISAIAH 63:19;
DEUTERONOMY 28:10; 1 SAMUEL 12:22; DANIEL 9:19;
PSALM 79:9–10; PROVERBS 18:10

By this we know love,
because He laid down His life for us.

Father, the love of Christ passes knowledge. Greater love has no one than this, than to lay down one's life for his friends. I know the grace of my Lord Jesus Christ, that though He was rich, yet for my sake He became poor, that I through His poverty might become rich. If You, Lord God, so loved me, I ought to love others. Enable me to be kind to others, tenderhearted, forgiving others, even as You in Christ forgave me. Help me bear with others, and forgive others, if anyone has a complaint against another; even as Christ forgave me. For even the Son of Man did not come to be served, but to serve, and to give His life a ransom for many. Christ suffered for me, leaving me an example, that I should follow His steps.

I ought to wash another's feet. For Jesus has given me an example, that I should do as He has done. I also ought to lay down my life for the brethren.

The path is clear, but walking it isn't easy, Lord.
Help me love and serve as Jesus did.

1 JOHN 3:16; EPHESIANS 3:19; JOHN 15:13;
2 CORINTHIANS 8:9; 1 JOHN 4:11; EPHESIANS 4:32;
COLOSSIANS 3:13; MARK 10:45;
1 PETER 2:21; JOHN 13:14–15; 1 JOHN 3:16

He knows the way that I take; when He has tested me,
I shall come forth as gold.

You, Lord God, know my frame. You do not afflict willingly, nor grieve the children of men.

Your solid foundation stands, having this seal: "The Lord knows those who are His," and, "Let everyone who names the name of Christ depart from iniquity." But in a great house there are not only vessels of gold and silver, but also of wood and clay, some for honor and some for dishonor. Therefore if I cleanse myself from the latter, I will be a vessel for honor, sanctified and useful for You, my Master, prepared for every good work.

You will sit as a refiner and a purifier of silver; and as You will purify the sons of Levi, so purge me as gold and silver, that I may offer to You an offering in righteousness. You will refine me as silver is refined. I will call on Your name, and You will answer me. You will say, "This is one of My people"; and I will say, "The Lord is my God."

Lord, refine me and purge me of the dross
that I may be a vessel of honor for Your kingdom use.

JOB 23:10; PSALM 103:14; LAMENTATIONS 3:33;
2 TIMOTHY 2:19–21; MALACHI 3:3; ZECHARIAH 13:9

October

Call upon Me

in the day of trouble;

I will deliver you,

and you shall glorify Me.

The fruit of the Spirit is . . . self-control.

Lord Jesus, everyone who competes for the prize is temperate in all things. Now they do it to obtain a perishable crown, but I for an imperishable crown. Therefore I run thus: not with uncertainty. Thus I fight: not as one who beats the air. But I discipline my body and bring it into subjection, lest, when I have preached to others, I myself should become disqualified.

I will not be drunk with wine, in which is dissipation; but will be filled with the Spirit.

If I desire to come after You, Lord Jesus, I must deny myself, and take up my cross, and follow You.

Let me not sleep, as others do, but let me watch and be sober. For those who sleep, sleep at night, and those who get drunk are drunk at night. But let me who am of the day be sober. Denying ungodliness and worldly lusts, I should live soberly, righteously, and godly in the present age, looking for the blessed hope and Your glorious appearing, my great God and Savior Jesus Christ.

Keep me faithful to my training regimen, Jesus,
so I may be ready for Your return and,
in the meantime, honor You with my life.

GALATIANS 5:22–23; 1 CORINTHIANS 9:25–27; EPHESIANS 5:18;
MATTHEW 16:24; 1 THESSALONIANS 5:6–8; TITUS 2:12–13

The goat shall bear on itself all their iniquities
to an uninhabited land;
and he shall release the goat in the wilderness.

Righteous God, as far as the east is from the west, so far have You, Lord God, removed my transgressions from me. "In those days and in that time," You say, "the iniquity of Israel shall be sought, but there shall be none; and the sins of Judah, but they shall not be found; for I will pardon those whom I preserve." You will cast all my sins into the depths of the sea. Who is a God like You, pardoning iniquity?

All we like sheep have gone astray; I, too, have turned to my own way; and You, Lord God, have laid on Jesus the iniquity of us all. He shall bear my iniquities. Therefore You will divide Him a portion with the great, and He shall divide the spoil with the strong, because He poured out His soul unto death, and He was numbered with the transgressors, and He bore the sin of many, and made intercession for us transgressors. The Lamb of God takes away the sin of the world!

Thank You, Jesus, for dying for my sin—
and thank You, Father God,
for sacrificing Your Son for that specific purpose.

LEVITICUS 16:22; PSALM 103:12; JEREMIAH 50:20;
MICAH 7:19, 18; ISAIAH 53:6; ISAIAH 53:11–12; JOHN 1:29

To Him who loved us and
washed us from our sins in His own blood.

Father, many waters cannot quench love, nor can the floods drown it. Love is as strong as death. Greater love has no one than this, than to lay down one's life for his friends.

Jesus Himself bore my sins in His own body on the tree, that I, having died to sins, might live for righteousness—by whose stripes I was healed. In Jesus I have redemption through His blood, the forgiveness of sins, according to the riches of His grace.

I was washed, I was sanctified, I was justified in the name of the Lord Jesus and by Your Spirit, Lord God. I am part of a chosen generation, a royal priesthood, a holy nation, Your own special people, that I may proclaim Your praises, for You called me out of darkness into Your marvelous light. So by the mercies of God, I will present my body a living sacrifice, holy, acceptable to God, which is my reasonable service.

May every minute of my life
be an offering of thanks to You, Lord God!
May You be honored and glorified in all I say and do!

REVELATION 1:5; SONG OF SOLOMON 8:7, 6; JOHN 15:13;
1 PETER 2:24; EPHESIANS 1:7; 1 CORINTHIANS 6:11;
1 PETER 2:9; ROMANS 12:1

*Moses did not know that the skin of his face shone
while he talked with Him.*

Not unto us, Lord God, not unto us, but to Your name give glory. Lord, when did I see You hungry and feed You, or thirsty and give You drink? In lowliness of mind may I esteem others better than myself. May I be clothed with humility.

Jesus was transfigured before Peter, James, and John. His face shone like the sun, and His clothes became as white as the light. All who sat in the council, looking steadfastly at Stephen, saw his face as the face of an angel. The glory which You, Lord God, gave Jesus He has given me. With unveiled face, beholding as in a mirror Your glory, Lord God, I am being transformed into the same image from glory to glory, by Your Spirit.

I am the light of the world. A city that is set on a hill cannot be hidden. Nor do people light a lamp and put it under a basket, but on a lamp stand, and it gives light to all who are in the house.

*As I serve You, Lord God,
may my face reflect Your glory.*

EXODUS 34:29; PSALM 115:1; MATTHEW 25:37;
PHILIPPIANS 2:3; 1 PETER 5:5; MATTHEW 17:2; ACTS 6:15;
JOHN 17:22; 2 CORINTHIANS 3:18; MATTHEW 5:14–15

Call upon Me in the day of trouble;
I will deliver you, and you shall glorify Me.

Lord, my soul is cast down and it is disquieted within me. I will hope in You, Lord God; for I shall yet praise You, the help of my countenance and my God. Lord, You have heard the desire of the humble; You will prepare my heart; You will cause Your ear to hear. For You, Lord, are good, and ready to forgive, and abundant in mercy to me when I call upon You.

Jacob said to his household, "Let us arise and go up to Bethel; and I will make an altar there to God, who answered me in the day of my distress and has been with me in the way which I have gone." Bless the Lord, O my soul, and forget not all His benefits.

I love You, Lord, because You have heard my voice and my supplications. Because You have inclined Your ear to me, I will call upon You as long as I live. The pains like death surrounded me, and the pangs as of Sheol laid hold of me; I found trouble and sorrow. Then I called upon Your name, Lord God.

Keep me mindful of Your faithfulness
when my soul is cast down.

PSALM 50:15; PSALM 42:11; PSALM 10:17; PSALM 86:5;
GENESIS 35:2–3; PSALM 103:2; PSALM 116:1–4

The Lord God Omnipotent reigns!

Lord God, I know that You can do everything. The things which are impossible with men are possible with You. You do according to Your will in the army of heaven and among the inhabitants of the earth. No one can restrain Your hand or say to You, "What have You done?" There is no one who can deliver out of Your hand; You work, and who will reverse it? Abba, Father, all things are possible for You.

Jesus asked the blind men, "Do you believe that I am able to do this?" They said, "Yes, Lord." Then He touched their eyes, saying, "According to your faith let it be to you." "Lord, if You are willing, You can make me clean." Then Jesus put out His hand and touched the leper, saying, "I am willing; be cleansed." You are a mighty God. All authority has been given to Jesus in heaven and on earth.

Some trust in chariots, and some in horses; but I will remember Your name, O Lord my God. I will be strong and courageous; I will not be afraid nor dismayed,

I am blessed to be Your child,
omnipotent, omniscient, all-loving God!

REVELATION 19:6; JOB 42:2; LUKE 18:27; DANIEL 4:35;
ISAIAH 43:13; MARK 14:36; MATTHEW 9:28–29;
MATTHEW 8:2–3; ISAIAH 9:6; MATTHEW 28:18;
PSALM 20:7; 2 CHRONICLES 32:7

The humble He teaches His way.

Jesus taught, "Blessed are the meek."

King Solomon saw that the race is not to the swift, nor the battle to the strong, nor bread to the wise, nor riches to men of understanding, nor favor to men of skill. A man's heart plans his way, but You, Lord God, direct his steps.

Unto You I lift up my eyes, O You who dwell in the heavens. Behold, as the eyes of servants look to the hand of their masters, as the eyes of a maid to the hand of her mistress, so my eyes look to You, Lord God. Cause me to know the way in which I should walk, for I lift up my soul to You.

O my God, You will judge my enemies. For I have no power against this great multitude coming against me; nor do I know what to do, but my eyes are upon You.

If I lack wisdom, I will ask You, God, who gives to all liberally and without reproach, and it will be given to me.

When the Spirit of truth has come, He will guide me into all truth.

May I be teachable, Lord—willing to have You guide me,
grant me wisdom, and direct my steps.

PSALM 25:9; MATTHEW 5:5; ECCLESIASTES 9:11;
PROVERBS 16:9; PSALM 123:1–2; PSALM 143:8;
2 CHRONICLES 20:12; JAMES 1:5; JOHN 16:13

I will not fear. What can man do to me?

Mighty Lord, who shall separate me from the love of Christ? Shall tribulation, distress, persecution, famine, nakedness, peril, or sword? Yet in all these things I am more than a conqueror through Jesus who loved me.

I will not be afraid of those who kill the body, and after that have no more that they can do. But Jesus has shown me whom I should fear: Fear Him who, after He has killed, has power to cast into hell; yes, Jesus says fear Him!

I am blessed when I am persecuted for righteousness' sake, for mine is the kingdom of heaven. I am blessed when they revile and persecute me, and say all kinds of evil against me falsely for Jesus' sake. I will rejoice and be exceedingly glad, for great is my reward in heaven. None of these things move me; nor do I count my life dear to myself, so that I may finish my race with joy. I will speak of Your testimonies, Lord God, before kings, and will not be ashamed.

May I fear You and You alone, Lord,
and therefore be bold in my witness to Your truth,
Your mercy, and Your grace.

HEBREWS 13:6; ROMANS 8:35, 37; LUKE 12:4–5;
MATTHEW 5:10–12; ACTS 20:24; PSALM 119:46

You are God, ready to pardon,
gracious and merciful.

Lord God, You are not slack concerning Your promise, as some count slackness, but are longsuffering toward me, not willing that I should perish but that I should come to repentance. Your longsuffering is salvation.

Paul said that he obtained mercy, so that in him first Jesus Christ might show all longsuffering, as a pattern to those who are going to believe on Him for everlasting life. Whatever things were written before were written for my learning, that I through the patience and comfort of the Scriptures might have hope.

Lord God, do I despise the riches of Your goodness, forbearance, and longsuffering, not knowing that Your goodness leads me to repentance? I rend my heart, and not my garments; I return to You, Lord God, for You are gracious and merciful, slow to anger, and of great kindness; and You relent from doing harm.

Loving people with Your love, Lord,
means extending the kind of patience, kindness, forgiveness,
and grace that You have extended to me.
Enable me to love like that.

NEHEMIAH 9:17; 2 PETER 3:9; 2 PETER 3:15; I TIMOTHY 1:16;
ROMANS 15:4; ROMANS 2:4; JOEL 2:13

The whole family in heaven and earth.

You Lord, are the one God and Father of all, who is above all, and through all, and in us all. I am Your Son through faith in Christ Jesus. In the fullness of the times You might gather in one all things in Christ, both which are in heaven and on earth—in Him.

Jesus is not ashamed to call us brethren. He said, "Here are My mother and My brothers! For whoever does the will of My Father in heaven is My brother and sister and mother." He said, "Go to My brethren and say to them, 'I am ascending to My Father and your Father.'"

Your revelation reveals that under the altar are the souls of those who had been slain for Your word and for the testimony which they held. A white robe was given to each and it was said that they should rest a little while longer, until both the number of their fellow servants and their brethren, who would be killed as they were, was completed. Oh, Lord, may they not be made perfect apart from us.

Ascended Lord, give me grace to live according to Your Word and courage to endure to the end.

EPHESIANS 3:15; EPHESIANS 4:6; GALATIANS 3:26;
EPHESIANS 1:10; HEBREWS 2:11; MATTHEW 12:49–50;
JOHN 20:17; REVELATION 6:9, 11; HEBREWS 11:40

Be not far from Me, for trouble is near.

How long, O Lord? Will You forget me forever . . . and hide Your face from me? How long shall I take counsel in my soul, having sorrow in my heart daily? Do not hide Your face from me; do not turn Your servant away in anger; You have been my help; do not leave me nor forsake me, O God of my salvation.

I shall call upon You, and You will answer me; You will be with me in trouble; You will deliver me and honor me. You, Lord God, are near to me when I call upon You in truth. You will fulfill the desire of those who fear You; You also will hear my cry and save me.

You will not leave me an orphan; You will come to me. Actually You are with me always, even to the end of the age.

You are my refuge and strength, a very present help in trouble. My soul silently waits for You; from You comes my salvation. My soul waits silently for You alone, for my expectation is from You.

Thank You, Lord, that You are never far from me and that You deliver me from my troubles.

PSALM 22:11; PSALM 13:1–2; PSALM 27:9; PSALM 91:15;
PSALM 145:18–19; JOHN 14:18; MATTHEW 28:20;
PSALM 46:1; PSALM 62:1, 5

God was in Christ reconciling the world to Himself,
not imputing their trespasses to them.

I t pleased You, Father God, that in Jesus all the fullness
should dwell, and by Him to reconcile all things to Yourself.
Mercy and truth have met together; righteousness and peace
have kissed.

Lord God, You know the thoughts that You think toward
me, thoughts of peace and not of evil. And You say, Lord, that
though my sins are like scarlet, they shall be as white as snow;
though they are red like crimson, they shall be as wool.

Who is a God like You, pardoning iniquity?

Now I acquaint myself with You, and I am at peace. I work
out my own salvation with fear and trembling; for it is You who
works in me both to will and to do for Your good pleasure. Lord,
You will establish peace for us, for You have also done all our
works in us.

Lord God, thank You for sending Your Son
to bridge the gap between holy You and sinful me. Thank You
for that work of reconciliation and peacemaking.

---

2 CORINTHIANS 5:19; COLOSSIANS 1:19–20; PSALM 85:10;
JEREMIAH 29:11; ISAIAH 1:18; MICAH 7:18; JOB 22:21;
PHILIPPIANS 2:12–13; ISAIAH 26:12

*From the first day that you set your heart to understand,
and to humble yourself before your God, your words were heard.*

You, Lord God, are the High and Lofty One who inhabits eternity, whose name is Holy. You dwell in the high and holy place, with those who have a contrite and humble spirit, to revive the spirit of the humble, and to revive the heart of the contrite ones. The sacrifices You welcome are a broken spirit, a broken and a contrite heart—these, O God, You will not despise. Though You, Lord God, are on high, yet You regard the lowly; but the proud You know from afar. So I humble myself under Your mighty hand, Lord God, that You may exalt me in due time. You resist the proud, but give grace to the humble. Therefore I submit to You.

You, Lord, are good, and ready to forgive, and abundant in mercy to all who call upon You. Give ear, O Lord, to my prayer; and attend to the voice of my supplications. In the day of my trouble I will call upon You, for You will answer me.

*May my knowing You,
Almighty God, keep me humble before You
and a humble servant to Your people.*

DANIEL 10:12; ISAIAH 57:15; PSALM 51:17; PSALM 138:6;
1 PETER 5:6; JAMES 4:6–7; PSALM 86:5–7

Christ died and rose and lived again,
that He might be Lord of both the dead and the living.

Father God, it pleased You, Lord God, to bruise Your Son Jesus; You have put Him to grief. When You make His soul an offering for sin, He shall see His seed, He shall prolong His days, and Your pleasure shall prosper in His hand. He shall see the travail of His soul, and be satisfied. By His knowledge Your righteous Servant shall justify many of us, for He shall bear our iniquities. Ought not the Christ to have suffered these things and to enter into His glory? We judge thus: that if One died for all, then all died; and He died for all, that I who live should live no longer for myself, but for Him who died for us and rose again.

Let all the house of Israel know assuredly that You, Almighty God, have made Jesus, whom was crucified, both Lord and Christ. He indeed was foreordained before the foundation of the world, but was manifest in these last times for me who through Him believe in God.

Your Son suffered and died
that I might know forgiveness and life eternal!
I praise You, heavenly Father,
for Your amazing plan of salvation!

ROMANS 14:9; ISAIAH 53:10–11; LUKE 24:26;
2 CORINTHIANS 5:14–15; ACTS 2:36; 1 PETER 1:20–21

God is my defense.

You, Lord God, are my rock and my fortress and my deliverer; the God of my strength, in whom I will trust; my shield and the horn of my salvation, my stronghold and my refuge; my Savior. You, Lord, are my strength and my shield; my heart trusted in You, and I am helped; therefore my heart greatly rejoices, and with my song I will praise You.

When the enemy comes in like a flood, Your Spirit will lift up a standard against him. We may boldly say: "The Lord is my helper; I will not fear. What can man do to me?"

You are my light and my salvation; whom shall I fear? You are the strength of my life; of whom shall I be afraid?

As the mountains surround Jerusalem, so You, Lord God, surround Your people from this time forth and forever. Because You have been my help, therefore in the shadow of Your wings I will rejoice.

For Your name's sake, lead me and guide me.

Almighty God, I praise You for Your power and strength—
which You exercise on behalf of Your people.
Thank You for being my help, my protection, and my defense.

PSALM 59:9; 2 SAMUEL 22:2–3; PSALM 28:7;
ISAIAH 59:19; HEBREWS 13:6; PSALM 27:1; PSALM 125:2;
PSALM 63:7; PSALM 31:3

Not lagging in diligence,
fervent in spirit, serving the Lord.

L ord, whatever my hand finds to do, I will do it with my might; for there is no work in the grave. Whatever I do, I do it heartily, as to You, Lord God, and not to men, knowing that from You I will receive the reward of the inheritance; for I serve my Lord Christ. Whatever good I do, I will receive the same from You, Father God.

Jesus said He must work the works of You who sent Him while it is day; the night is coming when no one can work. He once asked, "Did you not know that I must be about My Father's business?" Zeal for Your house, Lord, has eaten Him up.

I seek to be more diligent to make my calling and election sure, for if I do I will never stumble. I aim to show the same diligence to the full assurance of hope until the end, not become sluggish, but imitate those who through faith and patience inherit the promises. May I run in such a way that I may obtain it.

May I serve You, Lord, with all that I am—
and to You be the glory!

ROMANS 12:11; ECCLESIASTES 9:10; COLOSSIANS 3:23–24;
EPHESIANS 6:8; JOHN 9:4; LUKE 2:49; JOHN 2:17;
2 PETER 1:10; HEBREWS 6:11–12; 1 CORINTHIANS 9:24

In Your name they rejoice all day long,
and in Your righteousness they are exalted.

In You, Lord God, I have righteousness and strength. To You men shall come, and all shall be ashamed who are incensed against You. In You all the descendants of Israel shall be justified, and shall glory. Counted righteous, I am glad in You, Lord, and I rejoice; made upright in heart, I shout for joy!

Your righteousness, Lord, apart from the law is revealed, being witnessed by the Law and the Prophets, even Your righteousness, through faith in Jesus Christ, to all and on all who believe. To demonstrate at the present time Your righteousness, that You might be just and the justifier of those who have faith in Jesus.

I rejoice in You, Lord, always. Again I will rejoice! Whom having not seen I love. Though now I do not see You, yet believing, I rejoice with joy inexpressible and full of glory.

Lord God, the salvation You provided me
in Christ is a reason for joy
no matter what the circumstances of life.
May my joy point others to You even as it sustains me.

PSALM 89:16; ISAIAH 45:24–25; PSALM 32:11;
ROMANS 3:21–22, 26; PHILIPPIANS 4:4; 1 PETER 1:8

*One of the soldiers pierced His side with a spear,
and immediately blood and water came out.*

Lord, this is the blood of the covenant which You have made with me. The life of the flesh is in the blood, and You have given it upon the altar to make atonement for my soul. It is not possible that the blood of bulls and goats could take away sins.

So Jesus said, "This is My blood of the new covenant, which is shed for many." With His own blood He entered the Most Holy Place, having obtained eternal redemption. I know peace with You, God, through the blood of His cross.

I was not redeemed with corruptible things, like silver or gold, but with the precious blood of Christ, as of a lamb without blemish and without spot . . . manifest in these last times for me.

When You, Lord, sprinkle clean water on me, and I am clean, You cleanse me from all my idols. So let me draw near with a true heart in full assurance of faith, having my heart sprinkled from an evil conscience.

*Thank You for sending Your Son to die for me
that I might be cleansed by His blood!*

JOHN 19:34; EXODUS 24:8; LEVITICUS 17:11; HEBREWS 10:4;
MARK 14:24; HEBREWS 9:12; COLOSSIANS 1:20;
1 PETER 1:18–20; EZEKIEL 36:25; HEBREWS 10:22

The Lord will be your confidence,
and will keep your foot from being caught.

Lord, surely the wrath of man shall praise You; with the remainder of wrath You shall gird Yourself. The king's heart is in Your hand, Lord, like the rivers of water; You turn it wherever You wish. When my ways please You, You make even my enemies to be at peace with me.

I wait for You, Lord, my soul waits, and in Your word I do hope. My soul waits for You, Lord, more than those who watch for the morning—yes, more than those who watch for the morning. I sought You, Lord, and You heard me, and delivered me from all my fears.

You, eternal God, are my refuge, and underneath are the everlasting arms; You will thrust out the enemy from before me, and will say, "Destroy!" I am blessed for I trust in You, Lord, and my hope is in You.

What then shall I say to these things? If God is for me, who can be against me?

Your Word reveals wonderful reasons
for me to be confident in You. I praise You, Lord God, for being
my Refuge, my Strength, and my Deliverer.

PROVERBS 3:26; PSALM 76:10; PROVERBS 21:1;
PROVERBS 16:7; PSALM 130:5–6; PSALM 34:4;
DEUTERONOMY 33:27; JEREMIAH 17:7; ROMANS 8:31

*I delight in the law of God
according to the inward man.*

Lord, I love Your law! It is my meditation all the day. Your words were found, and I ate them, and Your word was to me the joy and rejoicing of my heart. I sat down in his shade with great delight, and his fruit was sweet to my taste. I have treasured the words of Your mouth more than my necessary food.

I delight to do Your will, O my God, and Your law is within my heart. Jesus said, "My food is to do the will of Him who sent Me, and to finish His work."

Your statutes, Lord God, are right, rejoicing my heart; Your commandment is pure, enlightening my eyes. More to be desired are they than gold, yea, than much fine gold; sweeter also than honey and the honeycomb. Enable me to be a doer of the word, and not a hearer only, deceiving myself. For if I am a hearer of the word only and not a doer, I am like a man observing his natural face in a mirror.

*Lord God, enable me to remember and do
what Your Word commands and know the joy of doing so.*

ROMANS 7:22; PSALM 119:97; JEREMIAH 15:16;
SONG OF SOLOMON 2:3; JOB 23:12; PSALM 40:8; JOHN 4:34;
PSALM 19:8, 10; JAMES 1:22–23

*Of His fullness we have all received,
and grace for grace.*

Father, You said of Jesus, "This is My beloved Son, in whom I am well pleased." And Father, what manner of love You have bestowed on me, that I should be called Your child!

You have appointed Your Son heir of all things. If I am Your child, then I am an heir—Your heir and a joint heir with Christ, if indeed I suffer with Him, that I may also be glorified with Him.

Father, Jesus and You are one. You are in Him, and He in You. You are His Father and my Father, His God and my God. Jesus in us, and You, Lord God, in Him; that we may be made perfect in one.

The church, which is Jesus' body, is the fullness of Him who fills all in all.

Having these promises, let me cleanse myself from all filthiness of the flesh and spirit, perfecting holiness in the fear of You, Lord God.

*You bless me richly, Lord—grace upon grace.
May I live with a clear sense
of Your very real presence with me.*

JOHN 1:16; MATTHEW 17:5; 1 JOHN 3:1; HEBREWS 1:2;
ROMANS 8:17; JOHN 10:30, 38; JOHN 20:17;
JOHN 17:23; EPHESIANS 1:22–23; 2 CORINTHIANS 7:1

O God, my heart is steadfast.

You, Lord God, are my light and my salvation; whom shall I fear? You are the strength of my life; of whom shall I be afraid?

You will keep me in perfect peace; my mind is stayed on You, because I trust in You. I will not be afraid of evil tidings; my heart is steadfast, trusting in You, Lord. My heart is established; I will not be afraid until I see my desire upon my enemies.

Whenever I am afraid, I will trust in You. In the time of trouble You shall hide me in Your pavilion; in the secret place of Your tabernacle You shall hide me; You shall set me high upon a rock. And now my head shall be lifted up above my enemies all around me; therefore I will offer sacrifices of joy in Your tabernacle; I will sing, yes, I will sing praises to You, my Lord.

Now may You, the God of all grace, who called me to Your eternal glory by Christ Jesus, after I have suffered a while, perfect, establish, strengthen, and settle me. To You be the glory and the dominion forever and ever.

My heart is confident, Lord,
because You are completely trustworthy and sure.
I praise You!

PSALM 108:1; PSALM 27:1; ISAIAH 26:3; PSALM 112:7–8;
PSALM 56:3; PSALM 27:5–6; 1 PETER 5:10–11

One's life does not consist
in the abundance of the things he possesses.

Lord, a little that a righteous man has is better than the riches of many wicked. Better is a little combined with fear of You, Lord, than great treasure with trouble. Godliness with contentment is great gain. Having food and clothing, with these I shall be content.

Give me neither poverty nor riches—feed me with the food allotted to me; lest I be full and deny You, Father God, and say, "Who is the Lord?" Or lest I be poor and steal, and profane Your name. Give me this day my daily bread.

I do not worry about my life, what I will eat or what I will drink; nor about my body, what I will put on. Life is more than food and the body more than clothing! When Jesus sent His disciples without money bag, knapsack, and sandals, did they lack anything? No, "Nothing." May my conduct be without covetousness; may I be content with such things as I have. For You Yourself have said, "I will never leave you nor forsake you."

Lord, Your truth runs so counter to the world's teachings.
Keep me aligned with You and content in You.

LUKE 12:15; PSALM 37:16; PROVERBS 15:16; 1 TIMOTHY 6:6, 8;
PROVERBS 30:8–9; MATTHEW 6:11; MATTHEW 6:25;
LUKE 22:35; HEBREWS 13:5

I have been cast out of Your sight;
yet I will look again toward Your holy temple.

Zion said, "The Lord has forsaken me, and my Lord has forgotten me." Can a woman forget her nursing child, and not have compassion on the son of her womb? Surely they may forget, yet You, Lord God, will not forget me.

I have forgotten prosperity. So I said, "My strength and my hope have perished from You, Lord." Awake! Why do You sleep, O Lord? Arise! Do not cast me off forever. Why do you say, O Jacob, and speak, O Israel: "My way is hidden from the Lord, and my just claim is passed over by my God"? With a little wrath, for a moment, You hid Your face but with everlasting kindness You have mercy on me.

When my soul is cast down and my soul is disquieted within me, I will hope in You, Lord God; for I shall yet praise You, the help of my countenance. I am hard-pressed on every side, yet not crushed; I am perplexed, but not in despair; persecuted, but not forsaken; struck down, but not destroyed.

I trust You will redeem me
and bring beauty out of ashes.

JONAH 2:4; ISAIAH 49:14–15; LAMENTATIONS 3:17–18;
PSALM 44:23; ISAIAH 40:27; ISAIAH 54:8;
PSALM 43:5; 2 CORINTHIANS 4:8–9

*Lo, I am with you always, even to
the end of the age.*

Lord Jesus, if two agree on earth concerning anything that we ask, it will be done for us by our Father in heaven. For where two or three are gathered together in Your name, Lord Jesus, You are there in our midst. I have Your commandments, Jesus, and keep them, for I love You. And I, loving You, will be loved by the Father, and You will love me and manifest Yourself to me.

One asked, "Lord, how is it that You will manifest Yourself to us, and not to the world?" And, Jesus, You said that if I love You, I will keep Your word; and Your Father will love me, and You and Your Father will come to me and make Your home with me.

Now to You, Lord Jesus, who are able to keep me from stumbling, and to present me faultless before the presence of Your glory with exceeding joy, to You my Savior, who alone are wise, be glory and majesty, dominion and power, both now and forever. Amen.

*Jesus, by the power of Your Spirit,
enable me to keep Your commands so that You may
know my love for You.*

MATTHEW 28:20; MATTHEW 18:19–20; JOHN 14:21;
JOHN 14:22–23; JUDE 24–25

The Lord reigns.

Lord God, You ask, "Do you not fear Me? Will you not tremble at My presence, who have placed the sand as the bound of the sea, by a perpetual decree, that it cannot pass beyond it? And though its waves toss to and fro, yet they cannot prevail; though they roar, yet they cannot pass over it." Exaltation comes neither from the east nor from the west nor from the south. You, God, are the Judge: You put down one, and exalt another.

You change the times and the seasons; You remove kings and raise up kings; You give wisdom to the wise and knowledge to those who have understanding. I will hear of wars and rumors of wars. I will not be troubled.

If You, Lord God, are for me, who can be against me? Are not two sparrows sold for a copper coin? And not one of them falls to the ground apart from Your will, my Father. The very hairs of my head are all numbered. I do not fear therefore; I am of more value than many sparrows.

*Almighty God who reigns over all history, all creation,
and all of my life, I praise You for Your power—and for Your love
which You let guide Your use of that power.*

PSALM 99:1; JEREMIAH 5:22; PSALM 75:6–7; DANIEL 2:21;
MATTHEW 24:6; ROMANS 8:31; MATTHEW 10:29–31

He Himself took our infirmities
and bore our sicknesses.

Lord, the law said the priest should command the leper to be cleansed to take two living and clean birds, cedar wood, scarlet, and hyssop. And the priest would command that one of the birds be killed in an earthen vessel over running water. He would take the living bird, the cedar wood, the scarlet, and the hyssop, and dip them and the living bird in the blood of the bird that was killed over the running water. And he would sprinkle it seven times on him who was to be cleansed from the leprosy, and pronounce him clean, and then let the living bird loose in the open field.

A man full of leprosy saw Jesus; and he fell on his face and, imploring Him, said, "Lord, if You are willing, You can make me clean." Jesus, moved with compassion, stretched out His hand and touched him, and said to him, "I am willing; be cleansed." As soon as He had spoken, immediately the leprosy left him, and he was cleansed.

Lord God, Jesus cared for my spiritual infirmity
by His once-for-all sacrifice. Thank You that He also heals
my body with compassion and in His perfect timing.

MATTHEW 8:17; LEVITICUS 14:4–7;
LUKE 5:12; MARK 1:41–42

He saw that there was no man,
and wondered that there was no intercessor;
therefore His own arm brought salvation for Him.

Father, with the psalmist I say, sacrifice and offering You did not desire, Lord God . . . burnt offering and sin offering You did not require . . . in the scroll of the Book it is written of me. I delight to do Your will, O my God, and Your law is within my heart. Jesus lay down His life that He may take it again. No one took it from Him, but He lay it down of Himself. He had power to lay it down, and He had power to take it again.

There is no other God besides You, Lord God, a just God and a Savior; there is none besides You. I look to You and am saved! For You are God, and there is no other. There is no other name under heaven given among men by which I must be saved.

I know the grace of my Lord Jesus Christ, that though He was rich, yet for my sake He became poor, that I through His poverty might become rich.

Almighty God, thank You for
being the Author of my salvation and my Intercessor.

ISAIAH 59:16; PSALM 40:6–8; JOHN 10:17–18;
ISAIAH 45:21–22; ACTS 4:12; 2 CORINTHIANS 8:9

He is altogether lovely.

Lord God, may my meditation be sweet to You. My Beloved is chief among ten thousand. Jesus is a chief cornerstone, elect, precious, and I believe on Him and will by no means be put to shame. You are fairer than the sons of men; grace is poured upon Your lips, Lord God, You have highly exalted Jesus and given Him the name which is above every name. It pleased You, Father God, that in Him all the fullness should dwell.

I have not seen Jesus yet I love Him. Though now I do not see Him, yet believing, I rejoice with joy inexpressible and full of glory.

I count all things loss for the excellence of the knowledge of Christ Jesus my Lord, for whom I have suffered the loss of all things, and count them as rubbish, that I may gain Christ and be found in Him, not having my own righteousness, which is from the law, but that which is through faith in Christ, the righteousness which is from You, Lord God, by faith.

Lord, Your Son is altogether lovely
and altogether worthy of my devotion. May I honor Him
by living a life of joy that glorifies Him.

SONG OF SOLOMON 5:16; PSALM 104:34;
SONG OF SOLOMON 5:10; 1 PETER 2:6; PSALM 45:2;
PHILIPPIANS 2:9; COLOSSIANS 1:19;
1 PETER 1:8; PHILIPPIANS 3:8–9

*It is good that one should hope
and wait quietly for the salvation of the Lord.*

H ave You, Lord, forgotten to be gracious? Have You in anger shut up Your tender mercies? I said in my haste, "I am cut off from before Your eyes"; nevertheless You heard my supplications when I cried out to You.

Shall You, God, not avenge me, Your own elect, who cries out day and night to You, though You bear long with me? You will avenge me speedily. I wait for You, Lord, and You will save me.

I rest in You, Lord, and wait patiently for You; I do not fret because of him who prospers in his way, because of the man who brings wicked schemes to pass.

I will not need to fight in this battle. I position myself, stand still and see Your salvation, Lord God.

Let me not grow weary while doing good, for in due season I shall reap if I do not lose heart. I see the farmer wait for the precious fruit of the earth, waiting patiently for it until it receives the early and latter rain.

*As I wait for You to work in my life,
keep me doing good for Your kingdom and
confident of Your salvation.*

LAMENTATIONS 3:26; PSALM 77:9; PSALM 31:22;
LUKE 18:7–8; PROVERBS 20:22; PSALM 37:7;
2 CHRONICLES 20:17; GALATIANS 6:9; JAMES 5:7

"Not by might nor by power, but by My Spirit,"
says the Lord of hosts.

Lord, who has directed Your Spirit, or as Your counselor has taught You?

God, You have chosen the foolish things of the world to put to shame the wise, and You have chosen the weak things of the world to put to shame the things which are mighty; and the base things of the world and the things which are despised You have chosen, and the things which are not, to bring to nothing the things that are, that no flesh should glory in Your presence.

The wind blows where it wishes, and I hear the sound of it, but cannot tell where it comes from and where it goes. So is everyone who is born of the Spirit . . . born, not of blood, nor of the will of the flesh, nor of the will of man, but of You, Lord God.

Jesus' Spirit remains among us; I do not fear! The battle is not mine, but God's.

You, Lord, do not save with sword and spear; for the battle is Yours.

Your Spirit, Lord, saves, guides, protects,
and brings victory to Your purposes.
Thank You for making His power available
to me for life's battles.

ZECHARIAH 4:6; ISAIAH 40:13; 1 CORINTHIANS 1:27–29;
JOHN 3:8; JOHN 1:13; HAGGAI 2:5;
2 CHRONICLES 20:15; 1 SAMUEL 17:47

November

*When I
sit in darkness,
the Lord will be a
light to me.*

Blessed is the man who listens to me,
watching daily at my gates, waiting at the posts of my doors.

Lord, as the eyes of servants look to the hand of their masters, as the eyes of a maid to the hand of her mistress, so my eyes look to You, my God, until You have mercy on me.

You commanded a continual burnt offering throughout the generations at the door of the tabernacle of meeting, where You would meet Your people to speak with them. In every place where You record Your name You will come to Your people, and You will bless us.

Where two or three gather together in Jesus' name, He is there in our midst.

The hour is coming, and now is when the true worshipers will worship You, Father God, in spirit and truth; for You are seeking such to worship You. Lord, You are Spirit, and when I worship You I must worship in spirit and truth.

I will pray always with all prayer and supplication in the Spirit. I will pray without ceasing.

Keep me listening for Your voice, Lord, as I pray, worship,
and enjoy Your presence with me.

PROVERBS 8:34; PSALM 123:2; EXODUS 29:42;
EXODUS 20:24; MATTHEW 18:20; JOHN 4:23–24;
EPHESIANS 6:18; 1 THESSALONIANS 5:17

Always pursue what is good.

Lord, for to this I was called, because Christ also suffered for me, leaving me an example, that I should follow His steps: who committed no sin, nor was deceit found in His mouth; who, when He was reviled, did not revile in return; but committed Himself to You, Lord God, who judges righteously. I consider Jesus who endured such hostility from sinners against Himself, lest I become weary and discouraged in my soul.

I lay aside every weight, and the sin which so easily ensnares me, and I run with endurance the race that is set before me, looking unto Jesus, the author and finisher of my faith, who for the joy that was set before Him endured the cross, despising the shame, and has sat down at the right hand of Your throne, Lord God.

Finally, whatever things are true, whatever things are noble, whatever things are just, whatever things are pure, whatever things are lovely, whatever things are of good report, if there is any virtue and if there is anything praiseworthy—I will meditate on these things.

*May the meditations of my heart
enable me to look to You, Lord God,
and pursue what is good.*

1 Thessalonians 5:15; 1 Peter 2:21–23; Hebrews 12:3;
Hebrews 12:1–2; Philippians 4:8

The ways of the Lord are right; the righteous walk in them,
but transgressors stumble in them.

To those of us who believe in You, Jesus, You are precious; but to those who are disobedient, You are a stone of stumbling and a rock of offense. The way of the Lord is strength for the upright, but destruction will come to the workers of iniquity.

He who has ears to hear, let him hear! Whoever is wise will observe these things, and they will understand the Lord's lovingkindness. The lamp of the body is the eye. If therefore my eye is good, my whole body will be full of light. If I want to do God's will, I shall know concerning the doctrine, whether it is from Him. Whoever has, to him more will be given, and he will have abundance.

I who am of God hears God's words; others do not hear, because they are not of God. Some are not willing to come to You, Jesus, that they may have life. Your sheep hear Your voice, and You know them, and they follow You.

Jesus, help me hear Your voice so that I might follow You,
honor You, and know You better.

HOSEA 14:9; 1 PETER 2:7–8; PROVERBS 10:29; MATTHEW 11:15;
PSALM 107:43; MATTHEW 6:22; JOHN 7:17; MATTHEW 13:12;
JOHN 8:47; JOHN 5:40; JOHN 10:27

Now for a little while, if need be,
you have been grieved by various trials.

F ather, Your Word encourages me to not think it strange concerning the fiery trial which is to try me, as though some strange thing happened to me; but I rejoice to the extent that I partake of Christ's sufferings, that when His glory is revealed, I may also be glad with exceeding joy. The exhortation speaks to me as to a son: "My son, do not despise the chastening of the Lord, nor be discouraged when you are rebuked by Him." Now no chastening seems to be joyful for the present, but painful; nevertheless, afterward it yields the peaceable fruit of righteousness to those of us who have been trained by it.

I do not have a High Priest who cannot sympathize with my weaknesses, but was in all points tempted as I am, yet without sin. For in that Jesus Himself has suffered, being tempted, He is able to aid those of us who are tempted. God, You are faithful, who will not allow me to be tempted beyond what I am able.

Thank You, Lord, that when trials and temptations come,
You are with me to strengthen me, comfort me, and guide me.

---

1 PETER 1:6; 1 PETER 4:12–13; HEBREWS 12:5;
HEBREWS 12:11; HEBREWS 4:15;
HEBREWS 2:18; 1 CORINTHIANS 10:13

Take for yourself quality spices. . . .
And you shall make from these a holy anointing oil.

God, You commanded that the temple's anointing oil shall not be poured on man's flesh; nor shall Israel make any other like it, according to its composition. It is holy, and it shall be holy to me. There is One Spirit . . . diversities of gifts, but the same Spirit.

You, God, have anointed Jesus with the oil of gladness more than His companions. You anointed Jesus of Nazareth with the Holy Spirit and with power. You, Lord God, do not give the Spirit by measure.

I have received of Jesus' fullness. As the same anointing teaches me concerning all things, and is true, and is not a lie, and just as it has taught me, I will abide in Him. You, Lord God, are the One who has anointed me, who also has sealed me and given me the Spirit in my heart as a guarantee.

The fruit of Your Spirit is love, joy, peace, longsuffering, kindness, goodness, faithfulness, gentleness, self-control. Against such there is no law.

Lord, Your anointing is for a purpose:
Please use me to do the work You call me to do.

EXODUS 30:23, 25; EXODUS 30:32; EPHESIANS 4:4;
1 CORINTHIANS 12:4; PSALM 45:7; ACTS 10:38; JOHN 3:34;
JOHN 1:16; 1 JOHN 2:27; 2 CORINTHIANS 1:21–22;
GALATIANS 5:22–23

When Christ who is our life appears,
then you also will appear with Him in glory.

Jesus, You are the resurrection and the life. Because I believe in You, though I may die, I shall live. God has given me eternal life, and this life is in You, His Son. I who have You have life; he who does not have You does not have life.

For You, Lord Jesus, will descend from heaven with a shout, with the voice of an archangel, and with the trumpet of God. And the dead in You will rise first. Then we who are alive and remain shall be caught up together with them in the clouds to meet You in the air. And thus we shall always be with You, our Lord. We comfort one another with these words. When You are revealed, I shall be like You, for I shall see You as You are. My human body is sown in dishonor, it is raised in glory. It is sown in weakness, it is raised in power.

If You, Jesus, go and prepare a place for me, You will come again and receive me to Yourself; that where You are, there I may be also.

What a glorious hope I have in You, Lord Jesus!

COLOSSIANS 3:4; JOHN 11:25; 1 JOHN 5:11–12;
1 THESSALONIANS 4:16–18; 1 JOHN 3:2;
1 CORINTHIANS 15:43; JOHN 14:3

*Oh, that men would give thanks to the Lord for His goodness,
and for His wonderful works to the children of men!*

Lord God, I have tasted and seen that You are good; I am
blessed for I trust in You! How great is Your goodness, which
You have laid up for those who fear You.

This people You have formed for Yourself shall declare Your
praise. You have predestined me to adoption as a son by Jesus
Christ to Himself, according to the good pleasure of Your will,
to the praise of the glory of Your grace, by which You have made
me accepted in the Beloved. I who first trusted in Christ should
be to the praise of Your glory, Lord God.

How great is Your goodness and beauty! You, Lord, are good
to all, and Your tender mercies are over all Your works.
All Your works shall praise You, O Lord, and Your saints shall
bless You. We shall speak of the glory of Your kingdom, and talk
of Your power, to make known to the sons of men Your mighty
acts, and the glorious majesty of Your kingdom.

*May the praises I lift to You, Lord God,
help others come to know You and Your gracious,
life-giving love!*

PSALM 107:8; PSALM 34:8; PSALM 31:19; ISAIAH 43:21;
EPHESIANS 1:5–6, 12; ZECHARIAH 9:17; PSALM 145:9–12

Let us who are of the day be sober,
putting on the breastplate of faith and love,
and as a helmet the hope of salvation.

Lord, I gird up the loins of my mind, and will be sober, and rest my hope fully upon the grace that is to be brought to me at the revelation of Jesus Christ. I stand therefore, having girded my waist with truth, having put on the breastplate of righteousness. I have the shield of faith with which I will be able to quench all the fiery darts of the wicked one. And I take the helmet of salvation, and the sword of the Spirit, which is Your Word, Lord God.

You will swallow up death forever, and You will wipe away tears from my face; the rebuke of Your people You will take away from all the earth; for You, Lord God, have spoken. And I will say in that day: "Behold, this is my God; I have waited for Him, and He will save me. This is the Lord; I will be glad and rejoice in His salvation."

Faith is the substance of things hoped for, the evidence of things not seen.

The battle rages.
Thank You for providing the armor,
the strength, and the faith I need!

1 THESSALONIANS 5:8; 1 PETER 1:13; EPHESIANS 6:14, 16–17;
ISAIAH 25:8–9; HEBREWS 11:1

I have given help to one who is mighty;
I have exalted one chosen from the people.

You, even You, are the Lord, and besides You there is no savior. There is one God and one Mediator between God and men, the Man Christ Jesus. There is no other name under heaven given among men by which we must be saved.

Your Son will be called "Mighty God." He made Himself of no reputation, taking the form of a bondservant, and coming in the likeness of men. And being found in appearance as a man, He humbled Himself and became obedient to the point of death, even the death of the cross. Therefore You, Lord God, have highly exalted Him and given Him the name which is above every name. I see Jesus, who was made a little lower than the angels, for the suffering of death crowned with glory and honor, that He, by Your grace, God, might taste death for everyone. As we children have partaken of flesh and blood, He Himself likewise shared in the same.

Thank You, merciful and mighty God,
for choosing Jesus to die on the cross for my sin, for by doing so,
He defeated death and the devil.

PSALM 89:19; ISAIAH 43:11; 1 TIMOTHY 2:5; ACTS 4:12; ISAIAH 9:6; PHILIPPIANS 2:7–9; HEBREWS 2:9; HEBREWS 2:14

*Fruitful in every good work
and increasing in the knowledge of God.*

Lord, I present my body a living sacrifice, holy, acceptable to You, my God, which is my reasonable service. And I will not be conformed to this world, but be transformed by the renewing of my mind, that I may prove what is Your good and acceptable and perfect will. Just as I presented my members as slaves of uncleanness, and of lawlessness leading to more lawlessness, so now I present my members as slaves of righteousness for holiness. In Christ Jesus neither circumcision nor uncircumcision avails anything, but a new creation. And as many as walk according to this rule, peace and mercy be upon us.

By this You, my Father God, are glorified, that I bear much fruit; so I will be Your disciple. Jesus chose me and appointed me that I should go and bear fruit, and that my fruit should remain, that whatever I ask You, Father, in Jesus' name, You may give me.

*As You transform my mind and
I discern Your perfect will, Lord God,
may I bear fruit that enriches Your kingdom
and glorifies You.*

COLOSSIANS 1:10; ROMANS 12:1–2; ROMANS 6:19;
GALATIANS 6:15–16; JOHN 15:8; JOHN 15:16

He led them on safely.

Mighty God, I traverse the way of righteousness, in the midst of the paths of justice.

You send an Angel before me to keep me in the way and to bring me into the place which You have prepared. In Your people's affliction, Lord, You were afflicted, and the Angel of Your Presence saved them; in Your love and in Your pity You redeemed them; and You bore them and carried them all the days of old.

They did not gain possession of the land by their own sword, nor did their own arm save them; but it was Your right hand, Your arm, and the light of Your countenance, because You favored them. So You lead Your people, to make Yourself a glorious name.

Lead me, O Lord, in Your righteousness because of my enemies; make Your way straight before my face. Oh, send out Your light and Your truth! Let them lead me; let them bring me to Your holy hill and to Your tabernacle. Then I will go to Your altar, to You my exceeding joy; and on the harp I will praise You, O God, my God.

Thank You, God, for faithfully leading me and providing for me just as You have always done for Your people.

PSALM 78:53; PROVERBS 8:20; EXODUS 23:20; ISAIAH 63:9; PSALM 44:3; ISAIAH 63:14; PSALM 5:8; PSALM 43:3–4

*Godly sorrow produces repentance leading to salvation,
not to be regretted.*

Father, Peter remembered the word of Jesus who had said to him, "Before the rooster crows, you will deny Me three times." So he went out and wept bitterly. If I confess my sins, You, Lord God, are faithful and just to forgive my sins and to cleanse me from all unrighteousness. The blood of Jesus Christ Your Son cleanses me from all sin.

My iniquities have overtaken me, so that I am not able to look up; they are more than the hairs of my head; therefore my heart fails me. Be pleased, O Lord, to deliver me; O Lord, make haste to help me!

So I, by Your help, God, return; I observe mercy and justice, and I wait on You, my God, continually.

The sacrifices You welcome, God, are a broken spirit, a broken and a contrite heart—these, O God, You will not despise. You heal the brokenhearted and bind up our wounds. You have shown me what is good; and what You require of me but to do justly, to love mercy, and to walk humbly with You, my God.

*Teach me, Lord, to do justly, love mercy,
and walk humbly with You.*

2 CORINTHIANS 7:10; MATTHEW 26:75; 1 JOHN 1:9;
1 JOHN 1:7; PSALM 40:12–13; HOSEA 12:6; PSALM 51:17;
PSALM 147:3; MICAH 6:8

Christ . . . loved the church and gave Himself for her, . . .
that He might sanctify and
cleanse her with the washing of water by the word.

Enable me, Lord, to walk in love, as Christ also has loved me and given Himself for me, an offering and a sacrifice to You for a sweet-smelling aroma.

I have been born again, not of corruptible seed but incorruptible, through Your Word which lives and abides forever. Sanctify me by Your truth. Your word is truth. Unless I am born of water and the Spirit, I cannot enter Your kingdom, Lord God. Not by works of righteousness which I have done, but according to Your mercy You saved me, through the washing of regeneration and renewing of Your Holy Spirit. Your word has given me life.

Your law, O Lord, is perfect, converting my soul; Your testimony is sure, making wise the simple; Your statutes are right, rejoicing my heart; Your commandment is pure, enlightening my eyes.

May I live my life, Lord God, according to Your Word,
sanctified by Your Spirit,
always rejoicing in Your mercy, and walking in Your love.

EPHESIANS 5:25–26; EPHESIANS 5:2; 1 PETER 1:23; JOHN 17:17;
JOHN 3:5; TITUS 3:5; PSALM 119:50; PSALM 19:7–8

You are my help and my deliverer;
do not delay, O my God.

Lord God, You order my steps as of a good man, and You delight in my way. Though I fall, I shall not be utterly cast down; for You uphold me with Your hand. In fearing You, Lord God, there is strong confidence, and Your children will have a place of refuge. Who am I that I should be afraid of a man who will die, and of the son of a man who will be made like grass? And I forget You, Lord God, my Maker.

You are with me to deliver me. I will be strong and of good courage, I will not fear nor be afraid; for You, my God, You are the One who goes with me. You will not leave me nor forsake me.

I will sing of Your power; yes, I will sing aloud of Your mercy in the morning; for You have been my defense and refuge in the day of my trouble. You are my hiding place; You shall preserve me from trouble; You shall surround me with songs of deliverance.

I praise You who are my Helper
and Deliverer, my Refuge and Hiding Place,
the source of peace and security.

PSALM 40:17; PSALM 37:23–24; PROVERBS 14:26;
ISAIAH 51:12–13; JEREMIAH 1:8; DEUTERONOMY 31:6;
PSALM 59:16; PSALM 32:7

God is faithful, by whom you
were called into the fellowship of His Son,
Jesus Christ our Lord.

Lord God, let me hold fast the confession of my hope without wavering, for You who promised are faithful. You have said: "I will dwell in them and walk among them. I will be their God, and they shall be My people." Truly my fellowship is with You, Father God, and with Your Son Jesus Christ. I rejoice to the extent that I partake of Christ's sufferings, that when His glory is revealed, I may also be glad with exceeding joy.

Being rooted and grounded in love, may I be able to comprehend with all the saints what is the width and length and depth and height—to know the love of Christ which passes knowledge; that I may be filled with all the fullness of God.

Whoever confesses that Jesus is the Son of God, God abides in him, and he in God. Those of us who keep His commandments abide in Him, and He in us.

Teach me, Lord, to live a life of love for You,
whose love for me is beyond description.

1 CORINTHIANS 1:9; HEBREWS 10:23; 2 CORINTHIANS 6:16;
1 JOHN 1:3; 1 PETER 4:13; EPHESIANS 3:17–19;
1 JOHN 4:15; 1 JOHN 3:24

Sanctify them by Your truth.
Your word is truth.

Father, I am already clean because of the word which Jesus has spoken to me. So I will let the word of Christ dwell in me richly in all wisdom.

How can a young man cleanse his way? By taking heed according to Your word, Lord God. With my whole heart I have sought You; oh, let me not wander from Your commandments!

When wisdom enters my heart, and knowledge is pleasant to my soul, discretion will preserve me; understanding will keep me.

My foot has held fast to Your steps, God; I have kept Your way and not turned aside. I have not departed from the commandment of Your lips; I have treasured the words of Your mouth more than my necessary food. I have more understanding than all my teachers, for Your testimonies are my meditation. If I abide in Your Word, I am Your disciple indeed. And I shall know the truth, and the truth shall make me free.

Your written Word gives life,
so I thank You for opening my heart to know its truth.

JOHN 17:17; JOHN 15:3; COLOSSIANS 3:16; PSALM 119:9–10;
PROVERBS 2:10–11; JOB 23:11–12; PSALM 119:99;
JOHN 8:31–32

Your thoughts are very deep.

Lord God, I ask that I may be filled with the knowledge of Your will in all wisdom and spiritual understanding. And may I, being rooted and grounded in love, be able to comprehend with all the saints what is the width and length and depth and height—to know the love of Christ which passes knowledge; that I may be filled with all Your fullness, Lord God.

Oh, the depth of the riches both of the wisdom and knowledge of You, my infinite God! How unsearchable are Your judgments and Your ways past finding out! Your thoughts are not my thoughts, Lord God, nor are my ways Your ways. For as the heavens are higher than the earth, so are Your ways higher than my ways, and Your thoughts than my thoughts. Many, O Lord my God, are Your wonderful works which You have done; and Your thoughts toward me cannot be recounted to You in order; if I would declare and speak of them, they are more than can be numbered.

I am humbled when I consider Your infinite love,
Your immeasurable wisdom, Your wonderful works, and Your
merciful thoughts toward sinners like me!

PSALM 92:5; COLOSSIANS 1:9; EPHESIANS 3:17–19;
ROMANS 11:33; ISAIAH 55:8–9; PSALM 40:5

He removes it by His rough wind
in the day of the east wind.

L et me fall into Your hand, Lord God, for Your mercies are great. You are with me to save me. You will correct me in justice, and You will not let me go altogether unpunished. You will not always strive with me, nor will You keep Your anger forever. You have not dealt with me according to my sins, nor punished me according to my iniquities. For You know my frame; You remember that I am dust. You will spare me as a man spares his own son who serves him.

God, You are faithful, You will not allow me to be tempted beyond what I am able, but with the temptation will also make the way of escape, that I may be able to bear it. When Satan asked for Peter that he might be sifted as wheat, Jesus prayed that Peter's faith should not fail. So do I need Your help.

You, Lord, have been a strength to the poor, and to the needy in his distress, a refuge from the storm, a shade from the heat;

Lord God, thank You for saving me, forgiving me,
and offering me an escape from temptation.

ISAIAH 27:8; 2 SAMUEL 24:14; JEREMIAH 30:11;
PSALM 103:9–10, 14; MALACHI 3:17; 1 CORINTHIANS 10:13;
LUKE 22:31–32; ISAIAH 25:4

By their fruits you will know them.

Father, I will let no one deceive me: he who practices righteousness is righteous, just as Jesus is righteous. Does a spring send forth fresh water and bitter from the same opening? Can a fig tree bear olives, or a grapevine bear figs? Thus no spring yields both salt water and fresh. Who is wise and understanding among you? Let him show by good conduct that his works are done in the meekness of wisdom. May I have my conduct be honorable among the Gentiles, that when they speak against me as evildoers, they may, by my good works which they observe, glorify God in the day of visitation.

Either make the tree good and its fruit good, or else make the tree bad and its fruit bad; for a tree is known by its fruit. A good man out of the good treasure of his heart brings forth good things, and an evil man out of the evil treasure brings forth evil things.

What more could have been done to Your vineyard, Lord, that You have not done in it?

God, please work in my heart that the fruit of my life—
the fruit of my words, my thoughts, my actions—
would bring glory and honor to You.

MATTHEW 7:20; 1 JOHN 3:7; JAMES 3:11–13;
1 PETER 2:12; MATTHEW 12:33; MATTHEW 12:35; ISAIAH 5:4

When I sit in darkness,
the Lord will be a light to me.

Lord, when I pass through the waters, You will be with me; and through the rivers, they shall not overflow me. When I walk through the fire, I shall not be burned, nor shall the flame scorch me. For You are the Lord my God, the Holy One of Israel, my Savior. You will bring the blind by a way they did not know; You will lead them in paths they have not known. You will make darkness light before them, and crooked places straight. These things You will do for them, and not forsake them.

Yea, though I walk through the valley of the shadow of death, I will fear no evil; for You are with me; Your rod and Your staff, they comfort me. Whenever I am afraid, I will trust in You. In You, God (I will praise Your word), in You I have put my trust; I will not fear. What can flesh do to me? You, Lord, are my light and my salvation; whom shall I fear? You, Lord, are the strength of my life; of whom shall I be afraid?

Lord God, these truths about You
are a source of encouragement, reassurance,
strength, and boldness.

MICAH 7:8; ISAIAH 43:2–3; ISAIAH 42:16; PSALM 23:4;
PSALM 56:3–4; PSALM 27:1

*The one who comes to Me
I will by no means cast out.*

When I cry to You, Lord, You will hear, for You are gracious. You will not cast me away, nor shall You abhor me, to utterly destroy me and break Your covenant with me; for You are the Lord my God. You will remember Your covenant with me in the days of my youth, and You will establish an everlasting covenant with me.

Lord, You say, "Come now, and let us reason together." Though my sins are like scarlet, they shall be as white as snow; though they are red like crimson, they shall be as wool. Let the wicked forsake his way, and the unrighteous man his thoughts; let him return to You, Lord, and You will have mercy on him; and to our God, for You will abundantly pardon. The dying thief said, "Lord, remember me when You come into Your kingdom." And Jesus said to him, "Assuredly, I say to you, today you will be with Me in Paradise."

A bruised reed You will not break, Almighty God, and smoking flax You will not quench.

*Great are Your mercy, grace, and forgiveness.
Thank You for Your abundant pardon
and Your faithfulness to Your covenant promises.*

JOHN 6:37; EXODUS 22:27; LEVITICUS 26:44; EZEKIEL 16:60;
ISAIAH 1:18; ISAIAH 55:7; LUKE 23:42–43; ISAIAH 42:3

Praying in the Holy Spirit.

Lord God, You are Spirit, and those of us who worship You must worship in spirit and truth. I have access by one Spirit to You, my heavenly Father.

Jesus prayed, "O My Father, if it is possible, let this cup pass from Me; nevertheless, not as I will, but as You will."

Your Spirit, Lord, helps in my weaknesses. For I do not know what I should pray for as I ought, but the Spirit Himself makes intercession for me with groaning which cannot be uttered. Now You, Lord, who search the heart know what the mind of the Spirit is, because He makes intercession for the saints according to Your will. This is the confidence that I have in You, Lord, that if I ask anything according to Your will, You hear me. When the Spirit of truth has come, He will guide me into all truth.

I pray always with all prayer and supplication in the Spirit, being watchful to this end with all perseverance and supplication.

Lord God, thank You for sending Your Spirit
who gives me access to You,
who intercedes for me, and who guides me into truth.

JUDE 20; JOHN 4:24; EPHESIANS 2:18; MATTHEW 26:39;
ROMANS 8:26–27; 1 JOHN 5:14; JOHN 16:13; EPHESIANS 6:18

Whoever listens to me will dwell safely,
and will be secure, without fear of evil.

L ord, You have been our dwelling place in all generations.
I dwell in the secret place of the Most High and shall abide
under the shadow of the Almighty. Your truth shall be
my shield and buckler.

My life is hidden with Christ in You, Lord God. He who
touches me touches the apple of Your eye. I stand still, and see
Your salvation. You, Lord, will fight for me, and I shall hold my
peace. You, God, are my refuge and strength, a very present help
in trouble. Therefore I will not fear.

Jesus comforted His disciples, "Be of good cheer! It is I; do
not be afraid." The resurrected Jesus asked, "Why are you troubled?
And why do doubts arise in your hearts? Behold My hands and
My feet, that it is I Myself. Handle Me and see, for a spirit does
not have flesh and bones as you see I have." I know whom I have
believed and am persuaded that You are able to keep what I
have committed to You.

Thank You for the safety and
security You provide, Lord God.

———————

PROVERBS 1:33; PSALM 90:1; PSALM 91:1;
PSALM 91:4; COLOSSIANS 3:3; ZECHARIAH 2:8;
EXODUS 14:13–14; PSALM 46:1–2; MATTHEW 14:27;
LUKE 24:38–39; 2 TIMOTHY 1:12

*My mother and My brothers are
these who hear the word of God and do it.*

Lord Jesus, both He who sanctifies and those who are being
sanctified are all of one, for which reason You, Lord, are not
ashamed to call us brethren, saying, "I will declare
Your name to My brethren; in the midst of the assembly I will
sing praise to You." In You, Jesus, neither circumcision nor
uncircumcision avails anything, but faith working through love.
I am Your friend, Jesus, if I do whatever You command me.
Blessed are we who hear the word of God and keep it!

Not everyone who says to You, "Lord, Lord," shall enter the
kingdom of heaven, but he who does the will of Your Father in
heaven. Your food, Jesus, is to do the will of Him who sent You.

If I say that I have fellowship with You, and walk in darkness,
I lie and do not practice the truth. Whoever keeps God's word,
truly the love of God is perfected in him. By this we know that
we are in Him.

*Lord Jesus, throughout this day—throughout my life—
may I follow Your Word and do God's will,
relying on You each step of the way.*

LUKE 8:21; HEBREWS 2:11–12; GALATIANS 5:6; JOHN 15:14;
LUKE 11:28; MATTHEW 7:21; JOHN 4:34; 1 JOHN 1:6; 1 JOHN 2:5

Having been set free from sin,
you became slaves of righteousness.

Lord God, I cannot serve You and mammon. When I was a slave of sin, I was free in regard to righteousness. What fruit did I have then in the things of which I am now ashamed? For the end of those things is death. But now having been set free from sin, and having become a slave of God, I have my fruit to holiness, and the end, everlasting life.

Jesus, You are the end of the law for righteousness to everyone of us who believes.

If I serve You, Jesus, let me follow You; and where You are, there I, Your servant, will be also. If I serve You, Your Father will honor me. I take Your yoke upon me and learn from You, for You are gentle and lowly in heart, and I will find rest for my soul. For Your yoke is easy and Your burden is light.

O Lord my God, masters besides You have had dominion over me; but by You only I make mention of Your name. I will run the course of Your commandments, for You shall enlarge my heart.

Heavenly Father, may I find fulfillment and even joy
in being a slave to Your righteous and holy standards.

ROMANS 6:18; MATTHEW 6:24; ROMANS 6:20–22;
ROMANS 10:4; JOHN 12:26; MATTHEW 11:29–30;
ISAIAH 26:13; PSALM 119:32

The Lord delights in you.

You, Lord God, who created me, say, "Fear not, for I have redeemed you; I have called you by your name; you are Mine." Can a woman forget her nursing child, and not have compassion on the son of her womb? Surely they may forget, yet You will not forget me. You have inscribed me on the palms of Your hands; my walls are continually before You.

Lord, You order my steps as of a good man, and You delight in my way. Your delight was with the sons of men. You take pleasure in those who fear You, in those who hope in Your mercy. You, the Lord of hosts, say that I shall be Yours on the day that You make us Your jewels. And You will spare me as a man spares his own son who serves him.

I, who once was alienated and an enemy in my mind by wicked works, yet now You have reconciled in the body of Your flesh through death, to present me holy, and blameless, and above reproach in Your sight.

May I never be numb to the amazing truth
that You delight in me—and may I respond to that delight
by living a life that honors You!

ISAIAH 62:4; ISAIAH 43:1; ISAIAH 49:15–16; PSALM 37:23;
PROVERBS 8:31; PSALM 147:11; MALACHI 3:17;
COLOSSIANS 1:21–22

The glory which You gave Me I have given them.

The prophet Isaiah saw You, Lord, sitting on a throne, high and lifted up, and the train of Your robe filled the temple. Above it stood seraphim. And one cried to another and said: "Holy, holy, holy is the Lord of hosts; the whole earth is full of His glory!" These things Isaiah said when he saw Your glory and spoke of You. On the likeness of the throne was a likeness of a man high above it. Like the appearance of a rainbow in a cloud on a rainy day, so was the appearance of the brightness all around it. This was the appearance of the likeness of Your glory, Lord God.

Moses said, "Please, show me Your glory." But You said, "You cannot see My face; for no man shall see Me, and live." No one has seen You at any time, Lord God. The only begotten Son, who is in Your bosom, He has declared You. You, who commanded light to shine out of darkness, have shone in my heart to give the light of the knowledge of Your glory in the face of Jesus Christ.

You will be glorified for eternity, Lord.
Help me live so I glorify You now!

JOHN 17:22; ISAIAH 6:1–3; JOHN 12:41; EZEKIEL 1:26, 28;
EXODUS 33:18, 20; JOHN 1:18; 2 CORINTHIANS 4:6

As the body without the spirit is dead,
so faith without works is dead also.

Heavenly Father, not everyone who says, "Lord, Lord," shall enter the kingdom of heaven, but he who does Your will. I pursue holiness, without which I will not see You, Lord. I will add to my faith virtue, to virtue knowledge, to knowledge self-control, to self-control perseverance, to perseverance godliness, to godliness brotherly kindness, and to brotherly kindness love. For if these things are mine and abound, I will be neither barren nor unfruitful in the knowledge of my Lord Jesus Christ. For if I lack these things I am shortsighted, even to blindness, and have forgotten that he was cleansed from his old sins. Therefore, I will be even more diligent to make my call and election sure, for if I do these things I will never stumble.

By grace I have been saved through faith, and that not of myself; it is Your gift to me, Lord God, not of works, lest I should boast.

Guide me in the works You would have me do—
works that reveal my living faith
in You so that You might be honored.

JAMES 2:26; MATTHEW 7:21; HEBREWS 12:14;
2 PETER 1:5–10; EPHESIANS 2:8–9

We shall be satisfied with the goodness of Your house.

One thing I have desired of You, Lord, that I will seek: that I may dwell in Your house all the days of my life, to behold Your beauty, and to inquire in Your temple. I am blessed when I hunger and thirst for righteousness, for I shall be filled. You have filled the hungry with good things, and the rich You have sent away empty.

You satisfy the longing soul, and fill the hungry soul with goodness. You are the bread of life. He who comes to You shall never hunger, and he who believes in You shall never thirst.

How precious is Your lovingkindness, O God! Therefore we children of men put our trust under the shadow of Your wings. I am abundantly satisfied with the fullness of Your house, and You give me drink from the river of Your pleasures. For with You is the fountain of life; in Your light I see light.

The goodness of being in Your presence,
Lord God, satisfies now and will satisfy forever.
Great is my love for You!

PSALM 65:4; PSALM 27:4; MATTHEW 5:6; LUKE 1:53;
PSALM 107:9; JOHN 6:35; PSALM 36:7–9

The Lord of peace Himself
give you peace always in every way.
The Lord be with you all.

Thank You, Lord, for peace from Jesus who is and who was and who is to come. Your peace, Lord God, which surpasses all understanding, will guard my heart and mind through Christ Jesus.

The resurrected Jesus Himself stood in the midst of His disciples, and said to them, "Peace to you." Peace He leaves with me, His peace He gives to me; not as the world gives does He give to me. I will let not my heart be troubled, neither let it be afraid.

Jesus gave us the Helper, the Spirit of truth. The fruit of the Spirit is love, joy, peace. The Spirit Himself bears witness with my spirit that I am a child of God.

God, You said to Moses, "My Presence will go with you, and I will give you rest." Then Moses said to You, "If Your Presence does not go with us, do not bring us up from here. For how then will it be known that Your people and I have found grace in Your sight, except You go with us?"

All praise to You, Father God,
who gives us—by Your presence with us—
peace beyond description!

2 THESSALONIANS 3:16; REVELATION 1:4; PHILIPPIANS 4:7;
LUKE 24:36; JOHN 14:27; JOHN 15:26; GALATIANS 5:22;
ROMANS 8:16; EXODUS 33:14–16

December

Bear one another's

burdens,

and so fulfill the

law of Christ.

A man will be as a hiding place from the wind,
and a cover from the tempest.

As I have partaken of flesh and blood, Jesus Himself likewise shared in the same. "The Man who is My Companion," says the Lord of hosts. Jesus said, "I and My Father are one."

I who dwell in Your secret place, O Lord Most High, shall abide under Your shadow. There will be a tabernacle for shade in the daytime from the heat, for a place of refuge, and for a shelter from storm, and rain. You, Lord, are my shade at my right hand. The sun shall not strike me by day, nor the moon by night.

When my heart is overwhelmed, lead me to the rock that is higher than I. You are my hiding place; You shall preserve me from trouble. You have been a strength to the poor, a strength to the needy in his distress, a refuge from the storm, a shade from the heat; for the blast of the terrible ones is as a storm against the wall.

In times of need and during the struggles of everyday life, Lord,
You provide shelter and strength. Thank You, Father God.

Isaiah 32:2; Hebrews 2:14; Zechariah 13:7; John 10:30; Psalm 91:1; Isaiah 4:6; Psalm 121:5–6; Psalm 61:2; Psalm 32:7; Isaiah 25:4

*You have an anointing from the Holy One,
and you know all things.*

Lord God, You anointed Jesus of Nazareth with the Holy
Spirit and with power. It pleased You that in Him all the
fullness should dwell. Of Jesus' fullness I have received,
and grace for grace.

You, Lord God, anoint my head with oil. The anointing
which I have received from You abides in me, and I do not need
that anyone teach me but as the same anointing teaches me
concerning all things, and is true, and is not a lie, and just as it
has taught me, I will abide in You.

The Helper, the Holy Spirit, whom You, Father God, sent in
Jesus' name, He will teach me all things, and bring to my
remembrance all things that He said to me.

The Spirit also helps in my weaknesses. For I do not know
what I should pray for as I ought, but the Spirit Himself makes
intercession for me with groaning which cannot be uttered.

*Lord God, thank You for Your Spirit who teaches me Your truth,
helps me remember what He has taught me,
strengthens me in my weaknesses, and prays for me!*

---

1 JOHN 2:20; ACTS 10:38; COLOSSIANS 1:19; JOHN 1:16;
PSALM 23:5; 1 JOHN 2:27; JOHN 14:26; ROMANS 8:26

I would seek God,
and to God I would commit my cause.

O Lord, is anything too hard for You? I commit my way to You, trust also in You, and You shall bring it to pass. I will be anxious for nothing, but in everything by prayer and supplication, with thanksgiving, let my requests be made known to You, Lord God. I cast all my care upon You, for You care for me.

When Hezekiah received the letter from the hand of the messengers, and read it, He went up to Your house, Lord, and spread it before You. Then He prayed to You.

So, it shall come to pass that before I call, You will answer; and while I am still speaking, You will hear. The effective, fervent prayer of a righteous man avails much.

I love You, Lord, because You have heard my voice and my supplications. Because You have inclined Your ear to me, therefore I will call upon You as long as I live.

Throughout Your Word, dear Lord, You remind me
of how much You love me. That love is reason enough for me
to pray always, rejoice always, and worry never!

JOB 5:8; GENESIS 18:14; PSALM 37:5; PHILIPPIANS 4:6;
1 PETER 5:7; ISAIAH 37:14–15; ISAIAH 65:24;
JAMES 5:16; PSALM 116:1–2

Where can wisdom be found?

Father God, if I lack wisdom, I ask You, who gives liberally and without reproach, and it will be given to me. But I will ask in faith, with no doubting. I trust in You, Lord, with all my heart, and lean not on my own understanding; in all my ways I acknowledge You, and You shall direct my paths. You alone are wise. I will not be wise in my own eyes.

Jeremiah feared and said, "Ah, Lord God! Behold, I cannot speak, for I am a youth." But You, Lord, said to him: "Do not say, 'I am a youth,' for you shall go to all to whom I send you, and whatever I command you, you shall speak. Do not be afraid of their faces, for I am with you to deliver you."

Whatever I ask You, Father, in Jesus' name You will give me. Until now I have asked nothing in His name. Ask, and I will receive, that my joy may be full. And whatever things I ask in prayer, believing, I will receive.

Genuine wisdom can be found only in You,
dear Lord, so teach me to turn to You for wisdom and
to trust without doubt or fear.

JOB 28:12; JAMES 1:5–6; PROVERBS 3:5–6;
1 TIMOTHY 1:17; PROVERBS 3:7;
JEREMIAH 1:6–8; JOHN 16:23–24; MATTHEW 21:22

*It is good for me that I have been afflicted,
that I may learn Your statutes.*

Though Jesus was Your Son, Lord God, yet He learned obedience by the things which He suffered. I suffer with Him, that we may also be glorified together. For I consider that the sufferings of this present time are not worthy to be compared with the glory which shall be revealed in us.

You know, Lord, the way that I take; when You have tested me, I shall come forth as gold. My foot has held fast to Your steps; I have kept Your way and not turned aside.

I shall remember that You, Lord God, led me all the way these forty years in the wilderness, to humble me and test me, to know what was in my heart, whether I would keep Your commandments or not. I should know in my heart that as a man chastens his son, so You, Lord God, chasten me. Therefore I shall keep Your commandments, Lord, to walk in Your ways and to fear You.

*May I learn more about Your faithfulness,
Your power, and even Your love from the hard times
You allow me to experience, Lord God.*

PSALM 119:71; HEBREWS 5:8; ROMANS 8:17–18;
JOB 23:10–11; DEUTERONOMY 8:2, 5–6

It is God who works in you.

Lord, I am not sufficient of myself to think of anything as being from myself, but my sufficiency is from You, Lord God. I can receive nothing unless it has been given to me from heaven. I cannot come to Jesus unless You, Father God who sent Him, draw me; and You will raise me up at the last day. You will give us, Your people, one heart and one way, that they may fear You forever.

I will not be deceived. Every good gift and every perfect gift is from above, and comes down from You, the Father of lights, with whom there is no variation or shadow of turning. Of Your own will, God, You brought us forth by the word of truth, that we might be a kind of firstfruits of Your creatures.

I am Your workmanship, created in Christ Jesus for good works, which You prepared beforehand that I should walk in them.

Lord, You will establish peace for me, for You have also done all my works in me.

You accomplish things through me,
You give every good gift to me, You have called me to be Your child!
I am blessed to be Yours, gracious God!

PHILIPPIANS 2:13; 2 CORINTHIANS 3:5; JOHN 3:27;
JOHN 6:44; JEREMIAH 32:39; JAMES 1:16–18;
EPHESIANS 2:10; ISAIAH 26:12

He made Him who knew no sin to be sin for us,
that we might become the righteousness of God in Him.

Y ou, Lord, have laid on Jesus the iniquity of us all. He
Himself bore my sins in His own body on the tree, that I,
having died to sins, might live for righteousness—by
whose stripes I was healed. As by one man's disobedience many
were made sinners, so also by one Man's obedience many of us
will be made righteous.

But when the kindness and the love of God our Savior
toward man appeared, not by works of righteousness which I
have done, but according to His mercy He saved me, through
the washing of regeneration and renewing of the Holy Spirit,
whom He poured out on me abundantly through Jesus Christ
my Savior, that having been justified by His grace I should
become heirs according to the hope of eternal life. There is
therefore now no condemnation to those of us who are in Christ
Jesus, who do not walk according to the flesh, but according to
the Spirit.

The Lord is our righteousness.

Lord, I am blessed by Your
kindness and love in many ways.
Thank You for loving me!

2 CORINTHIANS 5:21; ISAIAH 53:6; 1 PETER 2:24;
ROMANS 5:19; TITUS 3:4–7; ROMANS 8:1; JEREMIAH 23:6

Through love serve one another.

I f a man is overtaken in any trespass, we who are spiritual are to restore such a one in a spirit of gentleness, considering yourself lest you also be tempted. I must also bear others' burdens, and so fulfill the law of Christ.

If anyone among us wanders from the truth, and you turn him back, know that you who turn a sinner from the error of his way will save a soul from death and cover a multitude of sins. Since I have purified my soul in obeying the truth through the Spirit in sincere love of the brethren, I will love others fervently with a pure heart. I will owe no one anything except love, for he who loves another has fulfilled the law. I will be kindly affectionate to others with brotherly love, in honor giving preference to others. I will be submissive to others, and clothed with humility, for "You, God, resist the proud, but give grace to the humble."

I who am strong ought to bear with the scruples of the weak, and not to please myself.

Lord, help me serve by speaking to my brothers and sisters about their sin, loving them fervently, and—in humility—submitting and deferring to them.

GALATIANS 5:13; GALATIANS 6:1–2;
JAMES 5:19–20; 1 PETER 1:22; ROMANS 13:8;
ROMANS 12:10; 1 PETER 5:5; ROMANS 15:1

*To do righteousness and justice is
more acceptable to the Lord than sacrifice.*

Lord God, You have shown me what is good; and what You require of me—to do justly, to love mercy, and to walk humbly with You, my God. Have You as great delight in burnt offerings and sacrifices, as in my obeying Your voice? Behold, to obey is better than sacrifice, and to heed than the fat of rams. To love You with all my heart, with all my understanding, with all my soul, and with all my strength, and to love my neighbor as myself, is more than all the whole burnt offerings and sacrifices.

So I, by the help of my God, return; I observe mercy and justice, and wait on my God continually. Mary sat at Jesus' feet and heard His word. One thing is needed, and Mary chose that good part, which would not be taken away from her.

It is You, Lord God, who works in me both to will and to do for Your good pleasure.

*May my life be a pleasing sacrifice to You as I try to do justly,
love mercy, and walk humbly with You, Lord God.*

PROVERBS 21:3; MICAH 6:8; 1 SAMUEL 15:22; MARK 12:33;
HOSEA 12:6; LUKE 10:39, 42; PHILIPPIANS 2:13

*No one is able to snatch them
out of My Father's hand.*

Father, I know whom I have believed and am persuaded that You are able to keep what I have committed to You until that Day. You, Lord, will deliver me from every evil work and preserve me for Your heavenly kingdom. I am more than a conqueror through You who loved us. For I am persuaded that neither death nor life, nor angels nor principalities nor powers, nor things present nor things to come, nor height nor depth, nor any other created thing, shall be able to separate me from Your love, God, which is in Christ Jesus my Lord. My life is hidden with Christ in You, Almighty God.

Have You not chosen the poor of this world to be rich in faith and heirs of the kingdom which You promised to those who love You?

My Lord Jesus Christ Himself, and You, my God and Father, who have loved me and given me everlasting consolation and good hope by grace, comfort my heart and establish me in every good word and work.

*What security I find in Your love, Lord God!
You deliver me, preserve me, and strengthen me to serve You.
Please use me for Your kingdom.*

JOHN 10:29; 2 TIMOTHY 1:12; 2 TIMOTHY 4:18;
ROMANS 8:37–39; COLOSSIANS 3:3; JAMES 2:5;
2 THESSALONIANS 2:16–17

Do not let your good be spoken of as evil.

Lord God, I will abstain from every form of evil. I will provide honorable things, not only in Your sight, but also in the sight of men. This is Your will, that by doing good I may put to silence the ignorance of foolish men.

Let me not suffer as a murderer, thief, evildoer, or as a busybody in other people's matters. Yet if I suffer as a Christian, let me not be ashamed, but let me glorify You in this matter.

I have been called to liberty; only I will not use liberty as an opportunity for my flesh, but through love serve others. I will beware lest somehow this liberty of mine become a stumbling block to those who are weak. If I cause one of these little ones who believes in Jesus to sin, it would be better for me if a millstone were hung around my neck, and I were drowned in the depth of the sea. Inasmuch as I did it to one of the least of these Jesus' brethren, I did it to Him.

I can do good only in Your power, Lord.
Enable me to lovingly serve others.

ROMANS 14:16; 1 THESSALONIANS 5:22; 2 CORINTHIANS 8:21;
1 PETER 2:15; 1 PETER 4:15–16; GALATIANS 5:13;
1 CORINTHIANS 8:9; MATTHEW 18:6; MATTHEW 25:40

The Lord is in your midst.

Mighty God, I will fear not, for You are with me; I will not be dismayed, for You are my God. You will strengthen me, yes, You will help me, You will uphold me with Your righteous right hand. Use me to strengthen the weak hands, and make firm the feeble knees. I will say to those who are fearful-hearted, "Be strong, do not fear! Behold, your God will come with vengeance, with the recompense of God; He will come and save you." You, the Lord my God, in our midst, the Mighty One, will save; You will rejoice over me with gladness, You will quiet me in Your love, You will rejoice over me with singing. I wait on You, Lord; I will be of good courage, and You shall strengthen my heart.

I heard a loud voice from heaven saying, "Behold, the tabernacle of God is with men, and He will dwell with them, and they shall be His people. God Himself will be with them and be their God." And You, Lord God, will wipe away every tear from my eyes; there shall be no more death, nor sorrow, nor crying. There shall be no more pain.

Lord God, thank You for being with us now— and for eternity.

ZEPHANIAH 3:15; ISAIAH 41:10; ISAIAH 35:3–4;
EPHESIANS 3:17; PSALM 27:14; REVELATION 21:3–4

Be strong in the grace that is in Christ Jesus.

L ord, I will be strengthened with all might, according to Your glorious power. As I have therefore received Christ Jesus the Lord, so I walk in Him, rooted and built up in Him and established in the faith, as I have been taught, abounding in it with thanksgiving. I may be called a tree of righteousness, the planting of the Lord, that You may be glorified. My faith is built on the foundation of the apostles and prophets, Jesus Christ Himself being the chief cornerstone, in whom the whole building, being joined together, grows into a holy temple in the Lord, in whom I also am being built together for Your dwelling place, Lord God, in the Spirit.

I turn to You, God, and to the word of Your grace, which is able to build me up and give me an inheritance among all those who are sanctified. I will be filled with the fruits of righteousness which are by Jesus Christ, to Your glory and praise, almighty God.

I will fight the good fight of faith . . . not in any way terrified by my adversaries.

Strengthen me, Lord, to fight the good fight of faith—
and to You be the glory.

2 TIMOTHY 2:1; COLOSSIANS 1:11; COLOSSIANS 2:6–7;
ISAIAH 61:3; EPHESIANS 2:19–22; ACTS 20:32;
PHILIPPIANS 1:11; 1 TIMOTHY 6:12; PHILIPPIANS 1:28

Make His praise glorious.

Father, this people You have formed for Yourself; we shall declare Your praise. You will cleanse me from all my iniquity by which I have sinned against You, and You will pardon all my iniquities by which I have sinned and by which I have transgressed against You. Then it shall be to You a name of joy, a praise, and an honor before all nations of the earth. Let me continually offer the sacrifice of praise to You, that is, the fruit of my lips, giving thanks to Your name.

I will praise You, O Lord my God, with all my heart, and I will glorify Your name forevermore. For great is Your mercy toward me, and You have delivered my soul from the depths of Sheol. Who is like You, O Lord, glorious in holiness, fearful in praises, doing wonders? I will praise Your name, Lord God, with a song, and will magnify You with thanksgiving. The angels sing the song of Moses, Your servant, and the song of the Lamb, saying: "Great and marvelous are Your works, Lord God Almighty!"

My merciful, gracious, almighty, and all-loving God,
You alone are worthy of praise.
May my life be a song of praise to You!

PSALM 66:2; ISAIAH 43:21; JEREMIAH 33:8–9;
HEBREWS 13:15; PSALM 86:12–13; EXODUS 15:11;
PSALM 69:30; REVELATION 15:3

Bear one another's burdens,
and so fulfill the law of Christ.

Compassionate Lord, I will look out not only for my own interests, but also for the interests of others. Let this mind be in me which was also in Christ Jesus, who made Himself of no reputation, taking the form of a bondservant. Even the Son of Man did not come to be served, but to serve, and to give His life a ransom for many. He died for me, that I who live should live no longer for myself, but for Him who died for me and rose again.

When Jesus saw Mary weeping in sorrow, and the Jews who came with her weeping, He groaned in the spirit and was troubled. Jesus wept. I will rejoice with those who rejoice, and weep with those who weep.

I will have compassion for others; I will love as brothers, be tenderhearted, be courteous; not returning evil for evil or reviling for reviling, but on the contrary blessing, knowing that I was called to this, that I may inherit a blessing.

Thank You, Lord God, for the example of servanthood
You give me in Jesus—and for the power
to follow His example You give me through Your Spirit.

GALATIANS 6:2; PHILIPPIANS 2:4–7; MARK 10:45;
2 CORINTHIANS 5:15; JOHN 11:33, 35;
ROMANS 12:15; 1 PETER 3:8–9

Having loved His own who were in the world,
He loved them to the end.

Father, Jesus prays for me. He does not pray for the world but for those of us whom You, Lord God, have given Him, for we are Yours. And all His are Yours, and Yours are His, and He is glorified in us. Jesus does not pray that You should take us out of the world, but that You should keep us from the evil one. We are not of the world, just as Jesus is not of the world.

As You, God the Father, loved Jesus, He also has loved me; I abide in His love. Greater love has no one than this, than to lay down one's life for his friends. I am Jesus' friend if I do whatever He commands me. A new commandment Jesus gives to me, that I love others; as He has loved me, that I also love others.

You, Lord God, who have begun a good work in me will complete it until the day of Jesus Christ. Christ loved the church and gave Himself for her, that He might sanctify and cleanse her with the washing of water by the word.

Teach me to abide in Your love, Lord Jesus.

JOHN 13:1; JOHN 17:9–10, 15–16; JOHN 15:9;
JOHN 15:13–14; JOHN 13:34; PHILIPPIANS 1:6;
EPHESIANS 5:25–26

Revive us, and we will call upon Your name.

It is Your Spirit, Lord God, who gives life. The Spirit also helps in my weaknesses. For I do not know what I should pray for as I ought, but the Spirit Himself makes intercession for me with groaning which cannot be uttered. You who search the heart know what the mind of the Spirit is, because He makes intercession for the saints according to Your will. I will pray always with all prayer and supplication in the Spirit, being watchful to this end with all perseverance.

I will never forget Your precepts, for by them You have given me life. The words that Jesus speaks are spirit, and they are life. The letter kills, but the Spirit gives life. If I abide in Jesus, and His words abide in me, I will ask what I desire, and it shall be done for me. This is the confidence that I have in You, Lord God, that if I ask anything according to Your will, You hear us.

No one can say that Jesus is Lord except by the Holy Spirit.

Father God, keep me walking in the power of Your Spirit and according to the truth of Your Word.

PSALM 80:18; JOHN 6:63; ROMANS 8:26–27; EPHESIANS 6:18; PSALM 119:93; JOHN 6:63; 2 CORINTHIANS 3:6; JOHN 15:7; 1 JOHN 5:14; 1 CORINTHIANS 12:3

Let us therefore come boldly to the throne of grace,
that we may obtain mercy and
find grace to help in time of need.

Loving Father, I will be anxious for nothing, but in everything by prayer and supplication, with thanksgiving, let my requests be made known to You, Lord God; and Your peace, which surpasses all understanding, will guard my heart and mind through Christ Jesus. I did not receive the spirit of bondage again to fear, but I received the Spirit of adoption by whom I cry out, "Abba, Father."

You, Lord, did not say to the seed of Jacob, "Seek Me in vain." Having boldness to enter the Holiest by the blood of Jesus, by a new and living way which He consecrated for me, through the veil, that is, His flesh, and having a High Priest over the house of God, I draw near with a true heart in full assurance of faith, having my heart sprinkled from an evil conscience and my body washed with pure water. I may boldly say: "The Lord is my helper; I will not fear. What can man do to me?"

Lord God, may I never hesitate to go
boldly before You in prayer.
As a result may I know Your indescribable peace
and a rich relationship with You.

HEBREWS 4:16; PHILIPPIANS 4:6–7; ROMANS 8:15;
ISAIAH 45:19; HEBREWS 10:19–22; HEBREWS 13:6

Unto the upright there arises light in the darkness.

Merciful Lord, Your Word challenges me: Do I fear You, Lord? Do I obey the voice of His Servant? Who walks in darkness and has no light? Let those of us who do trust in Your name, Lord God, and rely upon You. Though I fall, I shall not be utterly cast down; for You, Lord, uphold me with Your hand. Your commandment is a lamp, and Your law a light.

Do not rejoice over me, my enemy; when I fall, I will arise; when I sit in darkness, my Lord will be a light to me. I will bear the indignation of the Lord, because I have sinned against Him, until He pleads my case and executes justice for me. He will bring me forth to the light; I will see His righteousness.

The lamp of the body is the eye. If therefore my eye is good, my whole body will be full of light. But if my eye is bad, my whole body will be full of darkness. If therefore the light that is in me is darkness, how great is that darkness!

May I walk in Your light, always fearing You,
always obeying Your commands, and always trusting in
Your righteousness and love.

PSALM 112:4; ISAIAH 50:10; PSALM 37:24; PROVERBS 6:23;
MICAH 7:8–9; MATTHEW 6:22–23

He chose us in Him before the foundation of the world.

Lord, I should be holy and without blame before You in love. You, my God, from the beginning, chose me for salvation through sanctification by the Spirit and belief in the truth, to which You called me for the obtaining of the glory of my Lord Jesus Christ. Whom You foreknew, You also predestined to be conformed to the image of Your Son, that You might be the firstborn among many brethren. Moreover whom You predestined, these You also called; whom You called, these You also justified; and whom You justified, these You also glorified. I am elect according to Your foreknowledge, Father God, in sanctification of the Spirit, for obedience and sprinkling of the blood of Jesus Christ.

You will give me a new heart and put a new spirit within me; You will take the heart of stone out of my flesh and give me a heart of flesh. You did not call me to uncleanness, but in holiness.

*By Your Spirit, Lord, may I live a life
that reflects my status as one of Your chosen children.
And keep my heart tender toward You, I pray.*

EPHESIANS 1:4; 2 THESSALONIANS 2:13–14;
ROMANS 8:29–30; 1 PETER 1:2; EZEKIEL 36:26;
1 THESSALONIANS 4:7

The days of your mourning shall be ended.

Eternal God, Your Word says, in the world I will have tribulation. The whole creation groans and labors with birth pangs together until now. And . . . I also who has the firstfruits of the Spirit, even I myself groan within myself, eagerly waiting for the adoption, the redemption of my body. I who am in this tent groan, being burdened, not because I want to be unclothed, but further clothed, that mortality may be swallowed up by life.

In the vision of the future You showed John the ones who come out of the great tribulation, and washed their robes and made them white in the blood of the Lamb. Therefore they are before Your throne, Lord God, and serve You day and night in Your temple. And You who sit on the throne will dwell among them. They shall neither hunger anymore nor thirst anymore; the sun shall not strike them, nor any heat; for the Lamb who is in the midst of the throne will shepherd them and lead them to living fountains of waters. And You, God, will wipe away every tear from their eyes.

Lord, I look forward to the day when You will
wipe away every tear from my eyes,
as well, when the days of my mourning shall be ended.

ISAIAH 60:20; JOHN 16:33; ROMANS 8:22–23;
2 CORINTHIANS 5:4; REVELATION 7:14–17

Your work of faith.

This is Your work, Lord God, that I believe in Him whom You sent.

Faith by itself, if it does not have works, is dead. Faith works through love. If I sow to my flesh I will of the flesh reap corruption, but if I sow to the Spirit I will of the Spirit reap everlasting life. I am Your workmanship, God, created in Christ Jesus for good works, which You prepared beforehand that I should walk in them. You gave Yourself for me, that You might redeem me from every lawless deed and purify for Yourself Your own special people, zealous for good works.

I thank You, God, because my faith grows exceedingly, and the love of every one of us abounds toward each other. I pray always that You, my God, would count me worthy of this calling, and fulfill all the good pleasure of Your goodness and the work of faith with power. It is You, God, who works in me both to will and to do for Your good pleasure.

Please continue to grow my faith and my love for You and Your people so that my works of faith will glorify You.

---

1 THESSALONIANS 1:3; JOHN 6:29; JAMES 2:17;
GALATIANS 5:6; GALATIANS 6:8; EPHESIANS 2:10; TITUS 2:14;
2 THESSALONIANS 1:3, 11; PHILIPPIANS 2:13

Let him take hold of My strength,
that he may make peace with Me.

God of Peace, the thoughts that You think toward me, are thoughts of peace and not of evil. "There is no peace," You say, "for the wicked."

In Christ Jesus I who once was far off have been brought near by the blood of Christ. For He Himself is my peace.

It pleased You, Father, that in Jesus all the fullness should dwell, and by Him to reconcile all things to Yourself, having made peace through the blood of His cross. Christ Jesus, whom You set forth as a propitiation by His blood, through faith, demonstrated Your righteousness over the sins that were previously committed, that You might be just and the justifier of those of us who have faith in Jesus. If I confess my sins, You are faithful and just to forgive me my sins and to cleanse me from all unrighteousness.

I will trust in You, Lord, forever, for in You is everlasting strength.

Lord God, thanks to Your Son's death on the cross,
I know peace with You.
I trust You for strength and forgiveness;
I trust You with my life.

ISAIAH 27:5; JEREMIAH 29:11; ISAIAH 48:22;
EPHESIANS 2:13–14; COLOSSIANS 1:19–20; ROMANS 3:24–26;
1 JOHN 1:9; ISAIAH 26:4

If you live according to the flesh you will die;
but if by the Spirit you put to death the deeds of the body,
you will live.

Holy God, the works of the flesh are evident, which are: adultery, fornication, and the like; those who practice such things will not inherit Your kingdom. But the fruit of the Spirit is love, joy, peace, longsuffering, kindness, goodness, faithfulness, gentleness, self-control. Against such there is no law. And those of us who are Christ's have crucified the flesh with its passions and desires. If I live in the Spirit, I will also walk in the Spirit.

Your grace, Lord God, that brings salvation has appeared to all men, teaching me that, denying ungodliness and worldly lusts, I should live soberly, righteously, and godly in the present age, looking for the blessed hope and glorious appearing of my great God and Savior Jesus Christ, who gave Himself for me, that He might redeem me from every lawless deed.

Enable me, Father, to walk in Your Spirit so that His fruit
will characterize my life. May the hope of Jesus' glorious return keep
me living a righteous and godly life in His honor.

ROMANS 8:13; GALATIANS 5:19, 21–25; TITUS 2:11–14

The kindness and the love of God our Savior
toward man appeared.

You, Father God, have loved me with an everlasting love. In this Your love was manifested toward me, that You have sent Your only begotten Son into the world, that I might live through Him. In this is love, not that I loved You, but that You loved me and sent Your Son to be the propitiation for my sins.

When the fullness of the time had come, You sent forth Your Son, born of a woman, born under the law, to redeem those of us who were under the law, that we might receive the adoption as sons. The Word became flesh and dwelt among us, and we beheld His glory, the glory as of the only begotten of the Father, full of grace and truth. Great is the mystery of godliness: You, Almighty God, were manifested in the flesh.

As we children have partaken of flesh and blood, Jesus Himself likewise shared in the same, that through death He might destroy him who had the power of death, that is, the devil.

It is a wonderful mystery: God in flesh, the perfect
and once-for-all sacrifice for humanity's sin! All praise to You,
the author of this amazing salvation plan!

TITUS 3:4; JEREMIAH 31:3; I JOHN 4:9–10; GALATIANS 4:4–5;
JOHN 1:14; I TIMOTHY 3:16; HEBREWS 2:14

Be steadfast, immovable,
always abounding in the work of the Lord.

L oving Lord, my labor is not in vain in You. As I have received Christ Jesus the Lord, so I walk in Him, rooted and built up in Him and established in the faith, as I have been taught, abounding in it with thanksgiving. If I endure to the end I shall be saved. The seeds that fell on the good ground are those people who, having heard the word with a noble and good heart, keep it and bear fruit with patience.

By faith I stand.

Jesus must work the works of You, Lord God, who sent Him while it is day; the night is coming when no one can work.

If I sow to my flesh I will of the flesh reap corruption, but if I sow to the Spirit I will of the Spirit reap everlasting life. And let me not grow weary while doing good, for in due season I shall reap if I do not lose heart. Therefore, as I have opportunity, let me do good to all, especially to those who are of the household of faith.

What a privilege to do Your kingdom work!
May I serve with love and know Your joy.

———————————

1 CORINTHIANS 15:58; COLOSSIANS 2:6–7;
MATTHEW 24:13; LUKE 8:15; 2 CORINTHIANS 1:24;
JOHN 9:4; GALATIANS 6:8–10

We do not look at the things which are seen, but at the things which are not seen. For the things which are seen are temporary, but the things which are not seen are eternal.

Lord, here I have no continuing city. I have a better and an enduring possession for myself in heaven.

I will not fear, for it is Your good pleasure, Father God, to give me the kingdom.

Now for a little while, if need be, I have been grieved by various trials. There the wicked cease from troubling, and there the weary are at rest.

I who am in this tent groan, being burdened. You, my God, will wipe away every tear from my eyes; there shall be no more death, nor sorrow, nor crying. There shall be no more pain, for the former things have passed away.

The sufferings of this present time are not worthy to be compared with the glory which shall be revealed in me. My light affliction, which is but for a moment, is working for me a far more exceeding and eternal weight of glory.

Thank You for keeping my eyes on my eternal future, on the glorious future Your people have in You, Lord God!

---

2 CORINTHIANS 4:18; HEBREWS 13:14; HEBREWS 10:34;
LUKE 12:32; 1 PETER 1:6; JOB 3:17; 2 CORINTHIANS 5:4;
REVELATION 21:4; ROMANS 8:18; 2 CORINTHIANS 4:17

Your sins are forgiven you.

Lord God, You will forgive my iniquity, and my sin You will remember no more. Who can forgive sins but You alone? You are He who blots out my transgressions for Your own sake; and You will not remember my sins. I am blessed, for my transgression is forgiven, and my sin is covered. I am blessed, for You do not impute my iniquity. Who is a God like You, pardoning iniquity?

You in Christ forgave me. The blood of Jesus Christ Your Son cleanses me from all sin. If I say that I have no sin, I deceive myself, and the truth is not in me. If I confess my sins, You are faithful and just to forgive me my sins and to cleanse me from all unrighteousness.

As far as the east is from the west, so far have You removed my transgressions from me. Sin shall not have dominion over me, for I am not under law but under grace. Having been set free from sin, I became a slave of righteousness.

Pardoned, forgiven, cleansed,
set free from sin, and loved by You—
Lord God, I am richly blessed!

MARK 2:5; JEREMIAH 31:34; MARK 2:7; ISAIAH 43:25; PSALM 32:1–2; MICAH 7:18; EPHESIANS 4:32; 1 JOHN 1:7–9; PSALM 103:12; ROMANS 6:14, 18

Understand what the will of the Lord is.

This is Your will, Lord God, my sanctification. I acquaint myself with You, and am at peace; thereby good will come to me. This is eternal life, that I may know You, the only true God, and Jesus Christ whom You have sent. I know that the Son of God has come and has given me an understanding, that I may know You who are true; and I am in You who are true, in Your Son Jesus Christ. This is the true God and eternal life.

May I be filled with the knowledge of Your will in all wisdom and spiritual understanding. May You, the God of my Lord Jesus Christ, the Father of glory, give me the spirit of wisdom and revelation in the knowledge of You, the eyes of my understanding being enlightened; that I may know what is the hope of Your calling, what are the riches of the glory of Your inheritance in the saints, and what is the exceeding greatness of Your power toward me who believes, according to the working of Your mighty power.

Lord God, enable me—
I pray—to know Your will and to do it!

———————————

EPHESIANS 5:17; 1 THESSALONIANS 4:3; JOB 22:21; JOHN 17:3;
1 JOHN 5:20; COLOSSIANS 1:9; EPHESIANS 1:17–19

Blameless in the day of our Lord Jesus Christ.

I, who once was alienated and an enemy in my mind by wicked works, yet now You, Lord God, have reconciled in the body of Your flesh through death, to present me holy, and blameless, and above reproach in Your sight—if indeed I continue in the faith, grounded and steadfast, and am not moved away from the hope of the gospel. I may become blameless and harmless, a child of God without fault in the midst of a crooked and perverse generation, among whom I shine as a light in the world.

Looking forward to these things, I will be diligent to be found by You in peace, without spot and blameless. I will be sincere and without offense till the day of Christ.

Now to You who are able to keep me from stumbling, and to present me faultless before the presence of Your glory with exceeding joy, to God my Savior, who alone is wise, be glory and majesty, dominion and power, both now and forever.

Keep me continuing in the faith, Lord,
steadfast in my belief, and steady in my gospel hope.
Empower to live a blameless life.

1 CORINTHIANS 1:8; COLOSSIANS 1:21–23; PHILIPPIANS 2:15;
2 PETER 3:14; PHILIPPIANS 1:10; JUDE 24–25

The Lord your God carried you, as a man carries his son,
in all the way that you went until you came to this place.

Father God, You bore me on eagles' wings and brought me to Yourself. In Your love and in Your pity You redeemed me; and You bore me and carried me all the days of old. As an eagle stirs up its nest, hovers over its young, spreading out its wings, taking them up, carrying them on its wings, so You alone led me.

Even to my old age, You are He, and even to gray hairs You will carry me! You have made, and You will bear; You will carry, and will deliver me. This is You, God, my God forever and ever; You will be my guide even to death.

I cast my burden on You, Lord, and You shall sustain me. I do not worry about my life, what I will eat or what I will drink; nor about my body, what I will put on. For You, my heavenly Father, know that I need all these things.

Thus far You, Lord God, have helped me.

Great is Your faithfulness. Immeasurable is Your love.
Infinite is Your grace. I am blessed to be Your child!

DEUTERONOMY 1:31; EXODUS 19:4; ISAIAH 63:9;
DEUTERONOMY 32:11–12;
ISAIAH 46:4; PSALM 48:14; PSALM 55:22;
MATTHEW 6:25, 32; 1 SAMUEL 7:12